The Perfect Practice Exam

The Perfect Practice Exam

The Skill of Legal Analysis

Christina Chong

Carolina Academic Press
Durham, North Carolina

LCCN: 2017938483
ISBN: 978-1-63284-320-3
eBook ISBN: 978-1-63284-321-0

Carolina Academic Press, LLC
700 Kent Street
Durham, North Carolina 27701
Telephone (919) 489-7486
Fax (919) 493-5668
www.cap-press.com

Printed in the United States of America
2021 Printing

This book is dedicated to my family and friends, for their encouragement during the creation of this book. A special thanks to Thomas Nakatsuchi, Jennifer Chong, Sally Chong, and Peter Chong; their endless support was integral to the completion of this series.

Contents

Essay Answers

The Perfect
Practice Exam

Writing Effective Examinations

The Three-Step Method

Student: "How do I improve?"
Professor: "You need *more* analysis."
Student: "What do you mean?"
Professor: "You are conclusory. You must explain your reasoning."

Law students often encounter the above conversation because lack of analysis is the main reason professors deduct points on essay exams. But what is legal analysis and how do you write *more*? Analysis is defined as a *detailed* examination of the elements or structure of something. However, regurgitating *more detail* about the law is not explaining your reasoning.

Legal analysis requires: (1) key words from the rule, (2) relevant facts, and (3) an inference. Most students successfully state the rules and facts, but fail to make inferences or fail to combine the three parts into one comprehensible thought. If you struggle with analysis, then use the sample templates below.

These [facts] show this [rule] is met because [inference].

This [rule] is met because [of these facts], which means [inference].

The sample templates will help you coherently present your thoughts, but filling in the brackets can be challenging. It is difficult to apply abstract legal concepts to real-world situations. If you experience writer's block, then use the following method. First, figure out what part of the applicable rule is at issue. Second, determine what facts are relevant to prove your argument. Third, explain why the facts you selected support your argument.

Before we breakdown the three steps in detail, you must learn where analysis belongs in an essay answer. Most law schools use IRAC to help students organize their responses. A definition of IRAC is below.

I: State the ISSUE raised by the facts.

R: Cite the applicable RULE.

A: ANALYZE the facts from both party's point of view.

C: CONCLUDE based on the arguments presented.

This book teaches you how to master the "A" in IRAC by applying the three-step method to the <u>Coffee Shop</u> scenario. The <u>Coffee Shop</u> exercises will focus on how to write *more analysis* in a non-legal and legal context.

Coffee Shop

Sally welcomed Thomas with a wave when he entered the coffee shop, but he frowned and ignored her gesture. Thomas called his friend, Jenn, and said, "This annoying girl waved to me." Thomas knew Jenn because they volunteer together at the Animal Shelter every Sunday. Thomas asked Jenn if she needed a ride to the shelter and Jenn said, "Yes." Thomas hung up and mumbled, "She is such a pain." Sally called Thomas's name and placed a drink on the counter. Thomas looked at the drink and saw the word "Peter" written in large, black letters. Thomas was in a rush so he took the drink and exited the coffee shop.

(1) Non-Legal Question

Is Thomas a nice or mean person? A mean person has several characteristics but is usually unpleasant or cruel. Nice people are different but generally pleasant or have good character.

(2) Legal Question

Did Thomas possess the necessary intent to be liable for taking Peter's coffee? Intentional interference requires a defendant to act with the desire to cause the consequences of his act or believe the consequences are substantially certain to result from his act.[1]

Step 1: Include the Key Words and Phrases from the Applicable Rule

First, identify the rule raised by the facts; this is called issue spotting. Next, identify the key words and phrases in the rule statement. A key word or phrase is an essential part of the applicable rule that you must explain using factual evidence to convince the judge or jury that your client should win.

---

1. Restatement (Second) of Torts § 8A (Am. Law Inst. 1965).

Let's do the non-legal example in <u>Coffee Shop</u>. The issue is whether Thomas is nice or mean. What are the key words of the definitions below?

Definitions	Key Words
A mean person has several characteristics but is usually unpleasant or cruel.	_____ _____
Nice people are different but generally pleasant or have good character.	_____ _____

The words *unpleasant, cruel, pleasant,* and *good character* are key words because factual evidence is required to establish if Thomas is pleasant (nice) or cruel (mean). If you are unsure whether a word is essential, then select other words in the definition and try to use factual evidence to explain your arguments. If you cannot develop an argument, then the word is not a key word.

For example, if you selected *several characteristics* or *people are different,* you would struggle to explain how having *several characteristics* shows Thomas is mean or how *people being different* shows Thomas is nice. In contrast, you can easily argue that Thomas is *unpleasant* because he ignored Sally's wave, which suggests he is mean. You can also argue that Thomas *has good character* because he volunteers at the Animal Shelter and agreed to give Jenn a ride, which suggests he is nice.

Let's apply this skill to the legal example involving torts. The issue is whether Thomas acted with intent. What are the key phrases in the rule statement below?

Applicable Rule	Key Phrases
Intentional interference requires a defendant to act with the desire to cause the consequences of his act or believe the consequences are substantially certain to result from his act.[2]	_____ _____ _____ _____ _____

The key phrases include "acts with the *desire to cause* the consequences" and "acts with *substantial certainty* that the consequences will result." Similar to the non-legal example, you can identify key phrases in a rule statement by eliminating unessential phrases. You cannot explain how *requiring a defendant to*

---

2. R. 2d of Torts § 8A, supra note 1.

act or how the *result from the defendant's act* shows Thomas's intent. Your analysis would make no sense.

Another way to determine a key word or phrase is to examine the facts provided. In <u>Coffee Shop</u>, facts about Thomas's internal thoughts were purposefully inserted for students to argue that Thomas *desired to interfere* or was *substantially certain* that taking the drink would interfere with Peter's lawful possession of the drink. The facts do not discuss any requirements *to act* or *the result of the act*; this suggests these phrases are probably not essential to determine Thomas's intent.

After you identify the key words and phrases in the rule statement, insert them into the brackets in the sample template. You may need to modify the sentence to follow the rules of grammar. Below are two examples.

Template	Fill in the brackets
These [facts] show this [rule] is met because [inference].	These [facts] show Thomas is [*unpleasant and cruel*] because [inference].
This [rule] is met because of these [facts], which means [inference].	Thomas [*desired to interfere*] because of these [facts], which means [inference].

When identifying key words and phrases, do not be afraid to divide the rule into multiple parts. The division of a rule is called imposing structure on a rule, which is advantageous because each key word or phrase can require different factual citations. If you divide the rule into parts, then it is easier to make accurate inferences. For example, if you analyzed *(1) desired to interfere* and *(2) substantially certain his act would interfere* in the same sentence, then your prose would be long and unclear. *Desire to interfere* analyzes whether Thomas wanted to take Peter's drink. *Substantially certain* analyzes if Thomas took the drink knowing it was likely to interfere with Peter's possession of the drink. The arguments are deceiving similar.

There are rare cases where you can address key words and phrases together. In the non-legal example, you can combine the key words because *unpleasant* and *cruel* have similar definitions. You can use the same facts and inferences to argue Thomas was *unpleasant* and *cruel*. However, as a default rule, take your analysis one key word or phrase at a time.

Although you cannot identify the applicable rule until you read the fact pattern, determining the key words and phrases of a rule prior to the exam helps you avoid common mistakes, such as identifying the incorrect key words and phrases or addressing too many key words and phrases in one thought. You should complete Step #1 before your exam, include the information in your outline, and take practice exams using the key words and phrases you selected.

Step 2: Quote Relevant Facts

Students do not quote facts in their answers because they assume the professor is familiar with the story. Although the professor wrote the exam, the professor is testing to see if you can identify the relevant facts. If you regularly forget to cite facts that support your arguments, then pretend you are writing a motion for the court. In practice, a judge or jury is not intimately familiar with your client's case. You must include the relevant facts to give your audience context.

A relevant fact is defined as evidence you need to prove your argument. A fact is relevant if you answer "YES" to any of the questions below.

1. Would my arguments or the outcome of the case change if this fact did not exist?
2. Does this fact support one party's argument more than another party's argument?
3. Is this fact ambiguous? If yes, can this fact be used by both parties to support their arguments?
4. Does this fact help explain any arguments related to the key words and phrases identified in Step #1?

Let's practice using the non-legal example from Coffee Shop. The issue is whether Thomas is *mean (unpleasant or cruel)* or *nice (pleasant or has good character)*. Check the boxes next to the relevant facts.

- ❏ A. Thomas frowned and ignored Sally's welcome.
- ❏ B. Thomas called Sally annoying because she waved to him.
- ❏ C. Thomas offered Jenn a ride to the Animal Shelter.
- ❏ D. Thomas volunteers at the Animal Shelter every Sunday.
- ❏ E. Thomas called Jenn a pain.
- ❏ F. Thomas took Peter's drink.

All six facts are relevant. We will use the four questions above to confirm this answer is correct.

1. If facts C and D did not exist, then the outcome of the case would change because Thomas would definitely be considered *unpleasant* and *cruel*.
2. Facts A, B, and F support an argument that Thomas is *unpleasant*.

3. Fact E is ambiguous because Thomas might be merely venting about a friend or actually believe Jenn is annoying. Reasonable people can differ on their interpretation of fact E.
4. All six facts relate to whether Thomas is *unpleasant, cruel, pleasant,* or *has good character.*

Let's apply the same skill to the legal scenario from <u>Coffee Shop</u>. The issue is whether Thomas *intended* to interfere with Peter's possession of the drink. Did Thomas act with the *desire to interfere* or *substantial certainty that the consequences would result?* Check the boxes next to the relevant facts.

❑ A. Sally called Thomas's name and placed a drink on the counter.
❑ B. Thomas saw the word "Peter" written in large black letters.
❑ C. Thomas was in a rush so he took the drink and exited the shop.

All three facts are relevant because they explain whether Thomas *desired to interfere* or *was substantially certain* that taking the drink would interfere with Peter's lawful possession of the drink. Facts B and C support the argument that Thomas was *substantially certain* the drink did not belong to him. Fact A supports Thomas's argument that he mistakenly believed the drink belonged to him.

Unlike Step #1, where you usually do not combine key words or phrases, you can combine several relevant facts into one thought. However, if your sentence structure will suffer or the facts support different arguments, then do not include multiple facts. Below are two examples using the sample templates.

Template	Fill in the brackets
These [facts] show this [rule] is met because [inference].	[*Thomas taking the drink with Peter's name on it*] shows Thomas is [unpleasant and cruel] because [inference].
This [rule] is met because of these [facts], which means [inference].	Thomas [desired to interfere] with Peter's lawful possession because [*Thomas saw the word "Peter" written in large, black letters on the drink*], which means [inference].

Step 3: Explain Why

The best way to ensure you explain why the relevant facts support your arguments is to make an inference, which is a conclusion based on factual evidence and reasoning. Students fail to make inferences because they believe the rule-fact connections are obvious. Although a professor can usually figure out your inference, the professor is testing your analysis skills and will not give points if your answer is missing the legal reasoning.

If you struggle with inferences, then pretend you are speaking to the judge or jury. In your closing statement, you would never state the key words of the rule and relevant facts without explaining the connections. You would explain how the facts support your argument and relate to the applicable rule. Explicitly stating the inference prevents the jury from developing alternative conclusions and encourages them to agree with your arguments. You do not skip inferences in practice; you should not skip inferences on your exams. Treat the professor like a layperson who struggles to understand the law and not a brilliant scholar.

If the concept of making an inference is still confusing, then consider the following scenario:

> You are a licensed attorney. A client comes for a consultation and tells you the facts of the case. You take notes, figure out the possible legal issues, and ask your research assistant to look up the law. The client provided the relevant facts (Step #2) and the law is publicly available (Step #1). **Why did the client hire you?**

Clients hire attorneys for their legal reasoning (Step #3), which is the ability to present arguments that connect facts to the law. Inferences are rarely in your lecture notes and outline because inferences are ideas in your head. Although the underlying legal reasoning of your ideas might come from precedent cases, your exams usually deal with different factual scenarios that require new connections. Most missing inferences are conclusions you consciously made when analyzing the facts, but never wrote on your paper.

Let's practice making inferences using the non-legal example in <u>Coffee Shop</u>. Fill in the blank below.

> Thomas taking the drink with Peter's name on it shows Thomas is unpleasant and cruel because _____
> _____.

Several different inferences can correctly fill in the blank, such as "a nice person would clarify the drink belong to him before taking it," or "a cruel person does not care if he inconveniences another person." Even though the explanations are obvious, you must still explicitly state your internal thoughts. You cannot skip the inference because reasonable minds can differ on whether taking a drink with another person's name on it is cruel. This skill is also applicable to legal scenarios. Fill in the blank below.

> Thomas desired to interfere with Peter's lawful possession because Thomas saw the word "Peter" written in large black letters on the drink, which means _____
>
> _____
>
> _____.

A possible inference is "Thomas knew the drink did not belong to him, but took it anyway." Your explanation is necessary because another person might assume Thomas's actions were an accident. You want to limit your audience's freedom to interpret the facts in a way that will conflict with your conclusion and hurt your case.

Law school exams test your ability to clearly make arguments because laypeople often struggle to comprehend implied inferences, and clients pay attorneys for their ability to develop explicit connections between laws and facts. Law school is not college. You do not receive As for repeating the professor's lecture. Thus, when in doubt, re-read your sentence and ask yourself "*Why?*" after the period. If you can answer "*Why?*" then you are missing an inference. Let's do another legal example.

> Thomas taking a drink with Peter's name on it shows Thomas was substantially certain his act would interfere with Peter's lawful possession because _____
>
> _____.

If you are unsure how to fill in the blank, then ask yourself *why* taking a drink with another person's name on it shows Thomas was *substantially certain* Peter would not receive his drink. A possible answer is "the drink obviously did not belong to Thomas and taking the drink means Peter would not receive his order."

Conclusion

The three-step method is a starting point for your legal analysis, but your exam-writing strategies will evolve and change as you complete more practice exams. You will encounter other obstacles, such as situations where the facts are the inference or where you must make an assumption. But do not worry, this book addresses common obstacles associated with analysis.

Facts as an Inference

An inference is required when reasonable minds differ about how the facts apply to the rule at issue. Sometimes an inference is not necessary because the facts are self-explanatory or there is only one plausible interpretation of the facts. Students are uncertain when to skip the inference because the explanations they subjectively believed were obvious are sometimes objectively ambiguous. Identifying when a fact is an inference is a difficult skill to master because everyone's views are different. The obviousness of a fact depends on a student's views, which does not always conform to the professor's opinion. But there are two universal situations where an inference is usually unnecessary.

1. A fact becomes the inference if the fact obviously explains why the rule is met or not met.
2. A fact becomes the inference if reasonable minds could not differ on how the fact applies to the rule.

To practice identifying when an inference is unnecessary, we will apply the three-step method to the battery example below.

Miko hit Ginger in the face. As a result, Ginger fell on top of Jewel. Both Ginger and Jewel suffered personal injuries. Miko is liable for battery if she intentionally caused harmful or offensive contact.[3] Direct contact with the victim is not required; it is sufficient that the defendant's voluntary act sets in motion a force that results in contact.[4] Did Miko make contact with Ginger and Jewel?

Step #1: The key phrases of the contact rule are *direct contact with the victim* and *the defendant set in motion a force that resulted in contact.*

Step #2: The relevant facts are "Miko hit Ginger in the face" and "Ginger fell on top of Jewel."

Step #3: Possible inferences include "Miko's hand or part of her body touched Ginger's face" and "Miko pushed Ginger into Jewel." To determine whether these inferences are necessary, you must determine if the universal situations apply to these arguments. Let's start with whether Miko made contact with Ginger.

---

3. R. 2d of Torts § 13 (AM. LAW INST. 1965).
4. *Id.*

1. The fact, "Miko hit Ginger in the face," obviously explains that Miko made *direct contact with the victim* because Miko hitting Ginger means Miko's hand made contact with Ginger's face.
2. Reasonable minds would agree that Miko made contact with Ginger because the common definition of hitting someone is touching them with your hand, another part of your body, or object.

In Ginger's case, the facts are the inference because both universal situations apply. You do not need to explain why hitting someone's face is *direct contact*. It is enough to write "*direct contact* was made because Miko hit Ginger in the face." An inference is unnecessary because reasonable minds would not differ in their interpretation of Miko's actions and the facts are obvious enough for the average reader to independently connect the facts and law.

However, the analysis of Miko's contact with Jewel is different. Let's apply the two universal situations.

1. The fact, "Ginger fell on top of Jewel," is not self-explanatory because it does not state whether Miko made physical contact with Jewel or whether Miko played a role in Ginger's motion.
2. Without an explanation, reasonable minds could interpret the fact differently because it is unclear if Ginger fell because she was clumsy or if Miko was the cause.

In Jewel's case, quoting the facts is not enough to explain how Miko *set in motion a force that resulted in contact* with Jewel. An inference is necessary because the average reader might not understand why Miko should be responsible for Jewel's injury if you only state "Ginger fell on top of Jewel." An example inference explaining Miko's contact with Jewel is below.

> Miko *set in motion a force that resulted in contact* with Jewel because Miko hit Ginger in the face. If Miko never hit Ginger, then Ginger would have never fallen on top of Jewel.

Most students incorrectly exclude the inference when analyzing if Miko made contact with Jewel because they feel the explanation is obvious. However, students forget the audience is a layperson on the jury and not the professor.

To avoid the trap of accidentally skipping inferences, envision a person who is your antithesis (the complete opposite of you). Pretend your antithesis knows nothing about the case, state the fact, and then determine whether your antithesis would understand the connections to the applicable law without further explanation. If the answer is no, then you need an inference to explain the relationship between the facts and law. If the answer is yes, then no inference is necessary. When in doubt, it is safer to explain your reasoning.

Assumptions Within Common Sense

In legal practice, clients will not always give you the complete story and it can take months to uncover all the relevant facts. Professors do not spend months drafting their final exams, which means law-school exams rarely include all the facts you need to write thorough analysis. If your professor drafts questions with relevant facts missing, then you must make assumptions to reach reasonable inferences and conclusions. However, making assumptions in legal writing is dangerous.

An assumption is considering something true without any proof. In law, assumptions cause confusion because our reader's assumptions do not always match our assumptions, and our assumptions are sometimes wrong. But assumptions are sometimes unavoidable. Thus, if you must make an assumption, then make sure it is within the realm of common sense. Let's call this a "common-sense assumption."

A common-sense assumption is an assumption that an average reader, with basic life experience and intelligence, would likely make and understand. Although the concept seems simple, students struggle to differentiate between making common-sense assumptions and changing the professor's fact pattern. If you struggle to balance assumptions with creative writing, then ask yourself the following questions before making an assumption. If your answer is "NO" to any of the questions, then your assumption is probably an overly imaginative argument that is outside the scope of common sense.

1. Would a reasonable, average, American person make this assumption?

   If a reasonable person would not make your assumption, then you likely examined the facts from a subjective perspective based on your unique life experiences. Never assume the reader shares your opinions and background. A common-sense assumption requires you to exam the situation from the objective viewpoint of an average, American person.

2. Is my assumption 99.9% likely to happen?

   If your assumption is unrealistic and unlikely to occur based on the facts, then your argument is likely too ambitious or weak. You should search for credible assumptions that will strengthen your argument.

3. Is my assumption based on facts explicitly included in the fact pattern?

A common-sense assumption is usually an unstated, subtle connection made between two explicitly stated facts. If your assumption requires adding facts to be plausible, then you are changing the exam to fit your argument rather than analyzing the facts presented by your professor.

Let's practice making assumptions using the intent rules from <u>Coffee Shop</u> and the battery example with Miko.

Intent requires a defendant to act with the *desire to cause* the consequences or with *substantial certainty* the consequences will result.[5] The day before Miko hit Ginger, the pair fought about Ginger's failure to return the highlighters that she borrowed from Miko. What are the common-sense assumptions related to whether Miko intentionally hit Ginger?

A reasonable person would assume that Miko *desired to* hit Ginger because Miko was upset. A common-sense assumption is "Miko was upset because Ginger failed to return her highlighters." However, some students will argue that "Miko was upset because Ginger prevented Miko from case briefing by keeping the highlighters, which caused Miko to fail her exams."

The first assumption is within common sense because an average, reasonable person would make the same assumption; and based on the facts explicitly provided, it is 99.9% likely that Miko is upset about the highlighters. The second assumption is too inventive because it jumps to conclusions without sufficient evidence to support the assumption. The professor did not provide facts about Miko's case briefing or exams. The student added these facts to strengthen the argument. But adding facts is not impressive; adding facts suggests you struggle with reading comprehension and creating reasonable inferences.

Common sense is tricky in law school because the exams often include imaginative situations that are unlikely to happen in real life. For example, a law-school professor can write about a summer camp for children where the campers pet tigers and ride elephants. Professors draft creative fact patterns to challenge their students' intellect, but the bizarre scenarios inadvertently cause students to ignore their common sense. If you encounter an unusual fact pattern, then remember that the audience never changes. Anything can happen in law-school world, but your arguments must always conform to society's norms and the facts presented.

---

5. R. 2d of Torts § 8A, supra note 1.

Factual Application Versus Factual Analysis

Law-school exams test two analytical skills: (1) factual application and (2) factual analysis. Both skills require an explanation of why the facts prove the rule was met or not met. However, in factual application, there is a clear winner; there is no counter argument or alternative explanation. Factual analysis is a debate between both sides about whose arguments are stronger and why. Factual analysis applies when the facts are ambiguous, or the fact pattern includes facts that support both sides.

If you can master differentiating factual application from factual analysis, then you can better control your timing and assumptions. A factual-application issue does not require a counter argument and should be addressed quickly. Your time and energy should be directed towards factual-analysis issues. Students who treat all issues as factual-analysis issues waste time brainstorming innovative counter arguments and often make unreasonable assumptions to create those arguments. Professors purposefully create factual-application issues to test your ability to identify when arguing both sides is futile. Below is an example of each analytical skill.

Factual Application

Let's use the battery example from the previous section.

> Miko hit Ginger in the face. As a result, Ginger fell on top of Jewel. Both Ginger and Jewel suffered personal injuries. Miko is liable for battery if she intentionally caused harmful or offensive contact.[6] Direct contact with the victim is not required; it is sufficient that the defendant's voluntary act sets in motion a force that results in contact.[7] Did Miko make contact with Ginger and Jewel?

If you argued that Miko did not make contact with Ginger when she hit Ginger's face, then you failed to identify that this was a factual-application issue. The element of contact is obviously met because no counter argument is present.

Jewel's case is similar. If you argued that Miko did not voluntarily set a force in motion that resulted in contact with Jewel, then you failed to identify this

---

6. R. 2d of Torts § 8A, supra note 3.

7. *Id.*

was a factual-application issue. As previously discussed, analysis of Jewel's case requires an inference, but whether an inference is necessary does not impact whether the issue itself requires factual application or factual analysis. It is obvious that Miko made contact with both Ginger and Jewel.

Factual Analysis

Unlike factual-application issues, factual-analysis issues are complex because they require you to anticipate the other side's arguments and explain why your argument is stronger. There are two common factual-analysis scenarios.

1. The exam includes facts that support each side's arguments on the issue.
2. The facts are ambiguous and can reasonably be interpreted to support each side's arguments.

In the first scenario, the facts used to support each side's arguments are different. In the second scenario, the facts used are the same, but both sides develop different inferences to support their positions. Let's practice using the battery example below.

> Miko and Ginger were waiting in line. The area was crowded with barely any space to move. Miko saw Ginger walking towards her. The pair previously fought about Ginger's failure to return the highlighters that she borrowed from Miko. As Ginger got closer, the crowd began to move up a staircase. Someone accidentally pushed Miko. Miko could have grabbed the adjacent rail to prevent her fall, but instead Miko reached her hands towards Ginger and hit Ginger in the face. Intent requires a defendant to act with the *desire to cause* the consequences or with *substantially certainty* the consequences will result.[8] Did Miko intend to hit Ginger?

Whether Miko intentionally hit Ginger is a factual-analysis issue; the question includes facts that support both sides and ambiguous facts with multiple interpretations. If you address factual-analysis issues haphazardly, then you will confuse your reader. You must address one side's argument at a time. For each argument, you must: (a) identify what facts support each side; (b) ask yourself why those facts support each side; and (c) use the three-step method to develop your analysis. In this example, both factual-analysis scenarios are present. Let's practice making arguments for each scenario.

---

8. R. 2d of Torts § 8A, supra note 1.

1. Factual-Analysis Scenario #1: The exam includes facts that support both sides.

   (a) What facts support each side's argument?

   Miko *did not* intend to hit Ginger.

   _____

   _____

   Miko *did* intend to hit Ginger.

   _____

   _____

Answer: A third party pushed Miko in a crowded area, which indicates Miko did not intend to hit Ginger. However, Miko reaching her hands towards Ginger and failing to grab the rail suggests Miko wanted to make contact with Ginger.

   (b) Why do these facts support each side?

   Miko *did not* intend to hit Ginger.

   _____

   _____

   Miko *did* intend to hit Ginger.

   _____

   _____

To answer question 1(b), you must make inferences. The possible answers are below.

   (b) Why do these facts support each side?

   Miko *did not* intend to hit Ginger.
   - Miko cannot control the actions of others. Miko hit Ginger by accident; someone falling down is not always thinking clearly.

   Miko *did* intend to hit Ginger.
   - Miko consciously decided not to grab the rail. Most people would grab the rail and not reach out their hands towards someone's face.

The first factual-analysis scenario was straightforward. However, unlike scenario #1, scenario #2 contains ambiguous facts that are more challenging to analyze. Let's practice identifying and using the ambiguous facts from the battery example.

2. Factual-Analysis Scenario #2. The exam contains ambiguous facts that can support both sides.

(a) What facts support arguments for both sides?

Miko *did/did not* intend to hit Ginger.

_____

_____

(b) Why do these facts support each side?

Miko *did not* intend to hit Ginger.

_____

_____

Miko *did* intend to hit Ginger.

_____

_____

In scenario #2, the common-sense reaction is to ask Miko if she intentionally failed to grab the rail because she wanted to hit Ginger. Students complain when professors fail to include facts about subjective intent, but many professors omit facts about intent on purpose because litigants do not always tell the truth. Miko could easily lie about her intent. An attorney's job is to make common-sense assumptions and interpret the facts in a way that convinces the jury to support their client's position. The answers to scenario #2 are below.

2. Factual-Analysis Scenario #2. The exam contains ambiguous facts that can support both sides.

(a) What facts support arguments for both sides?

Miko *did/did not* intend to hit Ginger.
   • Miko and Ginger previously fought about Ginger's failure to return Miko's highlighters. Miko reached her hands towards Ginger instead of grabbing the rail.

(b) Why do these facts support each side?

Miko *did not* intend to hit Ginger.
   • Miko might not care about the highlighters. The argument prior to their physical contact was a coincidence. Miko hitting Ginger was an accident.

Miko *did* intend to hit Ginger.
   • Miko was angry at Ginger for not returning the highlighters. Miko consciously decided not to grab the rail because

she wanted to hurt Ginger. Most people would grab an adjacent rail when falling down.

If you still struggle to identify whether an issue requires factual application or factual analysis, then try treating your exam like a trial. If an element is obviously met and you argue against it, then the judge will question your competency and it wastes the court's time.

You can also assess your conclusion to determine the strength of your arguments. If you argued both sides and one side's argument was significantly stronger than the other side's argument, then you might be writing a factual-analysis explanation for a factual-application issue. However, if both arguments are equal, then you correctly identified the factual-analysis issue.

How to Use This Book

First, complete the question within the time limit provided using the three-step method discussed above. Second, review the sample answer. The sample answers are an accurate reflection of how you should format and write your final exams. Third, compare your answer to the sample answer. You should pay attention to the similarities and differences in structure, issue spotting, and analysis.

Do not use this book to learn the law for your classes. This book uses common rules from statutes, cases, restatements, and the uniform commercial code, but your professor might teach different rules in his or her class. You should always use the rules from class if they conflict with the rules in this book. Remember that the focus of these practice questions is to improve your exam-taking skills, with an emphasis on analysis, and not to teach you substantive law.

Civil Procedure Questions

Question 1
(60 minutes)

Wild Water sells canoes nationally. Wild Water's state of incorporation and headquarters are in State B. In 2011, after 11 years of only selling canoes online, Wild Water opened a physical store to sell and rent canoes near Marsy River in State Z.

Six months ago, Wild Water opened a rental-return station in State Y for customers to return the canoes they rented in State Z. State Y and State Z are adjacent states. Patrons loved Wild Water's new rental-return station because patrons often rented canoes in State Z and canoed across the border to State Y, but were too tired to canoe back to State Z. The rental-return station collects the equipment and provides a shuttle ride back to State Z for $3 per a person, but does not sell or rent canoes.

Ellen is a resident of State Y. Ellen rented a canoe in State Z and canoed across the border to State Y. Ellen was tired. She decided to return the canoe in State Y and take the shuttle.

Damon is a Wild Water employee at the State Y rental-return location. He is enrolled in the local college's eight-year PhD program. Damon is a citizen of Country X and receives funding from Country X's government to study in America. Damon's sponsorship contract with Country X states "Country X will pay Damon's tuition if he returns to work for Country X's government after he completes his PhD." Damon started the PhD program in America three weeks ago.

During the return transaction, Damon dropped the canoe on Ellen's foot and broke her toes. Ellen sued Wild Water and Damon for negligence in the United States District Court in State Y. Both defendants file a motion to dismiss alleging there is no personal jurisdiction. State Y's long arm statute states, "A court of this state may exercise jurisdiction on any basis not inconsistent with the constitution of this state or of the United States." How should the court rule? Do not discuss service of process or in rem jurisdiction issues.

Question 2
(40 minutes)

Gaby and Hugo worked for Future Incorporated (Future) researching ways to save energy. After work hours, Gaby and Hugo used Future's research facilities to invent a robot that cleaned homes. Although they used Future's equipment, they paid for their own materials. Gaby designed the robot and Hugo created the technology. Their patents for the robot's technology and design were granted in January 2012. A month after the patents were granted, Future found the robot prototype, manufactured 500 robots, and sold them to various retailers at $120 per a robot. Future made a profit of $60,000 from the sale of the robots.

Future was incorporated in State D, its headquarters and research facilities are in State A, and its factories are in State B. Gaby is officially domicile in State Z, but has not returned to State Z for many years. Gaby spends the weekends in State B with her family where she owns a house, but she rents an apartment in State A during the weekdays for work. Hugo is domicile in State C and travels across the border to work in State A.

(1) Gaby and Hugo filed a claim against Future for patent infringement under 35 U.S. Code § 271 in the Superior Court of State A. Gaby and Hugo each claimed $60,000 in damages. Future timely filed a motion to remove the claims to State A's federal district court. The court granted the motion. Was the court correct? Do not address personal jurisdiction or venue issues.

(2) Assume the court's decision to remove the claims to State A's federal district court was proper. Gaby files a claim for breach of contract because Future agreed to pay Gaby royalties on the sales of any light bulbs sold using her energy-saving technology. Future owes Gaby $30,000 in royalty payments. Can the federal court exercise supplement jurisdiction over Gaby's claim?

Question 3
(60 minutes)

Draco is domicile overseas in Country X. American Tours (American) advertised its services in Country X. Draco saw the advertisements and purchased a tour of the United States. The negotiations, payment, and contract signing were completed at American's office in Country X. American's state of incorporation and principal place of business are in State A.

When Draco arrived at American's office in State A's Northern District, he learned the tour included a driving experience from State A to State B using a rental car. American's guides did not accompany clients on the driving tour to State B because the company wanted its clients to independently experience the states. American required its clients to rent cars from its partner, Roadies, a rental car company with a rental office in the Northern District of State A. Roadies's principal place of business and state of incorporation are in State B.

While driving through the Northern District of State B, Draco negligently hit Martin, a resident of State C, at a busy intersection. Martin called the State B police and filed a police report. Martin suffered personal injuries and could not afford to pay his medical bills. Martin sued Draco, American, and Roadies in the Superior Court of State B.

State B's statute of limitations requires a plaintiff to bring a personal injury claim two years from the date the injury was discovered. Martin filed the claim four days before the statute of limitations expired in State B. The federal statute of limitations requires personal injury claims to be brought within one year after the date the injury was discovered.

(1) The defendants filed a motion to remove the claim to the United States District Court, Northern District of State B. Assume the court granted the motion. Should the federal court apply State B's law or federal law to Martin's claim?

(2) American filed a motion to transfer the case to the United States District Court, Northern District of State A, which is where American's headquarters and sales offices are located. American has no offices in State B. Draco and Roadies opposed American's request to transfer. Will American's motion to transfer be granted? Assume venue is proper in State B, State A has personal jurisdiction over all the parties, and State A has subject matter jurisdiction over all claims.

(3) Assume the court granted American's motion to transfer and that there are no personal jurisdiction or subject matter jurisdiction issues. What law should be applied?

(4) Draco filed a forum non conveniens motion because he believes the best place to litigate is Country X. Should the court grant Draco's motion?

Question 4
(45 minutes)

Timeshare is an agreement where several individuals jointly own the right to use a property as a vacation home. Owner paid $6000 to Timeshare Corp (Timeshare) in exchange for the company's promise to sell Owner's timeshare interests. After two years, Timeshare had not sold Owner's interests. Owner filed a claim for breach of contract and fraud in the United States District Court. Owner's complaint stated the following information:

PARAGRAPH 1: Timeshare committed fraud and breached its contract because Timeshare agreed to sell Owner's timeshare interests, but failed for two years.

PARAGRAPH 2: Timeshare committed fraud and breached its contract because Owner already paid $6000, but Timeshare refused to refund the money after it failed to sell Owner's timeshare interests.

PARAGRAPH 3: Timeshare's unprofessional and poorly dressed employees caused the unsuccessful sale of Owner's timeshare interests.

PARAGRAPH 4: Owner requests a judgment against defendant for $6000 in damages.

(1) Timeshare filed a motion to dismiss under Rule 12(b)(6). Assume there are no issues with the court's jurisdiction. Should the court grant Timeshare's motion?

(2) Assume the judge denies Timeshare's motion. Timeshare files a motion to strike PARAGRAPH 3. Should the court grant Timeshare's motion?

(3) Assume the judge denies Timeshare's motion. Timeshare files a motion for a more definite statement. What should Timeshare include in its motion and should the court should grant Timeshare's motion?

(4) Assume the judge denies Timeshare's motion. Timeshare files an answer to Owner's complaint that states "Timeshare denies all allegations." Based on your analysis of prompt #1, #2, and #3, was Timeshare's answer appropriate?

Question 5
(60 minutes)

Classy Construction (Classy) was hired to complete the construction of a luxury apartment complex in State X. Nell and Mark were walking through Classy's construction site when a giant wrecking ball detached from its chain, fell down, and hit them. Nell and Mark suffered personal injuries. Nell filed a negligence claim against Classy in the United States District Court of State X. Assume there are no personal jurisdiction, subject matter jurisdiction, or venue issues.

Classy had rented the wrecking ball equipment from Blue Caterpillar (Blue). Classy notified Blue about the lawsuit and told Blue it would do everything to win the case. Classy asked Blue to send a new wrecking ball to the construction site. Blue immediately shipped the new equipment and wished Classy good luck on the lawsuit.

(1) After three months of discovery, Nell learned Blue had failed to properly maintain the wrecking ball equipment. Nell filed a motion to amend his complaint to (a) sue Blue instead of Classy and (b) add a claim against Blue under strict products liability for the wrecking ball's rusty chains. Blue argued that Classy was a necessary party because Classy was negligent. State X has a statute of limitations that allows relation back. Should the court grant Nell's motions?

(2) The media featured Nell's case because the local millionaire, Po, owned the luxury apartment complex. Po filed a motion for intervention. Po wanted to sue Blue and Classy for ruining his reputation. Should the court grant Po's motion?

(3) Mark did not want to be involved in the lawsuit or media chaos. Mark moved overseas, but planned to return after six months. Should Mark be joined as a necessary party?

(4) Nell's attorney filed the lawsuit against Classy without interviewing Mark or reviewing the security cameras. Nell's attorney only spoke with his client. Nell told his attorney that he had the legal right to be on the property when he was harmed. The security footage revealed that Mark and Nell were negligently playing on the wrecking ball equipment after work hours. Should sanctions be imposed against Nell's attorney?

Question 6
(60 minutes)

Lana was hospitalized for food poisoning after she ate at Burger Joint (Burger). Lana filed a lawsuit in the United States District Court of State X against Burger. Assume there are no personal jurisdiction, subject matter jurisdiction, or venue issues.

(1) Lana and Burger's attorneys met to discuss the discovery process and scheduled a deposition for Lana on May 9th. Lana was hospitalized for an unrelated illness the week before her deposition. Lana's attorney requested to postpone Lana's deposition, but Burger's attorney refused to modify the schedule. Burger's attorney arrived on May 9th to depose Lana in the hospital. The attorney aggressively asked Lana questions and ignored her requests to be left alone. Lana suffered a panic attack. Lana filed a motion for sanctions. Should the court impose sanctions on Burger?

(2) During discovery, Lana learned Burger used chemicals to enlarge its homegrown produce. Burger intended to present a document during trial that described the chemicals used on the food, but Burger never disclosed this document to Lana. As a result, Lana requested that Burger produce information on all the chemicals used on all its plants through the plants' entire lifespans and how often the plants were sprayed with these chemicals. Burger gave Lana access to thousands of disorganized paper records stored in its large warehouse. Lana filed a motion to compel a summary of the documents and not warehouse access. Should the court grant Lana's motion?

(3) A few years ago, Burger's attorney created a list of restaurants that purchased Burger's produce. After Lana filed the lawsuit, Burger's attorney marked the restaurants that never experienced food poisoning as a note to herself. Lana filed a motion to compel Burger to produce the list with the attorney's notes. Should the court grant Lana's motion?

(4) Burger's manager and attorney discussed potential restaurants as witnesses. Lana requested a recording of the conversation. The only people present were the manager, attorney, and the attorney's legal assistant. The assistant was taking notes for the attorney. Burger refused to produce the recording. Lana filed a motion to compel. Should the court grant Lana motion?

Question 7
(40 minutes)

Bruce published a children's book about two animals on a journey to save the world from a demon. The themes, scenes, and characters in Bruce's story were very similar to Ariel's drafted manuscript. Ariel's manuscript was only accessible to Ariel and her staff. Ariel sued Bruce for copyright infringement in the United States District Court of State X. Copyright infringement requires Ariel to prove (1) Bruce actually copied her work and (2) copying was a misappropriation of Ariel's work because she had the exclusive rights to distribute the work as the original creator.

During discovery, the parties learned that Ariel and Bruce had attended the same writer's convention a few years ago. Ariel and Bruce participated in a workshop where they were assigned to the same group. Their group collectively created the concept for a children's book as a workshop exercise. Ariel suggested that the group's storyline include two animals on a journey to save the world from being destroyed. Ariel's idea and several scenes were presented to all workshop attendees.

Ariel admitted, in her deposition, that she gave the convention members her blessing to use her idea, but did not intend for them to copy all the scenes. Bruce stated that he thought of the ideas on his own and never copied Ariel. Bruce claimed he did not remember Ariel's ideas from the convention. Bruce filed a motion for summary judgment. The court denied Bruce's motion.

At trial, Bruce testified that his friend worked with Ariel, but claimed his friend never spoke about Ariel's manuscript. Ariel believed Bruce's friend gave Bruce access to her ideas. Ariel filed for a motion for judgment as a matter of law. The court denied Ariel's motion.

The jury ruled in favor of Ariel. The jury gave Ariel 90% of Bruce's royalties because they determined it was her story. Bruce filed for a motion for a judgment non-withstanding the jury verdict. The court asked Ariel to take a lower judgment because the recovery was unfair. Ariel refused. The court granted Bruce's motion and ordered a new trial.

Discuss whether the court correctly granted each motion.

☆ don't do this one — not on the exam ☆

Question 8
(45 minutes)

Wanda works as the team lead for the retail department at Theme Park. Wanda applied for the manager position, but was denied the job. Wanda is a person of color. The promotion was given to Kathy, a White applicant. Federal Statute § 42 prohibits discrimination against persons based on age, race, and gender. Wanda filed a racial discrimination case against Theme Park because Kathy and Wanda were equally qualified, but Wanda was not chosen. Out of the 30 managers at Theme Park, there is only one minority manager even though 80% of the team leads and associates at Theme Park are minorities.

(1) The jury ruled in favor of Wanda. Theme Park appealed the decision on the basis that there is no legal requirement to chose a minority over a White person if the candidates are equally qualified. Theme Park believes the goal of the racial discrimination statute is to prevent companies from selecting unqualified White candidates over more qualified people of color. Should Theme Park's appeal be granted?

(2) Vu is also a person of color. Vu is the team lead of the food and beverage (F&B) department at Theme Park. Vu heard about Wanda's victory and felt he experienced similar discrimination when he applied for the F&B manager position. Vu was denied the promotion and the position was given to a White applicant. Vu filed a racial discrimination claim against Theme Park and alleged he was the prevailing party under the doctrines of res judicata and collateral estoppel. Is Vu correct?

(3) Wanda filed another lawsuit against Theme Park for its failure to give minorities access to manager training programs. Theme Park claims res judicata bars Wanda from filing the lawsuit. Is Theme Park correct?

Constitutional Law Questions

Question 1
(50 minutes)

Congress passed the Pollution Prevention Act (PPA) because pollution in the United States had dramatically increased over the past few years. The act required federal agencies to use the best pollution-control techniques available in all their operations. State agencies were not required to follow the PPA, but if a state adopted the PPA, then the state would receive an additional 10% in federal funding for the state's environmental programs.

Although 70% of the land in State Z was wetlands and grasslands, State Z thought the federal program was too strict. State Z adopted its own regulations that encouraged state agencies to consider the environment when making decisions, but State Z did not establish any concrete requirements. As a result, several agencies in State Z used substandard pollution-control techniques.

Erin is an environmental and animal rights activist who lives in State B. Erin regularly travels to State Z to observe animals in the wild. Since State Z reduced its pollution standards, Erin noticed more pollution and fewer animals. Erin is extremely distraught because she can no longer see the animals thrive in their natural habitats. Erin believes State Z's actions are encouraging the abuse of the earth.

Animal Activism (AA) is a State Z agency responsible for rehabilitating wild animals. The number of injured animals in State Z increased after State Z officially relaxed its pollution-control requirements. However, AA is unable to treat the injured animals because it lacks the necessary resources. AA wants more money and stricter pollution control, but needs to preserve its relationship with the state to ensure the agency is not shut down.

Erin sued State Z in federal district court for violating AA's and her constitutional rights. Erin requests injunctive relief. Erin wants State Z to adopt the PPAs required pollution-control techniques. Shortly after Erin filed the lawsuit, State Z gave AA an additional 15% in state funding.

State Z claims (1) the federal court has no power to review the case, (2) Erin has no standing, and (3) the PPA is an unconstitutional use of Congress's spending power because it violates the 10th Amendment. Discuss the merits of State Z's arguments.

Question 2
(30 minutes)

A well-known research study revealed that tobacco causes lung cancer and that lung cancer had been the leading cause of death in the United States for the past three years. In reaction to the study, Congress passed the Cancer Kills Act. The act required all stores selling cigarettes to pay an additional 8% in federal taxes on their annual cigarette sales. The act also stated that stores within four blocks of a middle school or high school must pay an additional 1% in federal taxes if the store fails to lock the cigarettes in a container behind the counter. The tax revenue would be used to research a cure for lung cancer. The average state sales tax in the U.S. is 8.45%.

To ensure cigarette sellers complied with the Cancer Kills Act, the act required state governments to regulate the stores within their borders by any reasonable means. If the state refused to regulate the program or did a poor job, then the state would lose half of the cancer research funding granted to the state by the federal government.

(1) State B claims the Cancer Kills Act is an unconstitutional use of the federal government's taxing and spending powers. Discuss the merits of State B's claim.

(2) The governor in State C makes annual visits to all the cigarette stores within State C's borders. During a visit to Greg's store, the governor realized Greg failed to put the cigarettes in a locked container behind the counter. Greg's store is two blocks from a high school. The governor fined Greg $1200 and prohibited Greg from selling cigarettes. Greg claims Congress unconstitutionally delegated its power to the state governor. Discuss the merits of Greg's claim.

Question 3
(45 minutes)

The president created the National Anti-Terrorist Center (NATC) to lead the fight against local and foreign terrorist activities. The president also proposed a bill that allowed the NATC to request any metadata related to user activity from all internet and phone service providers in the country. The president believed access to metadata would help the government identify threats in advance and timely deploy military protection to civilians.

A few months after Congress rejected the bill, the president issued an Executive Order that granted NATC access to metadata related to user activity from all internet and phone companies. Congress was silent about the president's order.

The president also entered an international treaty with Country A, B, and C to protect U.S. citizens from being detained overseas. The treaty stated that if any country to the treaty declares one of the other country's citizens a terrorist, then it must send the citizen back to his or her home country to be tried under the home country's laws. Congress was silent about the treaty.

(1) Bonnie, a dual-citizen of the U.S. and Country A, was declared a terrorist in the U.S. and detained in State X. Bonnie is not a citizen of State X, but a citizen of State Y. Without checking Bonnie's citizenship status, the state governor authorized her deportation to Country A to be tried under Country A's laws. (a) Bonnie sued the governor for pain and suffering caused by her deportation. (b) Bonnie also demanded the treaty be deemed unconstitutional. Discuss the merits of her claims.

(2) Bonnie worked for Digital, an internet provider. After Bonnie's arrest, NATC demanded that Digital send all Bonnie's user metadata to NATC immediately. Digital claimed the president's order was unconstitutional and it was not required to provide NATC with any metadata. Discuss the merits of Digital's claims.

Question 4
(60 minutes)

Congress passed the Dangerous Firearms Act (DFA). The DFA made it illegal for civilians to own any type of firearm without a license, required firearms to be sold in a hard case, and required owners to put their guns in a hard case whenever transporting the guns from one location to another. Anyone who violated the DFA would be fined $500 per a violation.

In State X, hunting was a common way to obtain food. To make life easier for its citizens, State X passed the Hunter's Act. Section 1 of the Hunter's Act allows State X residents to freely sell, buy, own, and use hunting rifles within state borders without a license. State X sells hunting rifles that include a trigger-identification system to prevent guns from being fired by anyone other than its authorized user. The trigger-identifications made the guns safer, but were rarely used by other manufacturers. Section 2 of the Hunter's Act made it illegal for anyone to sell or possess any type of rifle without a trigger-identification system within state borders. Anyone who violated the Hunter's Act would pay a fine of $100 and have their gun confiscated.

Chester, a resident of State X, purchased a hunting rifle while visiting State Z and registered it under the DFA. State Z does not sell hard cases. State Z only manufactures and sells rifles within its borders. State Z's guns have no trigger-identification system.

(1) While transporting the rifle from the store to his hotel in State Z, Chester did not put the rifle in a hard case. Chester was fined $500 by the federal government. Chester sued State Z to collect the $500 because State Z did not sell any hard cases. State Z claims the DFA is an unconstitutional use of Congress's legislative power under the Commerce Clause. Will State Z prevail?

(2) Chester entered State X borders with a State Z rifle. He was fined $100 and the border patrol confiscated his State Z rifle. Chester claims that Section 2 of the Hunter's Act violates the Commerce Clause. Is he correct?

(3) The rifles that State Y manufactures include state-of-the-art safety catches to prevent accidental discharge, but no trigger-identification system. State Y wants to sell its rifles in State X, but was denied access to the State X market under the Hunter's Act. State Y claims the Hunter's Act is unconstitutional because the DFA preempts the Hunter's Act. Is State Y correct?

Question 5
(35 minutes)

Victoria leased a building and parking lot from Greenwood Authority (Greenwood), an agency run by State Z. Victoria opened a private restaurant that only served vegan food. Her restaurant was the only vegan restaurant in State Z. The lease stated, "Greenwood is not responsible for repairing any damage caused by the tenant or natural disasters, but Greenwood will do annual inspections to remedy any normal wear and tear to the property." Greenwood provided no financial assistance and never interfered with Victoria's daily management of the restaurant.

To lower the unemployed rates of its citizens, State Z passed the Local Employment Act. The act required 50% of the employees of businesses operating within State Z to be State Z citizens. Currently, Victoria has a staff of nine people; four are State Z citizens and five are out-of-state citizens. Victoria wanted to hire an additional waiter, but refused to employ anyone who ate animal products. 97% of the population in State Z is omnivorous.

Victoria had two final candidates for the position, Terry and Jon. Terry is an international visiting student studying in State Z for a year. Terry is a vegan. Jon is an animal-rights activist, vegetarian, and State Z citizen. Victoria offered Terry the job after she learned Jon ate products from animal-derived substances.

State Z instructed Greenwood to ensure Victoria complied with the Local Employment Act by hiring another State Z citizen or firing one of her out-of-state employees. Greenwood forwarded the message to Victoria, but took no further action. Victoria fired Terry.

(1) Terry claims Greenwood violated his constitutional rights. Greenwood files for a motion to dismiss on the grounds that there is no state action. Should the court grant Greenwood's motion?

(2) Assume Greenwood's motion to dismiss was denied. Terry claims the Local Employment Act violates the Privileges and Immunities Clauses of the 14th Amendment and Article IV? Should the court declare the act unconstitutional?

Question 6
(90 minutes)

Over the past five years, the number of Asians immigrating to the United States had increased. Some citizens believed the increase was caused by mail-order brides resurfacing, a practice where women listed themselves in catalogs and were selected by men from another country for marriage. Citizens blamed Asian immigrants for the decrease in the percentage of American citizens being accepted to college. Citizens believed Asians created additional competition in higher education for Americans, but there is no statistically significant research to link the citizens' beliefs to immigration. State D passed the Asian Immigrant Act (AIA) that stated the following:

SECTION A: Asian immigrants between the ages of 18 and 30 cannot marry U.S. citizens unless the immigrant already received a college degree from a university accredited by the United States Department of Education.

SECTION B: Parents cannot teach their child a foreign language until the child reaches high school.

SECTION C: If an American citizen sponsors the immigration of a family member, then the citizen cannot live with the immigrant until the immigrant becomes a U.S. citizen unless the immigrant is the citizen's spouse or child.

Ron, an American citizen, fell in love with Lian. She was 28 years old, never previously visited America, and had a two-year old daughter. Ron sponsored the immigration of Lian and her daughter to America and they lived together in a single-story home. Ron and Lian were denied their marriage license under the AIA because Lian did not have a college education. Lian and her daughter were not allowed to live with Ron because he sponsored their immigration. Lian's daughter was eventually removed from her care and put in child protective services because Lian continued to teach her daughter Chinese.

Ron and Lian file a lawsuit claiming the AIA was unconstitutional under the 14th Amendment. Discuss the merits of their claim.

Question 7
(60 minutes)

Melinda was a teacher at Hope Elementary (Hope), which is a public school in State B. Melinda became pregnant after a one-night stand with a stranger. Hope had a rule that any teacher who became pregnant before marriage must resign or be immediately terminated. The school believed that teachers with children born out of wedlock were bad role models and sent a promiscuous message to the students.

Melinda had worked at Hope for many years and loved her job. She decided to get an abortion. However, to get an abortion from a licensed physician, State B required consent from the father and a one-page written reflection on why the mother wanted an abortion. State B also charged an extremely expensive fee. State B's population and government legislators supported pro-life campaigns. Melinda did not know how to contact the father, did not want to reflect, and was unable to afford the safe abortion on her teacher's salary. Melinda's only alternative was to get an illegal abortion from an unlicensed doctor. Illegal procedures have a high possibility of causing permanent damage to the uterus.

Hope heard rumors about Melinda's pregnancy and requested she resign. Melinda demanded a hearing to review her performance. Melinda always had exemplary reviews and was popular among the students and their parents. Melinda also wanted to keep living in the rent control apartment owned by the school. Hope denied her request and fired her. Hope told Melinda that she could continue living in the apartment, but would need to pay an additional $200 a month because she was no longer an employee at the school.

Melinda sued Hope for injunctive relief. She wants to be rehired and to reinstate her original monthly rent. Melinda claims the state's abortion laws and Hope Elementary's actions are unconstitutional under the 14th Amendment. How should the court rule?

Question 8
(60 minutes)

The entertainment industry suffers from an extreme lack of racial, gender, and religious diversity. To diversify the profession, State Z passed a law with the following provisions:

SECTION A: All casting notices must be posted on State Z's Labor & Workforce Employment Opportunities website. If the company fails to post the film's casting notices on the website, then the company will lose its permission to film within State Z's borders.

SECTION B: All casting notices must promote diversity. Notices will undergo a review by State Z's Diversity in Film Agency (DFA) before posting. If more than 60% of the casting notices from the film fail the DFA's review, then the company will lose its permission to film within State Z's borders.

SECTION C: If the company's casting notices pass the DFA's review, then State Z will give the company additional funding to hold an event that discusses how the film promotes diversity. The company can accept or deny the money.

The Church of Religions (Church) is a film organization focused on raising awareness about commonly-practiced religions. The casting notices from Church's first feature film passed the DFA's review and the organization received $10,000 from State Z to host a dinner discussing its views on the role of religion in film. Risky Studios (Risky) is a film studio that specializes in romantic films with graphic sexual scenes. Risky's casting notices requested only actors and actresses with sex appeal. Risky did not post its casting notices on the Labor & Workforce website and failed the DFA's review. Risky lost its filming permissions in State Z.

Risky filed a lawsuit claiming (1) Section C violates the Free Exercise and Establishment Clauses, (2) Section B, when applied to Risky's films, is overbroad, vague, and an unconstitutional content-based restriction, and (3) Section A is an invalid conduct regulation of speech. Discuss the merit of Risky's claims.

Contracts Questions

Question 1
(45 minutes)

Farmer hired Agent to sell 500 acres of Farmer's land and all the farming equipment on Farmer's property. Agent told Farmer he was a real estate expert, even though Agent had never sold a single property and was unlicensed. Agent learned his skills from online videos.

Agent provided Farmer with a standard form agreement that charged Farmer twice the normal commission rate of an entry-level real estate agent. The contract stated "Agent's duties are complete after the deal is closed." Farmer asked the Agent to explain the contract because Farmer had limited literacy. Agent told Farmer, "Don't worry. This form is just a formality." Farmer signed the contract.

Agent posted Farmer's land on the market. After six months, Agent arranged a meeting between Farmer and a potential buyer to discuss the terms of a purchase, but Buyer never showed up. Agent went to Buyer's home. When Buyer opened the door, Agent said, "You better close this deal with Farmer or you'll be sorry." Agent shoved the contract in Buyer's face and held out a pen. Buyer, who was only 17 years old, was scared by Agent's threats and immediately signed the contract. Buyer never paid Farmer any money.

Three weeks later, Buyer called Farmer and said she no longer wanted the land. Farmer asked Agent to continue selling the land, but Agent told Farmer that he no longer did real estate and claimed the deal closed when Buyer signed the contract. Farmer called Agent a fraud because Farmer believed Agent's duties were not completed until Farmer received the money from the sale.

(1) Farmer sued Buyer for breach of contract. What defenses can Buyer raise to defeat Farmer's claim? Only discuss affirmative defenses to contract formation.

(2) Agent filed a counter suit against Farmer for Agent's commission. What defenses can Farmer raise to defeat Agent's claim? Only discuss affirmative defenses to contract formation.

Question 2
(60 minutes)

Tim, an owner of a watch shop, emailed all the watch manufacturers in the state offering to purchase every Meko watch produced by the manufacturer over the next six months if the manufacturer gave Tim notice of the quantity produced on the 1st of each month.

WatchWorks emailed Tim, "We accept your offer. The cost is $10 per a watch. We will give you notice on the 14th of each month." Tim emailed, "Ok, but only if you deliver the watches to my shop on Z Street by the 28th of each month." WatchWorks never replied. ClockTime also replied to Tim's email. Tim entered into a valid written agreement with ClockTime.

On the 14th of the following month, WatchWorks did not give Tim notice of the quantity produced. A week before ClockTime's first delivery, Tim placed an advertisement in the newspaper offering to sell Meko watches at 50% off in exchange for antique watches. Tim considered any watch made before 1940 an antique watch. The following day, Customer went to the store and showed Tim a picture of his 1926 antique watch. Customer told Tim that the watch was at his parents' house, but he could bring the watch to the shop by next Friday. Tim gave the Customer a written note that stated "I will hold the 50% off Meko watch for Customer for two weeks."

On the way home, Tim was killed in a car accident. Tim's sole heir was his son. On the 28th of that month, ClockTime and WatchWorks delivered their first batch of watches to Tim's shop. Tim's son rejected WatchWorks's goods and accepted ClockTime's shipment. A week later, Customer returned on Friday to find Tim's son at the counter. Tim's son told Customer that he sold the Meko watch to someone else and offered to sell Customer a different watch at 50% off. Customer refused and demanded the original Meko watch for 50% off. Tim's son refused.

(1) Customer sued Tim's estate for breach of contract. Was there a valid contract? Do not address consideration.
(2) WatchWorks sued Tim's estate for breach of contract. Was there a valid contract? Do not address consideration.

Question 3
(45 minutes)

Pet Shop asked Marcie, a professional cat sitter, to foster Jumper, a cat from the adoption center, until they found him a permanent home. Marcie agreed, but said Pet Shop must give her a free cat tree once Jumper was adopted. Pet Shop said they would consider it.

A week later, Pet Shop emailed a contract to Marcie that agreed to her cat-tree terms, but added, "Marcie must keep Jumper in healthy condition." Marcie replied to Pet Shop's email with an updated contract that stated, "Marcie will receive free cat toys if Jumper has no medical problems." Pet Shop never responded to Marcie's email.

The following day, Marcie picked up Jumper from Pet Shop. After four weeks of fostering, Jumper ran away. Marcie put posters with her phone number on every street corner around town offering a $200 reward for the return of the cat. Jumper was missing for two weeks.

One Wednesday morning, Bella saw Jumper in the bushes. She remembered Marcie's reward posters and captured Jumper. Bella stopped by Marcie's house, but no one was home. Bella dropped a letter in Marcie's mailbox stating "I will come claim my reward after work on Friday because I found your cat!" On Thursday, before Marcie received Bella's letter, Marcie removed all her posters. Marcie realized she no longer wanted Jumper because he always scratched her furniture. On Friday afternoon, while walking to Marcie's house, Bella noticed the reward posters were removed. Bella assumed Marcie had received her letter. When Bella arrived, Marcie told Bella to keep Jumper and refused to give Bella the $200.

(1) Bella decided to adopt Jumper and sued Marcie for the reward money. Was there a valid contract between Bella and Marcie? Do not address consideration.

(2) Marcie sued Pet Shop for the free cat tree and toys. Was there a valid contract between Marcie and Pet Shop? Do not address consideration.

Question 4
(30 minutes)

Phil was a lifeguard at the city's community center. One summer afternoon, while on duty, Phil saved Sharon from drowning. Sharon owned a luxury car dealership that sold cars valued at $800,000 or more. Sharon was so grateful to be alive that she offered to give Phil any car from her dealership as payment for his services. Phil refused and said, "I was only doing my job." However, Sharon insisted until Phil finally agreed.

For the past year, Phil worked at the community center because the community center was only a few miles from his home and his only mode of transportation was a bicycle. After saving Sharon, Phil sold his bicycle and quit his lifeguard job. Phil intended to use his new car to find a better job in the neighboring town.

When Phil arrived at Sharon's dealership to claim his car, Sharon refused to let him take a car for free. She told Phil the car was a gift, but he needed to pay the taxes on the car. Phil refused. Phil sued Sharon for breach of contract.

(1) Sharon argues there was no valid consideration. Will Sharon prevail?

(2) Assume there is a valid contract and Sharon breached. Is specific performance an appropriate remedy?

Question 5
(50 minutes)

Rose went to Best Beds Warehouse to purchase a pillow-top mattress. John, the owner of Best Beds, obtained most of his inventory by burglarizing other mattress stores and reselling their products at a lower price. Rose knew John since they were children and decided to capitalize on his illegal operation.

Rose and John agreed that Rose would pay cash for a king-size mattress and John would deliver the mattress next week. John provided Rose with a confirmation memo with his company's logo printed on the bottom. The memo included a two-year warranty for free, but did not include the price of the mattress. The warranty allowed Rose to replace her bed with a new bed under any circumstances.

A few days later, John called Rose and told her that he needed to modify the contract because he incurred some unexpected costs. John said that under the new contract, Rose must pay $10 a month to keep the two-year warranty. Rose said that $10 a month was fine.

On delivery day, John's employee arrived with Rose's bed. She gave the employee $600, but the employee told her that the price was $1200. Rose told the employee she would work out the price with John. The employee accepted the $600 and left the bed with Rose.

The following day, John called Rose and demanded an additional $1800 because the actual market value of the bed was $2400. Rose refused to pay more than $1200, which was the price of similar beds sold at John's warehouse. Rose also said she was not going to pay $10 a month for the warranty.

(1) John sued Rose for breach of contract. Is there a valid contract?
(2) Assume the court ruled in favor of John. What remedies are available to him?

Question 6
(75 minutes)

Stephanie offered to pay Ronnie $80,000 a year if he agreed to relocate with her overseas to a village in the rainforest and be her bodyguard for the remainder of her life. Ronnie agreed, but only if Stephanie paid for all his packing expenses. Stephanie told Ronnie it would not be a problem and gave him a check for $80,000.

Ronnie hired his close friend, Lucy, to help with packing. Lucy and Ronnie executed a valid written contract that stated:

> Lucy promises to help Ronnie pack for his relocation in return for Ronnie's promise to sponsor Lucy's next visit to the village in the rainforest.[9]

Ronnie and Lucy signed the agreement, printed copies, and sent a copy to Stephanie who agreed to the terms. While packing, Ronnie told Lucy he was definitely going to cover her flight to the rainforest to show his thanks.

Ronnie and Stephanie moved the following day. A few weeks later, Lucy asked Ronnie to reimburse her for the rainforest airfare. Ronnie forwarded Lucy's email to Stephanie who told Lucy the contract only included room and board. Lucy argued with Ronnie until he finally agreed to pay for her flight, room, and board. Ronnie told Stephanie not to worry about sponsoring Lucy's trip because he took care of it.

During Lucy's trip, Ronnie and Lucy fall in love. After only a few months of work, Ronnie quit and left Stephanie to fend for herself in the rainforest. He moved back to the U.S. with Lucy.

Stephanie sued Ronnie for breach of contract and demanded that he return to the village. Ronnie filed a counter claim demanding that Stephanie pay for Lucy's flight. Who will prevail and what are the available remedies?

---

9. The plain meaning of sponsor is to provide funds for a project, activity, or the person carrying it out.

Question 7
(60 minutes)

On Monday, Samantha went to Hiro's electronics shop to purchase stereos for her dance party on Sunday. Samantha told Hiro, "I need a stereo that will play all types of CDs." Hiro convinced Samantha to purchase four of his Model A2 stereos for $450. Hiro told Samantha, "You shouldn't have any problems. These stereos can do anything related to music." Samantha paid in full and set up a delivery date for Saturday.

Samantha hired Lupita to cater her party. Samantha and Lupita executed a valid written agreement that stated "The amount of damages recoverable by either party in the event of a breach is $5000, as liquidated damages and not as a penalty." $5000 was twice the value of Lupita's catering services.

On Tuesday, Hiro delivered the four stereos. Samantha plugged in the stereos and discovered that one of them did not turn on. She immediately called Hiro and asked for a new stereo. Hiro apologized and agreed to deliver a new stereo by Saturday.

A couple days later, Samantha took out the MP3 CDs she wanted to play at the party and realized the A2 stereos only played audio CDs with songs in WAV format. Samantha called Hiro to complain that the stereo did not meet her needs. She demanded four stereos that played MP3s. Hiro told Samantha that he couldn't make the exchange because his store did not carry MP3 stereos. She requested a full refund, but Hiro said all sales are final and refused.

Samantha called all the electronic shops in the city, but no shop sold stereos that played MP3s. She called Lupita on Saturday and told Lupita that the party was cancelled because she did not have the music. Lupita was upset because she already purchased the food and completed the preparations for the party. Hiro never delivered the fixed stereo on Saturday.

(1) Samantha sued Hiro for breach of contract. Will she prevail? Do not discuss remedies.

(2) Lupita sued Samantha for breach of contract. Will she prevail? Do not discuss formation.

(3) Assume the court ruled in favor of Lupita. What remedies are available to her?

Question 8
(75 minutes)

In November, Pablo hired Contractor to build him an in-law unit in the backyard. Pablo agreed to pay $200,000 for the labor, if Contractor would pay for the materials. Pablo told the Contractor that he needed the unit to be completed by January 28th, which was the day his parents planned to move in. Contractor said it would not be a problem. They executed a valid written agreement that stated, "Pablo will pay Contractor $200,000 for the labor required to complete the in-law unit. This agreement contains the full statement of Pablo and Contractor's agreement."

On January 2nd, Contractor completed 75% of the project and spent $30,000 on materials and $60,000 on labor. However, Contractor told Pablo, "I might not be able to complete the in-law unit by January 28th because the heavy rains in December delayed construction by a month." Pablo panicked and called Joseph, who did last minute construction jobs, to complete the in-law unit by January 28th. Joseph agreed to help Pablo for $100,000 if Pablo paid Joseph in advance. Pablo agreed and paid Joseph in full.

The following day, Contractor told Pablo his calculations were mistaken and the unit would be completed by the 28th. Pablo told Contractor not to worry because he hired someone else to complete the unit. Contractor stopped working on the property. Pablo never paid Contractor any money for his services.

Joseph never came to work on the in-law unit and on January 28th, the in-law unit was incomplete. Pablo's parents were forced to stay in hotel and put their furniture in a storage unit. Pablo paid for their lodging and storage costs. After two months, Pablo's parents moved to Pablo's sister's house because the unit was still not finished. Today, the value of the incomplete in-law unit is $150,000. The value of a completed in-law unit is $250,000. The cost to complete the in-law unit is $40,000 in labor and materials.

(1) Contractor sued Pablo for breach of contract. Will Contractor succeed?

(2) Assume the court ruled in favor of Contractor. What remedies are available to Contractor?

(3) Pablo sued Joseph for breach of contract. Will Pablo succeed?

(4) Assume the court ruled in favor of Pablo and not Joseph. What remedies are available to Pablo?

Criminal Law Questions

Question 1
(60 minutes)

For many years, Desmond was the physician in a small mountain village. Desmond received training from the previous physician, but never went to medical school. Desmond was competent and qualified to diagnose patients in his village, but he wanted to do something different. Desmond moved to a city in State Z and started his own medical practice.

Blair was Desmond's patient. She suffered from depression because her relationship with her brother was deteriorating. Desmond prescribed her psilocybin mushrooms to help her develop a more positive outlook on life. The mushrooms were commonly used in his village, but patients often suffered from hallucinations within the first few hours after taking the drug. Desmond did not inform Blair about the side effects.

That evening, Blair went home and took the mushrooms before bed. Blair had an unusual reaction to the drug; Blair started sleepwalking. She went to her brother's home, kidnapped his pet ferret, and put the ferret in her shed. Blair woke up and did not remember anything. A couple days later, her brother found his ferret in the shed. The ferret's health was in poor condition.

State Z passed the following statute to discourage the operation of fraudulent medical practices, selling addictive drugs that impair the senses, and abuse of animals.

SECTION 100: Anyone who purposefully impersonates a doctor is subject to fines and jail time.

SECTION 200: Anyone in possession of marijuana, cocaine, ecstasy, morphine, or any other dangerous substance is subject to fines.

SECTION 300: Anyone who recklessly causes harm to someone's pet is subject to fines and jail time.

The plain meaning of doctor is a person skilled in the science of medicine, or a person who is trained and licensed to treat sick people. State Z's Drug

Enforcement Agency considers psilocybin mushrooms and the drugs listed in Section 200 controlled substances.

(1) Is Desmond guilty of violating Section 100?
(2) Is Blair guilty of violating Section 200 and 300?

Question 2
(45 minutes)

Greg lost his job, which caused extreme financial hardship. If Greg did not figure out how to pay the bills, then his wife intended to leave him. Greg decided to kidnap and hold someone for ransom. Greg asked Jared for help. Jared refused because he did not want anyone to get hurt. Jared knew Greg's temper was out of control. However, after Greg promised that he only wanted the money and would not hurt anyone, Jared agreed to help.

Greg and Jared grabbed a teenage boy at the mall, put in him the van, drove him to an abandoned warehouse, and locked him in a room. Greg and Jared could not send a ransom note to the boy's parents because the boy refused to share his contact information. After a week of unsuccessfully trying to get the boy to speak, Greg saw a missing persons report about the boy on the news. Greg panicked.

Greg told the boy, "You better tell me the information or I'm going to kill you." The boy refused and spit in Greg's face. Greg was frustrated. He grabbed his pocketknife and stabbed the boy in the stomach. The boy screamed and passed out from the pain. Greg told Jared they needed to leave the boy at the mall because the boy needed medical attention.

Jared and Greg left the boy in the parking structure and called 911. The paramedics arrived and took the boy to the hospital. The boy died because he loss too much blood.

(1) Are Jared and Greg guilty of battery, assault, and kidnapping? Do not discuss conspiracy liability or accomplice liability.
(2) Is Greg guilty of murder? Do not address causation or concurrence.
(3) Jared is charged with homicide. Is he guilty under the felony murder rule? Do not address causation or concurrence.

Question 3
(40 minutes)

A year ago, Bain flew through the front windshield during a car accident because he did not wear a seatbelt. After the accident, Bain suffered from post-traumatic stress. Alicia wanted to prank Bain to help him get over his trauma, but she mainly thought it would be entertaining to simulate his previous car accident. Alicia liked to play pranks and scare her friends.

Alicia asked Bain to join her on a joy ride in her new sports car. She promised Bain she would not drive fast. Bain agreed without hesitation. It is a felony to drive over 100 miles per hour on the highway.

Alicia rigged Bain's seatbelt to detach when she pressed a button. When they reached 105 miles per an hour, Alicia pressed the release button and Bain's seatbelt unlatched. Bain frantically tried to fix it, but he was unsuccessful. Bain was scared. As Alicia laughed and said, "Got ya!" the car spun out of control and hit the center divide.

Bain flew through the front windshield and suffered injuries, but miraculously he did not die. Bain stood up, looked at the car wreck, panicked, and immediately had a heart attack. Bain fell to the ground in pain. Another car on the highway was unable to stop and hit Bain. He died on impact.

Is Alicia guilty of homicide? Do not discuss voluntary manslaughter.

Question 4
(60 minutes)

Marie is an old, wealthy woman. Percy is Marie's in-home care provider. Percy intended to kill Marie after he convinced her to devise her fortune to him. Percy isolated Marie in her mansion and prevented her family from visiting. As a result, Marie became dependent on Percy. She believed her family no longer cared about her.

Marie was saving money for her funeral. Every month, she gave Percy money to deposit in her bank account, but Percy used the cash to pay off his gambling debt. Percy decided not to kill Marie because he enjoyed her company and she was helping him slowly pay off his debts.

One day, while Percy was out, Marie's daughter stopped by the mansion and asked Marie why she was avoiding the family. Marie was confused and confronted Percy when he returned. Percy told Marie, "We'll talk later," and quickly retreated to the kitchen.

Marie's daughter had brought a cake and left it on the kitchen counter. Percy saw the cake and sprinkled peanut oil on the icing because Marie was allergic to peanuts. Percy wanted Marie to believe her daughter did not care about her health. After Marie's daughter left, Percy served a piece of cake to Marie and she had a life-threatening reaction.

Percy did not intend for Marie to have an extreme reaction. He tried to find Marie's EpiPen, but failed. Percy told Marie that it was her daughter who poisoned the cake and that Marie's family could not be trusted. In her last breath, Marie said, "I can only trust you. Take this, sell it, and enjoy your life." Marie gave Percy her jewelry and died. Percy sold the jewelry for thousands of dollars.

Is Percy guilty of (1) embezzlement of Marie's funeral money, (2) larceny of Marie's jewelry, and (3) homicide of Marie. Do not discuss felony murder.

Question 5
(35 minutes)

Felicia is bipolar, suffers from obsessive-compulsive disorder, and has a disability that makes it difficult for her to understand social situations. Felicia worked with Rhonda and was obsessed with Rhonda's beautiful scarf. Felicia asked Rhonda, "Can I please have your scarf?" Rhonda thought Felicia was making a joke and replied, "Sure, if you can steal it from me." Rhonda laughed and walked away.

One day, Felicia noticed that Rhonda left the scarf in the office. Felicia thought to herself, "This is my chance to get the scarf." Felicia purchased black clothes and prepared to steal the scarf that evening. At 5:45 PM, Felicia used her employee ID to enter the office building, snuck into Rhonda's office, and stole the scarf.

The next day, Felicia wanted to show off her accomplishment. Felicia wore Rhonda's scarf to work. Rhonda saw Felicia and demanded that Felicia return her scarf. Felicia said, "No, I fulfilled your condition. This scarf is mine." Rhonda ignored Felicia and grabbed the scarf.

Felicia's bipolar disorder kicked in. Felicia screamed, "I'll kill you." She pushed Rhonda with extreme force. Rhonda fell and hit her head on the floor. Rhonda was unconscious. Felicia immediately felt horrible and called the paramedics. Felicia told the operator that she pushed Rhonda because she could not control her anger. Rhonda is in a coma.

(1) Is Felicia guilty of burglary?
(2) Is Felicia guilty of attempted murder?
(3) Felicia claims she is not guilty of burglary or attempted murder due to insanity. Will she succeed?

Question 6
(50 minutes)

Argo is an undercover police officer trying to infiltrate his Uncle Danny's drug-trafficking business. Argo asked Danny's son, Ben, to join the family business. Ben originally said no, but their mutual friend, Carl, convinced Ben it would be a good idea. Argo, Ben, and Carl joined the business. Argo was responsible for accounting and Carl sold the drugs. Danny only spoke to Ben about the trio's assignments.

Argo, Ben, and Carl were Danny's top sellers. Danny decided to give them a more challenging task. Danny told Ben the trio must intercept a newspaper delivery with drugs hidden in the newspaper bundles. Danny provided them with the guns, clothes, and vehicles that they needed to perform the job.

On the day of the heist, Ben told Argo and Carl, "I'm calling the police. What we are doing is wrong." Carl replied, "Go ahead." After Carl left, Argo told Ben not to worry because he was a police officer and would handle everything. Ben asked if he could do anything to help and Argo said no.

Argo and Carl drove to the interception point. When Carl got out of the car to steal the newspapers, Argo pulled out his gun and told Carl, "you are under arrest." Carl surrendered. Argo started to handcuff Carl, but Carl tried to grab Argo's gun. In the struggle, Carl accidentally killed Argo with the gun. Carl ran away.

(1) Are Ben, Carl, and Danny guilty of conspiracy to run an illegal drug-trafficking business?
(2) Is Carl guilty of solicitation?
(3) Assume Carl is found guilty of killing Argo. Are Ben and Danny guilty of homicide under conspiracy liability and accomplice liability?

Question 7
(60 minutes)

For the past month, Neil egged Mr. Liam's house every weekend. Matthew purchased the eggs and gave them to Neil. It is a misdemeanor to deface another person's property.

Mr. Liam purchased a bow and arrow to set a trap for the delinquents. If anyone entered Mr. Liam's front yard, then the arrow would activate. The following weekend, Matthew and Neil arrived to egg the house. As Neil opened the front gate, the arrow discharged and hit Neil in the chest. Neil fell to the floor and Matthew ran to his side.

Mr. Liam opened the front door and yelled, "Got you. Get off my property!" Matthew was not thinking clearly, grabbed the arrow from Neil's chest, and screamed, "You won't get me. Don't worry Neil! I'll protect you." Matthew threw the arrow at Mr. Liam and hit Mr. Liam in the arm. Mr. Liam fell to the ground. Matthew ran up to Mr. Liam and decided to steal his wallet. Matthew put his hand in Mr. Liam's pocket, but found no wallet.

Matthew grabbed Neil, who was already dead, and took him to Karen's house. Karen agreed to hide Matthew until everything settled down. Mr. Liam survived and told the authorities how to find Matthew. Eventually, after a few days of searching, Matthew was arrested.

(1) Mr. Liam is charged with the homicide of Neil. Discuss Mr. Liam's defenses.
(2) Is Matthew guilty of the attempted murder of Mr. Liam, robbery, and attempted robbery?
(3) Is Karen liable for Matthew's crimes as his accomplice?

Question 8
(60 minutes)

An avalanche trapped Penny, Rae, Sue, and Tracy in a cave. They had enough supplies for everyone to last a few days, but Penny and Rae believed there was a better chance of survival if one person sacrificed her life to save the other three. Sue and Tracy disagreed.

After one day, Tracy fell critically ill. Penny and Rae believed Tracy was going to die anyway and wanted to kill her. Penny grabbed her loaded gun, pointed it at Sue, and told Sue to kill Tracy or die in her place. Rae threw a needle with a deadly dose of morphine in Sue's direction. Sue feared for her life. Sue walked over to Tracy and administered the morphine. However, no one knew Tracy was already dead. Penny lowered the weapon.

The next day, they were rescued. For weeks, Sue had nightmares of Tracy's ghost. She started drinking at bars to make the guilt go away. One evening, Penny and Rae showed up at the bar. Sue was drunk and confronted them. Sue screamed, "I should have killed both of you and not Tracy." Sue grabbed a steak knife from the table and stabbed Rae. Penny ran out of the bar and Sue chased her, but Penny escaped. Rae died. Sue returned to the bar and was arrested.

(1) Is Sue guilty of killing Rae and attempting to kill Penny? Do not address causation, concurrence, depraved heart murder, involuntary manslaughter, or felony murder.

(2) Can Sue raise any defenses to her homicide of Tracy? Will they succeed?

(3) Is Penny guilt of conspiracy to commit murder and homicide of Tracy under accomplice liability?

Real Property Questions

Question 1
(60 minutes)

Wildwood was an extremely large parcel of unclaimed land on a remote island in the Pacific Ocean. In 1980, Cheng, an explorer, found the land while sailing. She claimed Wildwood by placing a flag on the land. When she returned home, Cheng's attorney drafted and recorded a deed to Wildwood and updated Cheng's will.

At the time of the grant, Cheng had no children. When Cheng wrote her will, Cheng's sister, Margaret, had two living children, Amelia and Deborah. Cheng's will stated, "After my death, Wildwood will go to my brother for life, and then to the children of my sister. However, if Amelia or Deborah ever sell the land, or use the land for a purpose other than exploring, such as residential or commercial purposes, then to my brother's son, Nick, for life, and then to Nick's heirs." Cheng loved nature and felt industrialization demolished natural habitats.

Sadly, in 1990, Cheng and her brother died in a car accident, which prompted Amelia to demand the distribution of Wildwood. In 1996, Amelia took possession of West Wildwood and built a three-story house for her family on the land. In 1997, Margaret gave birth to Phillip, and Deborah decided to live on East Wildwood, which was on the coastline of the island. When Deborah arrived, she discovered Theresa already occupied East Wildwood. Theresa had set up a small live-work coffee shop in 1986. Her coffee shop was visible from the ocean and regularly served sailors who passed by the island. When Theresa learned Deborah wanted to live on East Wildwood, Theresa asked Deborah to leave.

Amelia and Deborah immediately filed suit against Theresa claiming they owned Wildwood. Phillip joined the suit and claimed he owned 1/3 of Wildwood. Nick also joined the suit and claimed he was the sole owner of Wildwood. The statutory requirement for adverse possession is 10 years. Discuss the ownership interests of (1) Cheng in 1980, (2) Amelia, Deborah, Phillip, and Nick at the time of the grant, after C and B's death, and after Amelia built a home in 1996, and (3) Theresa.

Question 2
(60 minutes)

Michelle conveyed her two-story home, nicknamed Marshlands, to Garrett for life, and then if Elly graduated from college, to Elly, but if Elly did not graduate from college, then Garrett's children have the option to purchase the land. If Garrett's children refuse to purchase, then to Rachel. Garrett's children are Alice and Francis.

While living in Marshlands, Garrett failed to clean the home. The floors and walls became infested with mold. Garrett had several parties that ruined the grass in the front yard and broke the fence surrounding the house. Garrett also tore down the kitchen because it was old and the stoves were not working. Garrett installed a new granite kitchen where he could cook for his parties. Garrett's new kitchen increased the value of the home.

When Garrett died, Elly had not graduated from college. A year after Garrett's death, Michelle sold the land to Alice and Francis. The value of the home was only $300,000 because everything, except the kitchen, was in poor condition. However, Alice and Francis purchased the home for $600,000. Alice paid $80,000 and Francis paid $40,000 towards the down payment on Marshlands. Francis told Alice that she could live in the house because she technically owned more of the home. Francis never stepped foot in the house. Alice paid over $50,000 in repairs to make the home a livable space. Alice rented a room to a tenant for $2,000 a month. Alice devised her share in Marshlands to Rachel.

(1) Two years later, Elly graduated from college and demanded possession of Marshlands. Discuss the interests of the parties (a) at the time of the grant, (b) when Garrett died, (c) when Michelle sold the land to Alice and Francis, and (d) when Elly graduated from college. Who is the true owner?

(2) Assume Elly, Alice, Francis, and Rachel each had a valid future interest in Marshlands. If they sued Garrett's estate for damages incurred from his waste while he was on the property, will they succeed?

(3) Assume Francis and Alice were deemed the true owners. After Alice died, Rachel took possession of Marshlands. Francis sued Rachel for a portion of the rental proceeds and claimed he was the sole owner of Marshlands. Rachel refused to pay any rental proceeds and would not

vacate the property. Francis decided to stop paying the mortgage. Rachel demanded Francis financially contribute to the repairs that Alice originally made to the home and continue paying his share of the mortgage. How should the court rule on each issue?

Question 3
(45 minutes)

Katherine and Shane were engaged and purchased a condominium (condo) together. They evenly split the down payment on the condo and the deed included both their names. A month after closing the sale, the two moved into the home and got married.

Unfortunately, the couple ran into some hard times. They both moved out. Katherine unilaterally sold the condo to Max for $100,000. Max took possession of the condo and paid all the mortgages, taxes, and repairs on the property.

Two years later, Katherine and Shane reconciled and moved back into the condo because it held many memories. Luckily, Max did not live in the condo because he kept it as a spare home. The couple used Shane's key to move back into the condo. A year after they moved into Max's condo, Max got into a brawl at a bar that resulted in a four-year prison sentence.

During his imprisonment, Max lost his primary residence. When he was released, he returned to the spare condo where he found the couple living. During Max's incarceration, Katherine and Shane made improvements to the condo by installing a new built-in fireplace and a home stereo system that was latched onto the walls with hooks. Their improvements greatly increased the value of the condo.

Max was unsuccessful in evicting Katherine and Shane, but it did not matter because they moved out shortly due to disagreements. No one has paid the mortgage for the last six months.

(1) Max claims he rightfully owns the condo, including the new fireplace and home stereo system. Shane claims that he and Katherine share ownership because they are still married. The statutory period for adverse possession is five years. Who owns the land?

(2) Shane claims he is entitled to 50% of the proceeds from Katherine's sale of the condo to Max because Shane is Katherine's husband. Will he succeed?

(3) The bank sues Katherine for the mortgage payments. Will the bank succeed?

Question 4
(60 minutes)

On February 1, 2000, Landlord rented his two-bedroom, two-bath apartment to Tenant. They signed a written lease that included the following terms:

- The lease lasts for three years (ends on January 31, 2003).
- Rent is $1500 per a month and is due on the 1st of every month.
- Tenant cannot assign the lease without written consent from the landlord.
- Tenant is responsible for all repairs inside the apartment.

After two years, Tenant moved to Europe and transferred the remainder of the lease to Arthur. For the next 11 months, Arthur paid rent to Landlord on the 1st of every month. However, Arthur withheld rent when the plumbing in one of the bathrooms stopped working. Arthur immediately notified Landlord about the problem, but Landlord told Arthur that Arthur was responsible for the repairs. Since their altercation, Arthur paid no rent, but has lived on the property for three months.

Landlord sent a debt collector to Arthur's house every weekend to ask Arthur for the rent. This continued for a month, but Arthur never paid. Eventually, Arthur stopped answering the door. Landlord was upset and changed the locks. Arthur could not enter the apartment. While trying to get into the locked apartment, Arthur slipped on a loose wooden board in the hallway. Arthur fell and broke his wrist. A week later, on May 15, 2003, Arthur moved out. Neither party repaired the plumbing.

(1) Landlord claims Arthur renewed the lease and is responsible for another three years of rent. Landlord also sued Arthur for the unpaid rent. Discuss Landlord's claims and Arthur's defenses, if any.

(2) Landlord sued Tenant for all the unpaid rent from the original lease and Arthur's holdover tenancy. Landlord claims Tenant must pay rent on the renewed lease because Tenant never obtained written consent for the transfer and now Landlord is stuck with Arthur. Discuss Landlord's claims and Tenant's defenses, if any.

Question 5
(50 minutes)

Mia owned Shopacre, a parcel of land that she developed into a shopping center. In 1980, she built one giant building with three storefronts and a parking lot that surrounded the building. Mia retained the corner store on the right to sell clothing, but sold the other spaces. Charlie purchased the center store for his burger restaurant and the last space was sold to Jerry for his solo law practice.

Charlie, Mia, and Jerry agreed in writing that everyone could use the front and side parking lots for customer parking and product delivery, but must park their personal vehicles in the back parking lot. They also agreed that no one could add any structures to the roof of the building because it would block the view of the mountains from the parking lot. Mia ran a photo-taking station in the parking lot because the view was a popular spot for customers to take pictures.

Charlie and Mia entered an oral agreement that Charlie could use the back parking lot as a storage space for his personal belongings. Four years after they made the agreement, Charlie retired and sold his property to Sylvia, a professional hairdresser. Sylvia opened a salon. Before they closed the sale, Sylvia received a copy of the original agreement between Charlie, Mia, and Jerry, but she did not read it. Sylvia built a large billboard on the roof of her property advertising her services and built a storage shed for her equipment in the back parking lot. She eventually let her husband use the storage for his business. Sylvia also parked her car in the front parking lot without anyone's permission and never parked in the back lot.

Three years later, Jerry decided to go back to school and sold his property to Mia who created a warehouse for her clothing store. Mia realized she had fewer customers and determined that Sylvia was causing the problem.

Mia claims Sylvia has no right to be on any of her property and must remove the large billboard. Sylvia claims she has the right to (1) build a billboard, and (2) use the land for her storage, and (3) use all parking lots for parking and delivery. The prescriptive period is two years. Discuss their rights. Do not address real covenants and equitable servitudes.

Question 6
(60 minutes)

Luther purchased a plot of land that he intended to develop into a residential area. Luther divided the land into 20 lots, built a house on each lot, and created a homeowners' association. The houses were evenly distributed into four cul-de-sacs with five houses per a cul-de-sac. Luther sold 19 houses to people who agreed to only use the land for residential purposes. Richard purchased two of the 19 houses. Richard's two houses were adjacent to each other. Richard lived in one house and his sister, Janet, lived in the other.

Richard had a 10-year-old son, Sam, who loved to ride his bike. Janet, in a written note, allowed Sam to use her driveway to practice his BMX tricks. Eventually, Janet moved out and Richard wanted to sell the house. Martha wanted to purchase the home, but Richard said he would only sell the home to Martha if she promised to keep Sam's easement across her driveway for his bike riding. Martha said "Okay." Martha originally intended to allow Richard's son to use her driveway, but a few days after she moved into the home, she posted "No Trespassing" signs on her lawn. She was worried the bike would ruin her garden.

After two years of existence, the community's homeowners' association amended its written bylaws to require each property owner to pay $200 in annual dues to maintain the neighborhood's roads and to only paint their homes using pastel colors.

A year after the bylaws were amended, Luther sold the last home to Jasmin. She created a full-time music studio that attracted several customers. The customers monopolized the street parking in the cul-de-sac. Jasmin did not pay her maintenance dues and painted her house bright purple, blue, and pink to display her creative personality. Half of the community liked Jasmin's style and repainted their homes using bright colors.

(1) The homeowners' association immediately fined Jasmin $200, asked her to repaint her home to pastel colors, and told her that she could not run a music studio in the community. Does Jasmin need to comply with the requests?

(2) Richard claims Sam can ride his bike on Martha's driveway because Richard's sale to Martha was contingent upon Martha granting Sam an easement. Is he correct?

Question 7
(60 minutes)

For 10 years, Heidi owned a large factory on the outskirts of the city. When she opened the factory, Heidi built an adjacent, affordable daycare center where her staff could drop off their children. A new zoning ordinance stated that land outside the city was limited to industrial uses. The city wanted to protect children from pollutants by separating industrial and residential areas.

After Heidi heard about the ordinance, she applied for a use variance for the daycare center. The city board denied her request. The factory business is 100% of Heidi's household income. The lack of a childcare center caused Heidi's employees to seek other job opportunities, which made her factory seriously understaffed and hurt her production.

Heidi was a new, single mother of twins. She wanted to shorten her commute, which was currently two hours from the city, to make raising a family while working easier. Heidi started building a home on an undeveloped lot she owned near the factory. A week after construction began, the city took possession of Heidi's undeveloped lot. The city split the land into two lots. The government retained one lot to build a free legal aid center and returned the other lot to Heidi. The government told Heidi she could expand her factory, but could not build a home.

The long commute decreased the quality of Heidi's management and reduced her profits. Eventually, she was unable to pay the mortgage on the factory to the bank that gave her the original loan for the down payment. The bank's mortgage was properly recorded. Heidi took a second mortgage on the factory from a loan agency to pay the bank. The loan agency recorded the lien. After a few months, she defaulted on both loans.

The bank foreclosed on her property, but did not join the loan agency. The property was sold to Wesley. The foreclosure proceeds covered the foreclosure debt and the remaining surplus went to Heidi. The loan agency received nothing.

(1) After the sale, the loan agency immediately foreclosed on Wesley's property. Wesley claims the loan agency should sue Heidi because he owes it nothing. Who will prevail?

(2) Three months later, Heidi inherited a huge sum of money. She contacted the bank and offered to pay the foreclosure price to redeem her property. Will she succeed in repossessing the property?

(3) Heidi sued the city for unconstitutionally (i) lowering the utility of her land by denying her variance, (ii) using half of her undeveloped lot for the legal aid center, and (iii) restricting her use of the undeveloped lot. Assume the state followed all the correct notice and hearing procedures to pass the zoning ordinance. Discuss her rights and the city's defenses.

Question 8
(60 minutes)

Jim agreed to purchase Polly's Victorian home in State X. They signed a written contract that specified Jim would pay $500,000 to Polly for the Victorian home. State X is a race-notice jurisdiction.

Jim and Polly did not know that Carol had purchased the same Victorian home from the same seller as Polly. Carol had bought the Victorian home after Polly, but during the same month. Carol immediately recorded the deed, and moved in a couple days after the purchase. Polly never recorded the deed and did not move into the house. Jim was unaware that Polly did not live in the house. Polly sold the house to Jim five years after her original purchase of the home.

Before closing the sale with Jim, Polly died in a car accident. She had one daughter, Mary, and one son, Kent. In Polly's will, she devised the home to Mary, but a week before the closing, she gave Kent the physical deed and told him, "if anything happens to me, then you take care of the home." Kent completed the closing with Jim and transferred Jim a quitclaim deed. Jim recorded the deed. Jim has not made any immediate moving plans.

After Polly's death, Mary believed she was the owner and sold the home to Rebecca. Prior to the sale, while Carol was out of town, Mary showed the home to Rebecca. Mary used her mother's spare key to enter the home. Rebecca asked who lived in the house and Mary pretended to be the occupant. Mary drafted a replica of the deed and delivered a general warranty deed to Rebecca, who immediately recorded the interest. A week later, Rebecca arrived with a moving van and saw Carol occupying the home. Carol asked Rebecca to leave, but Rebecca refused and camped overnight on Carol's front yard.

(1) Kent claims Mary's sale to Rebecca is void because he was the true owner of the home. Is he correct?
(2) Jim sued Mary for possession of the home and Kent for unmarketable title. Will Jim succeed?
(3) Rebecca sued Carol for possession of the home and Carol sued Rebecca for trespass and nuisance. Who will win?
(4) Mary refused to help Rebecca litigate against Carol. Rebecca sued Mary for violating her deed. Will Mary win?

Torts Questions

Question 1
(45 minutes)

One rainy day, Kirk and Jessica offered a homeless man their meatball sandwich. However, the man was upset because he wanted money. The man hit the sandwich out of Jessica's hand. The sandwich flew towards Kirk's face. Kirk ducked because he was scared that the sandwich would hit him. The sandwich missed Kirk by an inch, but caused him to drop his umbrella.

The man grabbed Kirk's umbrella and ran away. Barry, the owner of the corner store, saw the man running and yelled "Stop Thief!" Barry threw a large rock at the man; Barry helped Kirk because Kirk had purchased the umbrella from Barry's store.

The rock hit the man in the head and knocked him down. The man was enraged, got up, and ran towards Barry with the umbrella raised. Barry punched the man in the face and the man fell down. The man was unconscious. When the man woke up, Barry said, "Follow me into the store or I'm going to call the police." The man said nothing and followed Barry into the store.

Barry put the man behind the counter and walked away to give the umbrella back to Kirk. Barry got into a conversation with Kirk that lasted 20 minutes. The man patiently sat behind the counter. Suddenly, the man fainted because the rock that hit him on the head caused internal bleeding. Barry returned and saw the man on the floor. Barry called 911 and the paramedics rushed the man to the hospital.

(1) Jessica sued the homeless man for battery. Is the homeless man liable?
(2) Kirk sued the homeless man for assault. Is the homeless man liable?
(3) The homeless man sued Barry for battery and false imprisonment. Is Barry liable?

Question 2
(45 minutes)

Dakota's art gallery rents rooms to artists to display their sculptures. Flik, a novice artist, planned to attend a convention where he would be a featured artist. The summer before the convention, Flik rented a space from Dakota for a week to display his newest chocolate sculpture. Flik wanted feedback from others to make improvements before the convention.

Dakota left a voice message on Flik's machine a day before his lease expired. Dakota reminded Flik that his sculpture would be thrown out if he did not pick it up by 10 AM the next morning. Flik never showed up. A week passed and Dakota did not know what to do. She kept the room at 55 degrees to prevent the chocolate from melting, but it cost her additional money. Dakota decided to shut off the air conditioning. The chocolate sculpture melted. The next morning, Dakota threw the sculpture in the dumpster.

Flik showed up that evening to pick up his sculpture. Dakota told him the sculpture was ruined. Flik was extremely upset because he spent half a year on the sculpture and the convention had several recruiters. Flik went to the dumpster and grabbed the chocolate to use for a future project. Flik missed the convention because he so depressed about losing his sculpture that he stopped eating regularly, lost weight, and gave up on his career in the arts.

Flik sued Dakota for (1) trespass to chattels and conversion, and (2) intentional infliction of emotional distress. Dakota counter sued for (3) trespass to land. Discuss their claims and defenses.

Question 3
(60 minutes)

Justin, a famous actor, was married five times within a span of three years. Justin met Carrie, a middle school teacher, and proposed to her behind closed doors in his mansion. Justin arranged a secret wedding with only their immediate family members in attendance because Justin did not want the media to get involved in his personal life.

The government prints a magazine called *The Future* that includes articles discussing problems in society. Reporter works for *The Future* and heard about the marriage from Carrie's brother. Reporter hid in the bushes at Justin's house and took pictures of the couple in wedding attire. Reporter used the photos as the graphic for the article titled "10 Reasons Why Popular Culture is a Bad Influence on Our Youth." The article and photo caption never mentioned Justin or Carrie by name, but it discussed the new generation's lack of commitment to marriage.

Anna, Justin's ex-wife, was talking to her best friend at the grocery market. Anna's friend asked her what she thought about the article. Anna whispered, "I don't think commitment is a problem in society. But I do think Carrie is in it for the money." A few teenagers heard Anna's statement and blogged about Carrie being a gold-digger. As a result, many magazines printed that Anna and Carrie were at war over Justin.

The bad publicity made it difficult for Carrie to have a normal life because people were always harassing her with questions. Carrie did marry Justin for the money, but she also enjoyed his company and loved him. Carrie's stress forced her to take time off from work to avoid people.

(1) Justin sued Reporter for defamation and invasion of privacy. Will he succeed?
(2) Carrie sued Anna for defamation. Anna claims she only spoke her opinion, which Anna believed was true. Will Carrie succeed?

Question 4
(50 minutes)

Albert and Belle converted their home into a bed and breakfast. Their business was popular among families because there was a giant trampoline in the backyard for children. The couple successfully ran the business for years until Albert passed away.

After Albert's death, Belle closed the bed and breakfast and only allowed close family and friends to stay overnight in her home. Belle refused occupants under 18 years old because she wanted children, but never had any with Albert. For the next five years, Belle never stepped into the backyard. The trampoline started to deteriorate. Belle put a small sign on the back door that said "Off Limits."

Wilder, a nine-year old boy who lived down the street, climbed the fence and used the trampoline on a daily basis. Belle never saw Wilder in the backyard because he always played in afternoon while she was grocery shopping. Wilder played unnoticed for two weeks until he accidentally left his jacket and notebook near the trampoline. Belle saw the items and thought it was strange, but never investigated further.

Demi, Belle's cousin, visited Belle for a couple days as a guest. During her visit, Demi saw Wilder on the trampoline. Demi did not see Belle's sign and went outside to watch Wilder. When Demi sat on a lawn chair, it broke because the screws were loose. Demi fell back and hit her head. Demi suffered a concussion. At the same time, the trampoline ripped and Wilder fell. Wilder scratched his legs on the rocky terrain under the trampoline. A state statute requires the use of rubber tile under any structures built for children.

(1) Demi sued Belle for negligence. Will she prevail? Do not discuss causation, damages, or affirmative defenses.
(2) Wilder sued Belle for negligence. Will he prevail? Do not discuss causation or damages, or affirmative defenses.

Question 5
(75 minutes)

Mark was babysitting Diego and Syaz, who were ten years old. Mark left the boys home alone to hang out with his friends because Mark forgot the boys were in the house. Mark is 20 years old and suffers from short-term memory loss.

After Mark left, Diego and Syaz went to the attic, opened the window, and climbed on the roof to play with a pile of leaves. Syaz snuck behind Diego and yelled "Boo!" Diego was startled, tripped on a branch, and fell off the roof into the pool. Diego thrashed around because he did not know how to swim.

Syaz ran to the backyard, grabbed a large pole, and stuck it into the water. Diego grabbed the pole and Syaz pulled him to the poolside. Diego was unable to move. When Syaz dragged Diego out of the water, Syaz accidentally knocked Diego's head on the wall. Diego passed out. Syaz did CPR, but broke one of Diego's ribs. Syaz called 911 and the ambulance took Diego to the hospital.

Dr. Z operated on Diego. Dr. Z is paralyzed from the waist down and has an elevated wheelchair to reach the operating tables. During the procedure, the wheelchair bumped into the table because Dr. Z's nurse failed to lock the wheelchair brake correctly. The bump caused Diego's broken rib to puncture his lung, which dramatically increased the length of his recovery. Diego also suffers from a disease that makes him heal slower than the average person. During Diego's next checkup, Dr. Z found a sponge in Diego's body. No one knows how the sponge appeared in Diego's body, but Diego must undergo another surgery to remove the sponge.

Diego sued Dr. Z, Syaz, and Mark for negligence. Discuss the strength of Diego's arguments below. Do not discuss affirmative defenses.

(1) Diego claims Dr. Z negligently increased his recovery time by puncturing his lung.
(2) Diego claims Dr. Z breached his duty because a sponge appeared in his body. Do not discuss causation or injury.
(3) Diego claims Syaz negligently caused his head injury and broken rib.
(4) Diego claims Mark failed to control Syaz, which ultimately lead to Diego's injuries.

Question 6
(60 minutes)

Dr. Vivian is an oral surgeon who works for D-Dental. Alex is her patient. Dr. Vivian told Alex that he needed his wisdom teeth extracted. She recommended receiving dental anesthesia that would make him unconscious during the procedure. Dr. Vivian began to explain the risks and instructions for anesthesia, but Alex stopped her. Alex said he knew the procedure already because he had a previous surgery. Dr. Vivian said okay, gave him a large packet of instructions, and told him to review it. Alex glanced at the packet and then signed the voluntary consent form.

The day of the procedure, Alex ate a breakfast buffet because he knew his diet would be restricted after the surgery. If Alex had read the packet or listened to Dr. Vivian's explanation, he would have known fasting was required to reduce the risk of inhaling stomach contents into the lungs. Before Dr. Vivian put Alex under anesthesia, she asked him if he ate anything that morning. Alex replied "a bit." Dr. Vivian proceeded with the surgery.

During the procedure, Alex is unable to control his gag reflex and his stomach contents regurgitated into his airways. Dr. Vivian worked to save Alex while her assistant informed Alex's wife, Noni, that there were complications with Alex's procedure. Noni fainted from the shock. Dr. Vivian saved Alex and finished the extraction. When Alex woke up, Dr. Vivian told him about the obstacles related to his surgery.

For the next couple months, Alex and Noni struggled to sleep and needed therapy. Noni had nightmares about Alex dying from the surgery. Alex was scared to sleep because he was worried he would never wake up.

(1) Is D-Dental liable for the torts committed by Dr. Vivian and her assistant?

(2) Assume D-Dental is liable for the torts of Dr. Vivian and her assistant. Alex sued D-Dental for negligent infliction of emotional distress. Alex claimed Dr. Vivian should have warned him not to eat before the surgery. Will he succeed?

(3) Assume D-Dental is liable for the torts of Dr. Vivian and her assistant. Noni sued D-Dental for negligent infliction of emotional distress. Will she succeed?

Question 7
(60 minutes)

AVX is a car manufacturing company. AVX developed a technology that kept cars within the lane whenever a driver started to drift. Bert, a truck driver, went to a car dealership that sold AVX technology. Bert told the dealership associate, "I need something to keep me safe whenever I fall asleep on the road." The associate suggested AVX's technology. Bert bought the technology. AVX sent the technology to the dealership with a defect in the program's code. The dealership did not know about the defect. The dealership's mechanic installed the lane-departure technology correctly, tested it, and verified it worked properly before returning Bert's truck.

Bert received a 40-page instruction manual that stated he must bring the truck in for maintenance every six months to ensure the lane-departure technology updated its maps. If Bert missed an update, then the technology would stop working. These instructions were on page 20 of the manual in 11-point font. The associate never explained the update process to Bert.

Some companies sold lane-departure technologies that automatically updated whenever connected to the internet. AVX did not create automatic updates because it would cost them three times more to manufacture the product. The manual also stated, in large font on the title page, "This lane-departure technology is a safety feature and should not be treated as an automatic-driver technology. Drivers must still keep their hands on the wheel and stay alert."

Bert did not read the manual and never brought the car in for maintenance. During the sixth month, the technology stopped working because of a program error that was amplified by the lack of an update. On the way to his next delivery, Bert decided to stop by his daughter's ballet recital. While driving, Bert took a very quick nap and allowed the car to drive itself on a straight road. However, the car veered out of control and Bert crashed. All the products ordered by FoodStar in Bert's truck were ruined. Bert works for Truck Company three out of seven days a week. Although Bert uses Truck Company's vehicle, Bert was not scheduled to begin work until after his daughter's ballet recital and receives no benefits.

FoodStar sued AVX, Car Dealership, and Truck Company. Discuss the merits of FoodStar's arguments.

(1) FoodStar claims AVX is strictly liable for its damages. Will FoodStar succeed? Do not discuss causation.

(2) FoodStar claims the car dealership is strictly liable for its damages because the associate should have warned Bert about the updates. Will FoodStar succeed? Do not discuss causation.

(3) FoodStar claims the defendants are joint and severally liable. Is FoodStar correct?

(4) FoodStar claims Truck Company is responsible for the torts committed by Bert. Is FoodStar correct?

Question 8
(45 minutes)

During the first week of Lunar New Year, Homeowner celebrates by setting off firecrackers every evening at 7:00 PM in his backyard. Homeowner's hometown in Asia made it a tradition to set off firecrackers every night to scare away the bad spirits and welcome the new year. Homeowner continued this tradition after immigrating to America. The firecrackers are loud, last for at least 5 minutes, and generate tons of smoke and sparks. Several neighbors found Homeowner's practice annoying because the smoke lingered and the noise was distracting. Garner sleeps at 2:00 PM everyday because he works the graveyard shift that begins at 12:00 AM. The firecrackers always woke up Garner.

One night, Homeowner forgot to put his dog, Butch, in the kennel before performing the firecracker ritual. Butch is a mix of a husky and gray wolf. When Homeowner set off the firecrackers, Butch was startled, grabbed an active firecracker, and ran into the front yard. Butch eventually dropped the firecracker, barked, and ran around frantically. Homeowner adopted Butch as a puppy and never saw Butch display any aggressive behavior, but Butch went into defense mode after hearing the firecrackers.

Garner woke up in a rage and ran over to Homeowner's house. Garner stepped on Homeowner's front yard and yelled, "Stop the firecrackers." Butch ran up to Garner and bit his arm. At the same time, a spark from the firecracker lit Garner's pants on fire. Homeowner panicked and ran into the house to grab a blanket. Homeowner hit Garner with the blanket to suppress the fire. The blanket had a rock lodged inside. The rock cut Garner's leg. Garner suffered burns on his leg and needed stitches for the dog bite and cut on his leg.

(1) What claims can Garner bring under strict liability and will they succeed?
(2) Garner sued Homeowner for nuisance. Will he succeed?
(3) The neighbors sued Homeowner for nuisance. Will they succeed?

Civil Procedure Answers

Answer 1

Ellen (E) vs. Wild Water (WW)

Personal Jurisdiction (PJ)

PJ is the power of the court to issue binding orders over a person. The court can exercise PJ over WW if the state's long arm statute and Constitution authorize PJ.

Statutory Basis (Long Arm Statute)

Here, State Y's long arm statute gives the court the broadest authority because the statute allows the court to "exercise jurisdiction on any basis not inconsistent with the constitution of this state or of the United States."

Constitutional Basis (Due Process)

The 14th Amendment requires notice and the opportunity to be heard.[10] Under *Pennoyer vs. Neff*, a state has jurisdiction over persons and property within its territory.[11] PJ is established if the defendant (1) is domiciled in the state, (2) appears in court or gives express consent, (3) is physically present in the state at the time of service, or (4) owns property in the state (in rem).[12] Here, no traditional notions of PJ apply because (1) WW is domicile in State B; a corporation's domicile is its state of incorporation and principal place of business (PPB).[13] No facts suggest (2) or (3) were met. (4) WW likely owns the rental station in State Y, but the prompt says to ignore in rem jurisdiction.

---

10. U.S. Const. Amend. XIV.
11. *Pennoyer v. Neff*, 95 U.S. 714, 722 (1877). See also *Burnham v. Superior Court*, 495 U.S. 604, 626–27 (1990), and *Ins. Corp. of Ireland v. Compagnie des Bauxites de Guinee*, 456 U.S. 694, 704 (1982).
12. *Pennoyer v. Neff*, supra note 11.
13. *Hertz Corp. v. Friend*, 559 U.S. 77, 87 (2010).

Modern Notions of PJ

PJ is established if (1) the defendant has sufficient minimum contacts with the state and (2) exercising PJ does not offend traditional notions of fair play and substantial justice.[14]

(1) Sufficient Minimum Contacts

General Jurisdiction

A court can assert general jurisdiction over a defendant if the defendant's activities are continuous and systematic where the defendant is essentially at home in the forum state.[15] A corporation is at home in its state of incorporation and PPB.[16]

Here, E will argue WW's contacts are systematic and continuous because WW ran a physical return station within State Y's borders for six months. Half a year is an extended amount of time and WW's presence in State Y is likely to continue. WW also conducted national e-commerce for 11 years, which means WW could have supplied canoes to State Y patrons.

WW will argue its domicile is B and not State Y. WW's six months in State Y is a short period of time compared to WW's 11 years of operation. Moreover, no facts confirm WW sold canoes to State Y citizens; E's argument is speculative. However, E's argument that general jurisdiction exists is stronger because WW is physically present in State Y and WW likely intended to continue business in State Y.

Specific Jurisdiction

The minimum contacts requirement is met if: (a) the defendant has contacts in the state, (b) the claim arises out of those contacts, and (c) the exercise of PJ would be fair and reasonable.[17] Here, (a) WW's contacts in State Y include its return station and shuttle services. (b) The claim arises out of WW's contacts because WW's employee broke E's toes on WW's property. E would not have been injured if WW did not open a business in State Y.

---

14. *International Shoe Co. v. Washington*, 326 U.S. 310, 316 (1945).

15. *Goodyear Dunlop Tires Operations, S.A. v. Brown*, 131 S. Ct. 2846, 2851 (2011).

16. *Hertz Corp. v. Friend*, supra note 13.

17. *International Shoe Co. v. Washington*, supra note 14. See also *Goodyear Dunlop Tires Operations, S.A. v. Brown*, supra note 15.

(c) Fair and Reasonable

Whether the exercise of PJ is fair and reasonable depends on (i) if the defendant purposefully availed itself to the privilege of conducting activities within the forum state, and (ii) if the defendant's conduct and contacts are such that it could reasonably anticipate being haled into that state court.

Purposeful Availment

Hanson v. Denckla held there are sufficient minimum contacts if the defendant invoked the benefits and protections of the state's laws.[18] Here, WW is protected by State Y's labor, property, and sales laws because it owns property, employs citizens, and charges $3 for shuttle services. WW financially benefits from conducting businesses in State Y.

Stream of Commerce

Asahi Metal Indus. Co. v. Superior Court held minimum contacts exist if the defendant purposefully directs its actions toward the forum state, such as placing a product into the stream of commerce for financial gain.[19] Here, WW will argue its products are not in State Y's stream of commerce because the return station does not sell or rent canoes. This is a weak argument because WW's 11-year national, online business likely put canoes into State Y's stream of commerce.

Contracts

McGee v. Int'l Life Ins. Co. held there are minimum contacts if the suit is based on a contract with a substantial connection to the state.[20] Here, WW likely entered a land sale contract or lease for the return station and created employment contracts with State Y residents. These contracts are substantially connected to E's injury in State Y because WW needed the contracts to run its canoe business.

WW will argue the rental contract with E occurred in State Z, which is not within State Y's borders. Although E intended to use WW's shuttle services, she never actually paid for or boarded the shuttle. However, WW's argument will fail because E's rental contract likely allowed E to return her canoe in State Y or State Z.

---

18. *Hanson v. Denckla*, 357 U.S. 235, 253 (1958).
19. *Asahi Metal Indus. Co. v. Superior Court*, 480 U.S. 102, 112 (1987).
20. *McGee v. Int'l Life Ins. Co.*, 355 U.S. 220, 223-24 (1957).

Haled Into Court

World-Wide Volkswagen Corp. v. Woodson held foreseeability alone is not enough for PJ.[21] The defendant must reasonably anticipate being haled into that state court.[22] Here, WW should have known it could be haled into court for tort, contract, employment, or property disputes because WW has a physical return station in State Y and WW put its products into the stream of commerce through national e-commerce.

The Internet

If the defendant conducts activities, such as sales through an interactive website, then the defendant could be subject to PJ.[23] If the website is purely passive, such as posting information, but no sales, then there is no PJ.[24] If there is some interactivity, such as information exchange, but no sales, then courts must look at the nature and extent of the site's interactivity.[25] Here, WW is subject to specific jurisdiction because its interactive website sells canoes online. A State Y citizen could have purchased canoes from WW's website during its 11 years of e-commerce because the Marsys river runs through State Y's borders.

Conclusion

Sufficient minimum contacts likely exists because WW availed itself to the benefits of State Y laws, knew it could be haled into court by opening a physical return station, had multiple contracts substantially connected to the state, and created an interactive website.

(2) Fair Play and Substantial Justice

A court considers five factors to determine if PJ is fair and reasonable: (a) the burden on the defendant, (b) the forum state's interest, (c) the plaintiff's interest in a convenient forum, (d) the interstate judicial system's interest in efficient resolution of controversies, and (e) the shared interests of the states in furthering substantive social policies.[26]

Here, (a) WW's burden is low because it is already physically present in State Y through its return station. WW can easily litigate in State Y. (b) State

---

21. *World-Wide Volkswagen Corp. v. Woodson*, 444 U.S. 286, 297 (1980).
22. *Id.*
23. *Zippo Mfg. Co. v. Zippo Dot Com, Inc.*, 952 F.Supp. 1119, 1126 (W.D. Pa. 1997).
24. *Pebble Beach Co. v. Caddy*, 453 F.3d 1151, 1160 (9th Cir. 2006).
25. *Zippo Mfg. Co. v. Zippo Dot Com, Inc.*, supra note 23 at 1124.
26. *Burger King Corp. v. Rudzewicz*, 471 U.S. 462, 476–77 (1985).

Y's interest is high because WW is providing State Y citizens with employment opportunities and services. (c) E is a resident of State Y, which makes traveling to State Y convenient. (d) A trial in State Y is more efficient because the incident happened in State Y, which means the evidence and witnesses are likely in State Y, and (e) State Y and State Z have an equal interest to protect their citizens from harm. Thus, State Y can exercise PJ over WW because both elements of *International Shoe* are met.

Federal Rules of Civil Procedure (FRCP): Rule 4(K)

Federal courts technically have jurisdiction over the entire U.S., but a federal court can only exercise PJ over a defendant if the state courts also have PJ over the defendant.[27] Without Rule 4(K), the federal courts would be overwhelmed by cases that should be heard elsewhere and the parties would suffer huge travel inconveniences. Here, the U.S. District Court of State Y has jurisdiction because the state court of State Y has PJ. In conclusion, the court should deny WW's motion to dismiss.

Ellen (E) vs. Damon (D)

Personal Jurisdiction

State Y has statutory authority. See rule and analysis above. (Ellen vs. Wild Water: Statutory Authority).

Constitutional Basis

See rule above. (Ellen vs. Wild Water: Constitutional Authority). An individual's domicile is where he or she physically resides and intends to remain indefinitely.[28]

Here, (2), (3), and (4) do not apply. (1) D will argue he is a citizen of Country X because he only intents to stay in State Y for eight years to finish his PhD. This is a strong argument because D has a contract with Country X's government to return to work after he completes his PhD. D will not remain indefinitely in State Y because he would suffer consequences for breaking the contract, especially after Country X paid his tuition. However, E will argue D started his program three weeks ago, which means D's permanent home will be in State Y for the next eight years. D may also break his contract with

---

27. Fed. R. Civ. P. 4(k).
28. *Mas v. Perry*, 489 F.2d 1396, 1399 (5th Cir. 1974).

Country X. E's argument is weaker because eight years is still a fixed term. Thus, D's domicile is Country X and there is no PJ under *Pennoyer*.

Modern Notions of PJ

See rules above. (Ellen vs. Wild Water: Modern Notions of PJ).

General Jurisdiction

Here, E will argue general jurisdiction exists because D will be studying and working for the next eight years in State Y; State Y is his home. However, D will argue he arrived in State Y only three weeks ago, which is a short period of time and likely not enough to be continuous. D is not at home in State Y because he is a citizen of Country X. Thus, there is no general jurisdiction.

Specific Jurisdiction

See rules above. (Ellen v. Wild Water: Specific Jurisdiction). Here, (a) D's contacts include studying and working in State Y, and (b) the claim arises out of D's employment contacts, because he dropped the canoe on E's foot while he was working.

Purposeful Availment

Here, D benefited from State Y's education and labor laws because he voluntarily came to State Y for school and work.

Contracts

Here, D had a substantial connection to State Y because E's injury directly related to D's employment contract within State Y. D would not have hurt E if he was not employed.

Haled Into Court

Here, D will be physically living and studying in State Y for eight years. It is foreseeable that D could be haled into court for employment, educational, or property disputes during that time. There is likely minimum contacts because D benefited from State Y laws.

(2) Fair Play and Substantial Justice

Here, (a) there is no burden on D to litigate because he lives in State Y, (b) State Y has a high interest in the lawsuit because D is living and working within State Y's borders. Analysis of (c), (d), and (e) are the same as above. (See Ellen vs. Wild Water: Fair Play and Substantial Justice). In conclusion, there is PJ under *International Shoe*.

FRCP: Rule 4 (K)

See rule and analysis above. (Ellen v. Wild Water: FRCP Rule (4)(K). The rule, analysis, and conclusion are same. The U.S. District Court in State Y has PJ over D and the court should deny D's motion to dismiss.

Answer 2

(1) Removal

Unless otherwise provided by Congress, if the federal court has original jurisdiction over the claim, then the defendant can remove any civil action brought in state court to the U.S. district court where the action is pending.[29] Here, Future Incorporated (F) validly moved to remove the claim to State A's federal district court because the action is pending in State A; Gaby (G) and Hugo (H) filed a patent infringement claim in the Superior Court of State A. The issue is whether the U.S. District Court of State A had original jurisdiction over the G and H's claim.

Subject Matter Jurisdiction

For an action to be brought, a federal court must have subject matter jurisdiction, which is the power to hear the claim.

Diversity Jurisdiction

U.S. district courts have original jurisdiction over all civil actions where (a) the matter in controversy exceeds $75,000, exclusive of interest and costs, and (b) the lawsuit is between citizens of different States; citizens of a State and citizens of a foreign state; or a foreign state and citizens of a State.[30]

(a) Amount in Controversy

Separate and distinct claims of two or more plaintiffs cannot be aggregated to satisfy the jurisdictional amount.[31] If their claims are combined into a single suit for convenience, then the demand of each plaintiff must independently meet the jurisdictional amount.[32] Aggregation is only allowed if a single plaintiff seeks to aggregate two or more of his own claims against a single defendant, or if two or more plaintiffs unite to enforce a single right in which they have a common and undivided interest.[33]

Here, G and H each claim $60,000 in lost profits, which is not enough to individually meet the jurisdictional requirement. However, they can aggregate their claims because they invented the robot together, which created an

---

29. 28 U.S.C. § 1441 (a) (2012).
30. 28 U.S.C. § 1332 (2012).
31. *Troy Bank of Troy, Ind., v. G.A. Whitehead & Co.*, 222 U.S. 39, 40-41 (1911).
32. *Id.*
33. *Snyder v. Harris*, 394 U.S. 332, 335 (1969).

indivisible right. G's design and H's technology contributed to the successful sales of the robots because G and H's skills were both required to complete the product. Thus, when aggregated, their claim is $120,000, which meets the jurisdictional amount.

Legal Certainty

A plaintiff's claim does not exceed $75,000 if, on the face of the pleadings, it is apparent to a legal certainty that the plaintiff cannot recover the amount claimed.[34] Here, F will argue G and H are each entitled to a maximum of $30,000 because F's total profit was only $60,000; F sold 500 robots for $120 per a robot. The $60,000 should be split between the inventors. Thus, G and H cannot meet the amount in controversy unless they claim additional punitive damages for F's patent infringement, which neither mentioned in the pleadings. An aggregated claim of $120,000 is unlikely recoverable.

(b) Complete Diversity

No party on one side of a lawsuit may be a citizen of the same state as any party on the other side.[35]

Future

A corporation is a citizen of the state of its incorporation and the state where it has its principal place of business.[36] A corporation's principal place of business is where a significant amount of the corporation's activities take place.[37] If there is no such state, then the principal place of business is its nerve center.[38] Here, F conducts business in State A and State B. However, State A is its principal place of business because F's headquarters and research facilities are in State A, which is likely where its executive and administrative functions are performed.[39] F has factories in State B, but the factory is likely where the instructions from State A's headquarters are executed. Thus, F is a citizen of State A and State D, which is its state of incorporation.

---

34. *St. Paul Mercury Indem. Co. v. Red Cab Co.*, 303 U.S. 283, 289 (1938).
35. *Strawbridge v. Curtiss*, 7 U.S. 267 (1806).
36. *Hertz Corp. v. Friend,* supra note 13 at 82.
37. *Id. at 87.*
38. *Id.*
39. *Id.*

Gaby and Hugo

An individual's domicile is where she physically resides and intends to remain indefinitely.[40] Here, G is officially domicile in State Z, but she likely changed her domicile to State A or State B because she had not returned to State Z for many years. Although G is likely living in her State A apartment for five work days, which is more than the weekend at her State B house, G probably intended to remain indefinitely in State B because G purchased a home and her family lived in State B. G's rented apartment in State A was probably a temporary home for work purposes. Thus, G likely changed her domicile from State Z to State B. H travels across the border to State A for work, but is domicile in State C.

Conclusion

F is a citizen of State D and A. G is a citizen of State B. H is a citizen of State C. Thus, no party is a citizen of the same state as a party on the other side. However, it is unlikely the amount in controversy is met. Thus, there is no diversity jurisdiction and the case cannot be removed to federal court unless there is subject matter jurisdiction under §1331.

Removal Based on Diversity of Citizenship

A claim brought solely on the basis of jurisdiction under §1332 cannot be removed if a defendant is a citizen of the state in which the action is brought.[41] Here, even if the court determined the amount in controversy was met, F is unable to remove the claim to federal court because F is a citizen of State A and the claim was brought in State A.

Federal Question

U.S. district courts have original jurisdiction over all civil actions arising under the Constitution, laws, or treaties of the United States.[42] A suit arises under the Constitution and laws of the U.S. if the plaintiff's complaint shows that her claim is based upon U.S. laws or the Constitution. It is not enough that the plaintiff alleges an anticipated defense.[43] Here, G and H filed a claim for patent infringement under the federal statute, 35 U.S. Code §271. Their claim was not based on F's anticipated defense, but on F's infringement of their design

---

40. *Mas v. Perry*, supra note 28.
41. 28 U.S.C. § 1441 (b) (2012).
42. U.S. Const. Art. III, § 2, cl. 1. See also 28 U.S.C. §1331 (2012).
43. *Louisville & Nashville R.R. Co. v. Mottley*, 211 U.S. 149, 152 (1908).

and technology patents. Thus, the federal court has subject matter jurisdiction over G and H's claim.

Exclusive Jurisdiction

U.S. district courts have original and exclusive jurisdiction over any civil action arising under any Act of Congress relating to patents, copyrights, and trademarks.[44] Exclusive jurisdiction means no state court can hear the case. Here, the Superior Court of State A cannot exercise any jurisdiction over G and H's claim because patent cases can only be brought in federal court. Thus, removal under §1331 is appropriate and the court correctly granted F's motion.

(2) Supplement Jurisdiction

If the U.S. district courts have original jurisdiction over a claim, then the district courts have supplemental jurisdiction over related claims.[45] A related claim must be derived from a common nucleus of operative fact as the main claim, which means the related claim would ordinarily be tried with the main claim in one judicial proceeding.[46]

Here, G will argue her $30,000 claim for royalties arose from her employment at F, which is derived from the same common nucleus of operative fact as the patent infringement claim because G also used F's facilities and equipment to create the cleaning robot.

However, F will argue G's energy-saving research is unrelated to G's robot. The lightbulb is a different product than the robot and the dispute involves events that are not connected to G's design of the robot. The breach of contract claim also does not involve H or the robot patents. Thus, the court is unlikely to exercise supplement jurisdiction over G's claim because the claims would not normally be tried together.

---

44. 28 U.S.C. § 1338 (2012).
45. 28 U.S.C. § 1367 (2012).
46. *United Mine Workers of Am. v. Gibbs*, 383 U.S. 715, 725 (1966).

Answer 3

(1) Applicable Law on Removal

Erie Doctrine

Congress has explicitly instructed federal courts to apply state substantive law and federal procedural law.[47] The Rules of Decision Act instructs courts to apply the law of the states unless Congress or the U.S. Constitution say otherwise.[48] The Rules of Enabling Act and Federal Rules of Procedure and Evidence allow the Supreme Court to prescribe general rules of practice and rules of evidence, but Congress stated these laws shall not abridge, enlarge, or modify any substantive right.[49] If the state's procedural laws conflict with federal procedural law, then the federal rule is applied.[50]

Procedural versus Substantive Law

Substantive law includes rules that govern the dispute, such as the rights and obligations of the parties, and effect the ruling of the case. Procedural law includes rules concerning the mechanisms of enforcing the substantive law. However, some procedural laws become substantive law because their impact on the case is extreme, such as the statute of limitations and choice-of-law codes. To determine whether a law is substantive or procedural, the courts use the outcome-determinative test.[51] If applying the federal law would change the outcome, then the court must apply state law.[52]

Here, the defendants will argue the statute of limitations is procedural because it impacts when the plaintiff must file a claim. Martin (M) likely filed his claim in state court because his claim would have been dismissed if he filed in federal court. M filed four days before the two-year statute of limitations expired in State B, but federal law required M to file his personal injury claim within one year after the date of injury. The statute of limitations is outcome determinative because the defendants would win under federal laws before the merits were ever litigated.

---

47. *Erie R. Co. v. Tompkins*, 304 U.S. 64, 78 (1938).
48. 28 U.S.C. § 1652 (2012).
49. 28 U.S.C. § 2072 (2012).
50. *Hanna v. Plumer*, 380 U.S. 460, 472-73 (1965).
51. *Guar. Trust Co. of N.Y. v. York*, 326 U.S. 99, 109-10 (1945).
52. *Id.*

Balancing Interests

In some cases, even if the state's law is procedural and outcome determinative, the courts must balance the interests of the state and federal courts.[53] If the federal interest is overwhelming pertinent and the federal law was obviously designed to govern the issue at hand, then the court must apply the federal procedural law.[54] Here, the defendants will argue the federal court has a strong interest to maintain efficiency. If State B's statute of limitations was applied, then plaintiffs would be encouraged to file their expired federal claims in state court and remove them to federal court. This creates a loophole for plaintiffs to litigate their claim in federal court and could overwhelm the federal system.

However, M will argue that the filing deadline is unlikely overwhelming pertinent to the lawsuit because the statute of limitations was not specifically designed by the federal court to govern car accidents. Thus, State B's laws should be applied to M's case. The court is likely to agree with M because the statute of limitations is outcome determinative and states have the right to govern tort claims that occur within their borders.

(2) Motion to Transfer

Change of Venue

A district court may transfer any civil action to any other district where the claim may have been brought or to any district to which all parties have consented.[55] Here, all parties did not consent because Roadies (R) opposed American Tours's (AT) transfer request. Thus, the court must analyze if the claim could have originally been brought in State A and if it is more convenient to litigate in State A instead of State B.

Residence Venue

If all defendants are residents of the same state, then a civil action can be brought in any judicial district where a defendant resides.[56]

---

53. *Byrd v. Blue Ridge Rural Elec. Coop., Inc.*, 356 U.S. 525, 549-51 (1958).
54. *Id.*
55. 28 U.S.C. § 1404 (2012).
56. 28 U.S.C. § 1391 (2012).

Draco's Residence

A defendant who is not a resident in the U.S. may be sued in any judicial district, and the joinder of such a defendant shall be disregarded in determining where the action may be brought with respect to other defendants.[57] Here, Draco (D) is not a resident in the U.S. because he lives overseas in Country X and merely came to America for tourism. Thus, D can be sued in State A or State B.

American's Residence

A corporation, if a defendant, is deemed to reside in any judicial district in which the corporation is subject to the court's personal jurisdiction with respect to the civil action in question.[58] Personal jurisdiction (PJ) is established if a defendant is domicile in the state.[59] A corporation's domicile is its state of incorporation and principal place of business.[60] Here, AT's state of incorporation and principal place of business are in State A, which means AT is subject to personal jurisdiction in State A. Thus, AT resides in State A.

Roadies' Residence

See rule above (Motion to Transfer: American's Residence). Here, R's state of incorporation and principal place of business are in State B. However, PJ is also established if the defendant has sufficient minimum contacts with the state and the lawsuit does not offend traditional notions of fair play and substantial justice.[61] State A likely has PJ over R because R purposefully availed itself to the benefits of State A by building a physical location in the Northern District of State A to rents cars.[62] R is running a business under the protection of State A's laws and benefiting financially from its partnership with AT, one of State A's businesses.

PJ is fair and reasonable because (a) the burden on R to litigate is low and (b) State A has an interest in the lawsuit because R is physically conducting business in the Northern District of State A.[63] Although (c) M is a citizen in State C, M can likely travel to State A because M opted to sue the defendants in State B,

---

57. *Id.*
58. *Id.*
59. *Id.*
60. *Hertz Corp. v. Friend,* supra note *13.*
61. *International Shoe Co. v. Washington,* supra note 14.
62. *Hanson v. Denckla,* supra note 18.
63. *Burger King Corp. v. Rudzewicz,* supra 26.

which is adjacent to State A.[64] (d) The judicial system likely prefers the lawsuit to be heard in State B, where the accident happened, but (e) all states have an interest in ensuring an interstate corporation is responsible for its torts.[65] Thus, for venue purposes, R resides in State A because its physical, rental-car operations are enough to make PJ fair and reasonable.

Residence Venue Conclusion

M's claim could originally be brought in the Northern District of State A because, for venue purposes, D, AT, and R are all residents of State A, and both AT and R reside in the Northern District.[66] However, the court must determine if it is more appropriate to litigate the claim in State A or State B.

Convenience and Justice Factors

The court considers the following private factors: (a) the accessibility of evidence; (b) the availability of compulsory process to secure the attendance of witnesses; (c) the cost of attendance for willing witnesses; and (d) all other practical problems that make a trial easy, expeditious, and inexpensive.[67]

Here, M will argue the factors favor litigating in State B because (a) the accident occurred at a busy intersection in State B, which means all the evidence is located in State B. Although the parties could request the police report from State B, if the claim was transferred to State A, then the jury could not easily visit the scene of the accident. (b)(c) Moreover, the State B police officer and witnesses likely live in State B, which means a trial in State A will increase their travel costs and inconvenience.

However, AT will argue that State A is more appropriate because (a) both AT and R's facilities are located in State A, and D picked up the car in State A, which means the evidence related to D's rental is located in State A. (b) The witnesses who dealt with D and knew about D's capability as a driver, such as AT's tour guides, are also located in State A. If the trial was in State B, then it would be costly for them to travel. (d) M is neither a resident of State A or State B and will need to travel regardless of the forum choice.

Based on the private factors, AT is likely to lose because M, as the plaintiff, selected State B instead of State A for personal convenience. In addition, the

---

64. *Id.*
65. *Id.*
66. 28 U.S.C. § 1391, supra note 56.
67. *In re TS Tech USA Corp.*, 551 F.3d 1315 (Fed. Cir., 2008).

lawsuit is about the car accident in State B and not the agreements made between AT, R, and D in State A.

The court also considers the following public factors: (a) the administrative difficulties flowing from court congestion; (b) the local interest in having localized concerns decided at home; (c) the forum's familiarity with the law that will govern the case; and (d) the avoidance of unnecessary conflicts of law.[68] Here, no facts about (a), (c), and (d) are provided, but (b) State B's local interest is higher than State A because the accident happened within State B's borders. The litigation is unrelated to R and AT's daily business operations in State A.

In conclusion, although M's claim could originally be brought in State A, AT's motion should be denied because State B is a more convenient forum.

(3) Applicable Law on Transfer

Transfer of Law

A transfer of venue should not defeat the advantages the plaintiff may obtain through his choice of forum.[69] If the original venue was proper, then the transferee court is obligated to apply the state law that would have been applied if there had been no change in venue.[70] If the original venue was not proper and the transfer is granted to cure the lack of venue or personal jurisdiction, then the court should apply the law of the receiving state.[71] Here, the applicable law will depend on whether M properly brought the claim in the Northern District of State B.

Event Venue

A civil action may be brought in a judicial district where a substantial part of the events giving rise to the claim occurred, or a substantial part of property that is the subject of the action is situated.[72] Here, although the car was rented in State A, the accident occurred on a busy intersection in the Northern District in State B. Thus, a substantial part of the events at issue occurred in State B, such as D's alleged negligent driving. The receiving state, State A, must apply State B laws because the U.S. District Court, Northern District of State B had proper venue over M's claim.

---

68. *Id.*
69. *Van Dusen v. Barrack,* 376 U.S. 612 (1964). See also 28 U.S.C § 1404, supra note 55.
70. *Id.*
71. 28 U.S.C. § 1406 (2012).
72. 28 U.S.C. § 1391, supra note 56.

(4) Forum Non Conveniens

Forum non conveniens provides a federal district court with the discretion to decline jurisdiction over an action when a more appropriate forum is available for the parties.[73] Forum non conveniens prevents the U.S. judicial system from becoming the court of the world.[74] To determine the most appropriate forum, the court considers: (a) the private interests of the litigants, such as access to evidence; (b) availability and cost of the compulsory process for attendance of unwilling witnesses; (c) possibility to view the premises; and (d) all other practical problems that make trial easy, expeditious, and inexpensive.[75]

Here, (a) D will argue AT advertised the tour in Country X and the negotiations, payment, and contract signing were completed in County X. (b) Thus, all the witnesses who interacted with D when he purchased AT's tour of the U.S. are in Country X. However, State B is likely a more appropriate forum because the sources of proof, such as the scene of the accident, and witnesses who saw the collision are in State B.

The court also considers the following public factors: (a) administrative difficulties flowing from court congestion; (b) local interest in having localized concerns decided at home; (c) interest in having the trial in a forum experienced with the law that governs the action; (d) avoidance of unnecessary conflicts of law; and (e) the unfairness of burdening citizens in an unrelated forum with jury duty.[76] See analysis above. (Motion to Transfer: Convenience and Justice Factors).

Here, (b) D will argue Country X has an interest in the lawsuit because AT provided services to a Country X resident. (c) However, this is a weak argument because the accident occurred in State B between D and M, which is unrelated to Country X's laws and the contract between AT and D. (e) A trial in Country X would burden Country X citizens who may never visit the U.S. and (d) Country X tort laws might conflict with State B laws. In conclusion, State B is the most appropriate forum and D's motion for forum non conveniens will be denied.

---

73. 28 U.S.C. § 1404, supra note 55. See also *Sinochem Int'l. Co. Ltd. v. Malaysia Int'l. Shipping Corp.*, 549 U.S. 422, 429 (2007).

74. *Monde Re v. Nak Naftogaz of Ukraine, 158 F. Supp. 2d 377, 382 (S.D.N.Y. 2001).*

75. *Gulf Oil Corp. v. Gilbert*, 330 U.S. 501, 507 (1947).

76. *Piper Aircraft Co. v. Reyno*, 454 U.S. 235, 241 n.6 (1981).

Answer 4

(1) 12(b)(6) Motion to Dismiss

To win a 12(b)(6) motion to dismiss, the defendant must show the plaintiff failed to state a claim upon which relief can be granted.[77] A valid claim for relief requires: (1) a short and plain statement of the grounds for the court's jurisdiction; (2) a short and plain statement of the claim showing the plaintiff is entitled to relief; and (3) a demand for the relief sought.[78] Here, there are no issues with the court's jurisdiction and Paragraph (P) #4 states Owner's (O) demand for $6,000 in damages. Thus, the issue is whether O's complaint states a short and plain statement that O is entitled to relief.

Breach of Contract Claim

When deciding whether to grant a motion to dismiss, the court accepts all allegations in the compliant as true, but does not accept mere legal conclusions as true.[79] Here, O's complaint does not contain mere legal conclusions because it explains why O believed Timeshare (TS) committed fraud and breached its contract. O stated that TS never sold the timeshare as promised, refused to refund the $6,000 to O, and likely failed because of its unprofessional staff.

Second, the court examines the remaining non-conclusory allegations to determine if the plaintiff plead enough facts to state a claim of relief that is plausible on its face.[80] A claim is plausible if the court can draw a reasonable inference that the defendant is liable for the misconduct alleged.[81] Here, TS will argue O's complaint does not include facts that will give TS notice on how to prepare its defense. O excluded the specific terms of the contract, such as TS's deadline to sell the property. Land sales can take years, especially if the property is not popular real estate. O also failed to include when or how TS failed to refund the money, and did not explain how unprofessional or poorly dressed employees prevented TS from selling O's property.

---

77. Fed. R. Civ. P. 12(b)(6).
78. Fed. R. Civ. P. 8.
79. *Ashcroft v. Iqbal*, 556 U.S. 662, 678-79 (2009).
80. *Bell Atl. Corp. v. Twombly*, 550 U.S. 544, 570 (2007).
81. *Ashcroft v. Iqbal*, supra note 79 at 678.

However, O will argue the court can reasonably infer TS breached the contract because the complaint states TS did not sell O's timeshare for two years, which is a long time for property to be on the market. O also paid TS the $6,000 in full and TS never refunded O's money. Finally, O does not need to further explain how unprofessionalism can hinder sales; it is common knowledge that appearances matter in business deals.

In conclusion, although O's complaint does not include specific facts, it gives TS notice of why O is suing TS for breach of contract. The plausibility standard departs from heightened code-pleading standards to a notice-pleading standard[82] where a plaintiff only needs to narrate the grievance enough to put the defendant on notice about the accusations.[83] TS's motion to dismiss the breach of contract claim will be denied.

Fraud Claim

When alleging fraud, a party must state with particularity the circumstances constituting fraud, but can allege malice, intent, or other conditions of a person's mind generally.[84] Rule 9 does not require the plaintiff to include detailed evidence, but requires more than Rule 8's notice-pleading standard of vague allegations.[85] Plaintiffs must, at least, include the person, time, place, and content of each misrepresentation.

Here, O will argue the complaint included the circumstances constituting fraud because it stated TS agreed to sell the timeshare, failed to sell the timeshare after two years, failed to refund O's money, and had unprofessional employees. The pleading suggests TS lied about its abilities and likely tricked customers to invest in services that TS could not deliver. However, TS will argue O did not state who misrepresented TS's ability to sell timeshare or when O felt TS misrepresented its services. O also failed to include the content of the fraudulent statement. Thus, O's allegations are likely too vague. The court will grant TS's motion to dismiss the fraud claim.

---

82. *Leatherman v. Tarrant Cnty. Narcotics Intelligence & Coordination Unit*, 507 U.S. 163, 168 (1993).

83. *Doe v. Smith*, 429 F.3d 706, 708 (7th Cir. 2005).

84. Fed. R. Civ. P. 9.

85. *Denny v. Carey*, 72 F.R.D. 574, 578 (E.D. Pa. 1976). See also *Denny v. Barber*, 576 F.2d 465, 470 (2d Cir. 1978).

(2) Motion to Strike

The court may strike any redundant, impertinent, or scandalous matter from a pleading.[86] However, the allegations are only stricken if their presence will prejudice the adverse party, are obviously false and unrelated to the subject matter of the action, or not essential to the claim for relief or defenses pled. Here, TS will argue that P #3 should be stricken because O did not explain how unprofessional and poorly dressed employees caused TS to breach the contract or misrepresent its ability to sell O's timeshare. P #3 presents TS in a negative light to evoke an emotional response from the jury, such as distrust, which might distract the jury from analyzing the facts.

However, O will argue the actions of TS's employees are important because the employees contributed to TS's inability to sell O's timeshare. TS's employees are agents of the corporation and may have misrepresented TS's services or discouraged potential buyers. Thus, it is unlikely the court will strike P#3 because the employee's actions are related to O's claims and should be investigated during discovery.

(3) Motion for a More Definite Statement

A party may move for a more definite statement if the pleading is so vague or ambiguous that the party cannot reasonably prepare a response.[87] The motion must point out the defects and the details desired.[88] Here, TS should argue O's complaint failed to explain the terms of the contract. O never plead the agreement stated that time was of the essence. O's complaint also failed to include when and who refused to refund O's $6,000, identify the employees who dressed poorly and behaved unprofessionally, and explain how TS's employees hindered potential sales.

The court will likely grant TS's motion because TS needs more information to reasonably prepare a response. However, the court is unlikely to order O to plead the contract terms because TS probably has a copy of the contract, and O's statement that TS failed to perform after two years is detailed enough for TS to infer that the long delay upset O.

---

86. Fed. R. Civ. P. 12(f).
87. Fed. R. Civ. P. 12(e).
88. *Lodge 743, Int'l Ass'n of Machinists, AFL-CIO v. United Aircraft Corp.*, 30 F.R.D. 142, 143 (D. Conn. 1962).

(4) Answer

When responding to the complaint, the defendant must (a) state, in short and plain terms, its defenses to each claim asserted against it; and (b) admit or deny the allegations asserted against it by the opposing party.[89] A denial must fairly respond to the substance of the allegation, but if a party intends, in good faith, to deny all the allegations of the pleading, then it may do so by a general denial that does not specifically deny each allegation.[90] If a party lacks knowledge or information sufficient to form a belief about the truth of an allegation, then the party must explicitly state the lack of information in the responsive pleading.[91]

Here, TS's answer was likely inappropriate because TS should have specifically addressed each allegation in P#1, P#2, and P#3 instead of generally denying all allegations. TS also made several arguments related to the lack of specificity in O's complaint and should have explained the knowledge it needed to properly deny or admit O's allegations. A general denial, after several motions requesting more information, suggests TS's answer was not made in good faith because TS did not know the full details of O's claim against it.

However, TS will argue its general denial was made in good faith because the denial was based on TS's understanding of the situation. It is possible TS thought specific denials were inappropriate because TS honestly believed it did not breach the contract or commit fraud.

---

89. Fed. R. Civ. P. 8.
90. *Id.*
91. *Id.*

Answer 5

(1) Amendments to Nell's (N) Complaint

Amendments Before Trial

A party can amend their responsive pleadings once within 21 days after service without the opposing party's written consent or the court's leave.[92] Here, N filed the motion to amend the complaint three months after he filed the original complaint. Thus, N's only option is to argue the strict liability claim against Blue Caterpillar (BC) relates back to the original complaint.

Amendments that Relate Back

The plaintiff can add to or amend the pleading if: (a) the plaintiff filed the original claim in a timely manner, (b) the law allows relation back, and (c) the amendment asserts a claim that arose out of the same transaction or occurrence in the original pleading.[93]

Here, (b) the applicable statute of limitations allows relation back and (a) no facts suggest N failed to file the original complaint in a timely manner. (c) BC will argue that BC's maintenance of the wrecking ball is unrelated to Classy Construction's (CC) use of the wrecking ball, but BC's argument will fail because both claims arose out of the same transaction. CC used the wrecking ball to build the luxury apartments and BC's failure to fix the rusty chains likely caused the wrecking ball to detach during CC's use. Thus, the strict liability claim against BC relates back to the original negligence claim against CC because the facts of each claim are essential to determine who is responsible for N's injuries.

Changing Party

The courts are allowed to permissively join parties if the new claim arises out of same transaction or occurrence and there is a logical relationship.[94] To change a defendant, (a) the plaintiff must file the motion to amend the pleading within 120 days of the initial serving of the summons and complaint, and (b) the party brought in by the amendment must receive enough notice of the action to prevent prejudice against the party when it defends the merits of

---

92. Fed. R. Civ. P. 15(a).
93. Fed. R. Civ. P. 15(c)(1)(B).
94. Fed. R. Civ. P. 20.

the claim.[95] (c) The party being brought in must also know or should know the action would have been brought against it, but for the mistake concerning the proper party's identity.[96]

Here, (a) N filed the motion within three months, which is less than 120 days. (b) However, BC will argue that it cannot defend the merits of the claim because BC does not have the details about N's injury, CC's use of the wrecking ball, or what occurred on the day of the accident. BC will also argue N should have identified the correct defendant before filing a lawsuit. BC's argument is weak because the court examines if the defendant knew the action would be brought against it and not if the plaintiff had knowledge; whether CC knew the identity of BC is irrelevant.[97] (c) BC had actual knowledge of the lawsuit because CC notified BC about N's claim. BC should have known it was the proper defendant because CC requested a new wrecking ball, which put BC on notice that BC's failure to maintain the equipment may have caused the wrecking ball to fall. Thus, N can amend the complaint to include BC.

Court's Discretion

Even if the moving party meets the requirements of Rule 15, the court still has discretion on whether to grant the amendment. A court considers the following factors to determine if an amendment should be permitted: (a) undue delay; (b) bad faith or dilatory motive; (c) repeated failure to cure deficiencies by amendments previously allowed; (d) undue prejudice to the opposing party, such as unfair surprise; and (e) futility.[98]

Here, (a) N filed the motion to amend the complaint after he discovered CC rented the wrecking ball from BC and that BC's poor maintenance produced rusty chains. Although the motion was made three months after the original complaint was filed, no facts suggest N delayed filing his motion. Discovery is a slow process and can take months. (b) N had no ulterior motives because he likely filed the request to ensure the right party was held responsible. (c) N did not repeatedly fail to cure because this was N's first motion to amend. (d) There is no undue prejudice to BC because CC gave BC notice of N's claim. The factors favor granting the amendment to change the defendant to BC and include the strict liability claim.

---

95. Fed. R. Civ. P. 15(c)(1)(C).

96. Id.

97. *Krupski v. Costa Crociere S. p. A.*, 560 U.S. 538, 548-49 (2010).

98. *Foman v. Davis*, 371 U.S. 178, 182 (1962).

Necessary Party

A necessary party must be joined as a party if feasible.[99] If joinder of the necessary party is not feasible, then the claim must be dismissed if the party is indispensable.[100] A party is a necessary party if the court could not accord complete relief among the existing parties; the judgment would impair the absent party's interest or ability to protect his interest if he did not participate in the litigation; or litigating the case without the absent party might impose double, multiple, or inconsistent obligations.[101]

Here, BC will argue CC is a necessary party because the wrecking ball was in CC's possession when it fell on N. If CC is not a party to the litigation, then CC cannot defend itself. CC will want to explain that BC's failure to maintain its equipment made the wrecking ball rust and fall, which means CC's use of the wrecking ball did not cause N's injuries. CC's role in the controversy is important because N can sue CC for negligent use of the wrecking ball and, if BC loses, then BC can sue CC for contribution. Multiple lawsuits against CC about the same controversy could impose inconsistent rulings that require CC to pay N and BC. Thus, CC is a necessary party. For efficiency purposes, the court should consolidate the claims against CC and BC into one trial.

Feasible

Here, unless including CC and BC would destroy subject matter jurisdiction, joinder is feasible because CC was an original party to the claim and defendants can join other parties under Rule 13.[102] BC will likely file a compulsory counter claim against CC because the court must determine the percentage of fault between CC's use of the wrecking ball, BC's failure to maintain the wrecking ball, and N's contributory negligence, if any.

(2) Intervention of Right and Permissive Intervention

A court must permit anyone to intervene if a statute gives them the unconditional right; or the party has a relevant interest in the subject matter of the suit and denying intervention may impair the party's ability to protect his interests.[103] If a statute gives a conditional right to intervene, then a court has the

---

99. Fed. R. Civ. P. 19.
100. Id.
101. Id.
102. Fed. R. Civ. P. 13.
103. Fed. R. Civ. P. 24(a).

discretion to allow intervention.[104] Here, no statutes related to intervention are provided. Thus, the court must weigh the following factors to determine if Po (P) has a right to intervene: (a) whether the proper procedures have been followed; (b) whether the nonparty has an immediate interest in the action and if the interest will be impaired; (c) if intervention will enlarge the issues in the litigation; (d) if the reasons for intervention outweigh any opposition by the parties already in the action; and (e) if the intervener will bring special expertise or a different perspective that will be helpful.[105]

Here, (a) there are no facts related to the procedures, but (b) P has an immediate interest in the litigation because the accident happened on P's property and N's injuries were allegedly caused by the company P hired to build his luxury apartments. P could be held vicariously liable for CC's actions. If P is not included in the litigation, then P cannot defend himself. P also has an interest to maintain his reputation as the owner of the property because people might assume P was negligent.

(c) The defendants will argue P's harm to his reputation enlarges the issues because P's claim is not directly related the wrecking ball's rust or why the wrecking ball fell on N. (d) The defendants will oppose P's intervention because CC and BC do not want liability to another party. However, P will argue the intervention outweighs any opposition because P would sue CC and BC in a separate lawsuit and the litigation would involve the same facts as N's claim. Thus, it is efficient to consolidate the actions. Finally, (e) P could add a different perspective about the defendants' operations and maintenance of the construction site. In conclusion, P has a right to intervene as the landowner of the property and employer of CC.

(3) Joinder of Mark (M)

Necessary Party

See rule above. (Amendments to Nell's Complaint: Necessary Party). Here, M is a necessary party because N and M were both injured by the same wrecking ball operated by the same companies on the same property. If M sued CC or BC, then the relevant facts in M's case will be nearly identical to the facts litigated in N's lawsuit. If M is not joined as a party, then M's subsequent

---

104. Fed. R. Civ. P. 24(b).
105. *S.F. v. State*, 128 Cal. App. 4th 1030, 1036 (2005).

lawsuits could impose different obligations on the defendants or raise issues related to collateral estoppel. Thus, M is a necessary party.

Feasible

Joinder of a party is feasible if the absent party is subject to personal jurisdiction (PJ); adding the party would not destroy subject matter jurisdiction (SMJ); the joined party does not object to venue; and it is efficient and possible to join the party.[106]

Here, there are no facts about PJ or SMJ. The issue is whether joining M is efficient and possible. For the next six months, joining M as a party is inefficient because M is overseas and cannot appear in court. Although M intends to return, M might suddenly decide to remain overseas and the lawsuit could be indefinitely delayed. However, if M's intent to return to America is enough to make joinder feasible, then M is likely required to participate in the litigation to resolve all related issues in one lawsuit.

Indispensable Party

If the court decides joinder is not feasible because M is living overseas, then the court must determine if M is an indispensable party. The factors to decide if a party is indispensable include: (a) extent to which a judgment rendered in the person's absence might prejudice the person or existing parties; (b) extent to which prejudice could be lessened or avoided by protective provisions in the judgment, shaping of relief, or other measures; (c) the adequacy of the remedy that can be granted in the party's absence; and (d) whether the plaintiff would have an adequate remedy if the action were dismissed for non-joinder.[107]

Here, (a) the defendants might be prejudiced because they will not have M's version of the story, which is important because M was present at the time of N's injury. The defendants could also be subject to multiple lawsuits because M could sue them in the future. (c) However, the court can give N an adequate remedy without M's presence because N and M's personal injuries are distinct and separate. (d) The plaintiff may obtain a remedy through insurance, but if N's insurance claim is denied, then N would have no other way to collect his medical bills beyond a court order or the defendants' voluntary payment.

(b) The factors used to determine if prejudice can be avoided include: (i) plaintiff's interests in forum; (ii) defendant's interests in a packaged deal

---

106. Fed. R. Civ. P. 19(b).
107. *Provident Tradesmens Bank & Trust Co. v. Patterson*, 390 U.S. 102, 108-11 (1968).

to avoid multiple lawsuits, inconsistent relief, or sole responsibility he shares with another; (iii) outsider's interests in participating; and (iv) the court and public's interest in complete, consistent, efficient dispute resolution.[108] Here, (i) there are no facts about the appropriate forum. (ii) If M is not joined, then the defendants are subject to multiple litigation. The plaintiff will argue that a lawsuit from M is unlikely because M is not interested in the media chaos or the lawsuit. M specifically moved overseas to avoid the controversy. (iii) Outside parties, such as witnesses, would prefer one lawsuit to avoid testifying multiple times, and (iv) the court is already overburdened and would want to avoid multiple lawsuits about the same incident.

In conclusion, the court must require M's joinder because more factors suggest M is an indispensable party. M's interests are deeply connected to the facts of N's case and it does not make sense to separately litigate claims with overlapping issues.

(4) Sanctions

Sanctions exist to deter frivolous pleadings and prevent bad conduct. Courts want attorneys to critically evaluate the merits of the claim, but do not want to discourage attorneys from advancing novel legal theories. When an attorney presents a signed pleading, written motion, or other paper to court, the attorney certifies that the paper was prepared to the best of the attorney's knowledge,[109] and that the attorney made reasonable inquiries before filling the pleading.[110]

Although N's claims were warranted by existing law and not filed for an improper purpose, N's allegation that the defendants were solely responsible for N's injury may not have evidentiary support. A reasonable attorney would have watched the security camera footage before filing a lawsuit because a video recording is likely more reliable than a human's memory. The security footage would have revealed that N may have caused his own harm. N's attorney should have also interviewed M, who was present at the time of the accident, to learn more about N's claims. A reasonable attorney would not rely solely on his client's statements because clients can lie.

---

108. *Id.*
109. Fed. R. Civ. P. 11.
110. *Id.*

However, N's attorney will argue a reasonable attorney can trust his client. No attorney is expected to conduct a full investigation before filing a lawsuit because the facts will be revealed during discovery. By speaking to his client, he acted reasonably under the circumstances. Thus, the court is unlikely to impose sanctions because, even if N contributed to his injuries, BC and CC could have still played a role in causing N's harm. N's claims are not frivolous because the lawsuit will determine who is responsible for N's injuries.

Answer 6

(1) Sanctions on Burger Joint (BJ)

Meet and Confer

Before discovery begins, parties must confer about their proposed discovery plans and set a schedule.[111] After the schedule is established, the deadlines can only be changed with judicial approval upon showing of good cause.[112] When determining whether to grant a request to reschedule, the court considers the (a) explanation for the untimely motion, (b) importance of amendment, (c) potential prejudice in allowing the amendment, and (d) availability to cure such prejudice.[113]

Here, Lana's (L) request to modify the schedule will likely be granted because, (a) although L filed the motion a week before her deposition, L did not purposefully delay her motion to reschedule. L could not predict that she would be hospitalized. (b) BJ properly deposing L is critical to the case because she is the plaintiff. The court does not want L distracted by her illness when answering questions. (c) L will argue BJ suffers no prejudice because L can be deposed after she is discharged from the hospital. BJ will argue that postponing L's deposition would delay the discovery process and make it difficult for BJ to continue its investigation. (d) However, BJ's argument is weak because the court can easily change the trial date and extend the time for discovery. Thus, BJ should have agreed to reschedule L's deposition and could be subject to sanctions.

Depositions

All parties must have notice of the deposition with the date, time, place, and deponents name and address.[114] A deposition cannot be conducted in bad faith to badger or humiliate the witness.[115] Here, BJ gave L notice that she would be deposed on May 9th, but L's deposition was likely to harass L. BJ's lawyers aggressively deposed L in the hospital while L was sick. L asked the attorneys to leave, but BJ ignored her request. Thus, BJ is subject to sanctions.

---

111. Fed. R. Civ. P. 26(f).
112. Fed. R. Civ. P. 16.
113. *Fahim v. Marriott Hotel Servs., Inc.*, 551 F.3d 344, 348 (5th Cir. 2008).
114. Fed. R. Civ. P. 30. See also Fed. R. Civ. P. 31.
115. *Id.*

Sanctions

If a party fails to cooperate during discovery, then the party could be subject to sanctions that require compliance or will ensure the party does not profit from its failure to comply.[116] Parties rarely get money sanctions because the court wants to discourage parties from filing a motion every time they cannot resolve an issue.[117] But, if the motion is granted, then the party can get reasonable expenses unless the movant filed without attempting in good faith to resolve the issue or the opposing party's action is substantially justified.[118]

Here, L tried to resolve the issue in good faith. L did not skip the deposition or request an unreasonable extension. L gave BJ notice of her illness and asked to reschedule her deposition to after her hospitalization. BJ might benefit from its failure to cooperate because BJ triggered L's panic attack in the hospital; L may withdraw her claim due to fear or stress. Thus, BJ could be required to pay reasonable fees associated with L's motion and provide L with a later deposition date at a more appropriate location.

(2) Information About Chemicals

Mandatory Disclosures

A party must disclose things that will support its claim, such as individuals with discoverable information and documents that the party intends to use for its claim or defense.[119] The party must make these mandatory disclosures without waiting for a discovery request.[120] Here, BJ's intended defense included the document describing the chemicals used to enlarge its produce. BJ violated Rule 26 because BJ failed to disclosed the document to L and waited for L to make a discovery request. BJ must produce the document about the chemicals.

Motion to Compel

Any party may request from another party documents or tangible things within the scope of discovery for inspection, copy, test, or sample.[121] The scope of discovery is very broad and includes any non-privileged information

---

116. Fed. R. Civ. P. 37.

117. *Id.*

118. *Id.*

119. Fed. R. Civ. P. 26 (a). See also *Cummings v. Gen. Motors Corp.*, 365 F.3d 944, 953-54 (10th Cir. 2004).

120. *Id.*

121. Fed. R. Civ. P. 34.

that is relevant to any party's claim or defense.[122] The discoverable information does not need to be admissible at trial, but must reasonably lead to the discovery of admissible evidence.[123]

Here, L's request for information about the chemicals used on the plants is relevant because L suffered from food poisoning, which could have been caused by the chemicals on BJ's produce. The document will help L uncover if the chemicals were safe to use on human food. However, BJ might argue that information about the chemicals is not relevant because food poisoning is not caused by agricultural mistakes, but by failure to properly maintain and prepare food. BJ's argument is weak because L's food poisoning could have multiple causes and the chemicals may have played a role in her injury. L's request is within the scope of discovery and BJ must produce the document unless one of the protective measures apply.

Protective Measures

A motion to compel must describe, with reasonable particularity, each item or category of items to be inspected. The party must know exactly what the other party is requesting.[124] The court may issue an order to protect any party from discovery requests that cause annoyance, embarrassment, or an undue burden.[125] The court can limit discover requests on its own, or when a party makes a motion. To determine whether to grant a motion to compel, the court considers many factors, such as (a) if the request is unreasonably cumulative or duplicative; (b) if the information can be obtained from another source that is less inconvenient, burdensome, or expensive; (c) if the party seeking discovery had amble opportunity to obtain the information; (d) if the burden and expense of discovery outweighs its likely benefit; (e) the quantity of information requested; (f) if the failure to produce would result in the information no longer being available; (g) the importance of the issues at stake; (h) the parties' resources; and (i) the accessibility of the information stored.[126]

Here, L described the items with reasonable particularity because she specifically requested information on all the chemicals used on all of BJ's plants throughout their lifetime and how often the chemicals were used on the plants. L will argue that her request is valid because (b) she cannot obtain the

---

122. Fed. R. Civ. P. 26 (b).
123. *Id.*
124. Fed. R. Civ. P. 34.
125. Fed. R. Civ. P. 26 (c).
126. *Id.*

information elsewhere since she does not have access to BJ's records, (c) she never had the opportunity to get the information earlier in the discovery process, and (g) the list of chemicals is important to her case because the chemicals likely caused her food poisoning. (a) L's request is also not duplicative or cumulative because it is her first request related to the chemicals in BJ's food.

However, (d) BJ will argue that the burden to produce all the records for every plant for its entire lifespan would be expensive and burdensome because the plants likely had long lifespans and BJ had several plants. (e) The vast quantity of information requested by L is evidenced by BJ's warehouse full of records. (i) BJ will also argue the accessibility of the information is limited because it requires someone to filter through all the documents in the warehouse, which could take a long time. Moreover, the benefit of providing information on BJ's entire inventory of crops is low because every plant was not used in L's food. L's request is overinclusive. At most, BJ should be required to produce information on the chemicals used on the plants included in the meal that allegedly caused L's food poisoning.

In conclusion, L will need to narrow the scope of her request, but (h) BJ, as a company with more resources and access to produce the requested information, will be required to comply with L's request.

(3) List of Restaurants

Scope of Discovery

See rule above. (Information About Chemicals: Motion to Compel). Here, BJ will argue the list of restaurants is irrelevant because L ate food at BJ's location and not other restaurants. A list of restaurants that purchased BJ's food would not help L's case. However, L has a stronger argument because the list will help L determine if food poisoning was a common occurrence at the restaurants that used BJ's food. If food poisoning was common, then the cause could be related to BJ's use of chemicals on the crops and not the food preparation at each location. The list provides potential witnesses that can reasonably lead to more discoverable information. Thus, because the scope of discovery is broad, it is likely the court will find the list is relevant and BJ will be required to produce the list unless an exception applies.

Attorney Work Product

Documents and tangible things created in anticipation of litigation or for trial are not discoverable.[127] Here, L will argue the list of restaurants is not attorney work product because, although BJ's attorney prepared the list, the document was prepared years ago, which was before L suffered from food poisoning and filed a lawsuit. Thus, the list is discoverable.

Mental Impressions

An attorney's work product, such as oral statements or memoranda, are not discoverable because work product is susceptible to inaccuracy and untrustworthiness; this includes mental impressions, conclusions, opinions, or legal theories of the attorney.[128]

Although L can likely access the list, BJ will argue the attorney's personal notes about the restaurants were prepared in anticipation of litigation and are not discoverable. BJ's attorney marked the restaurants as a note to herself, which suggests she was memorializing her mental thoughts on the paper when reviewing the list. The markings were the attorney's best guess of what restaurants experienced food poisoning. Thus, to get a list with the attorney's markings, L must prove (a) there is a substantial need for the materials, (b) it is essential for L to prepare her case, and (c) a substantial equivalent cannot be obtained without undue hardship or prejudice to L's case.[129]

Here, (a) BJ already knows the names of the restaurants selling its produce and L likely needs the list to start her investigation. (b) L will argue the attorney's markings are essential to prepare her case because the notes narrow down the list of restaurants that L should interview. (c) L cannot obtain the information from another source because most companies do not publicize their client lists. It would be burdensome for L to independently figure out the restaurants that purchased BJ's food and consumers that suffered from food poisoning. Denying L's request would waste resources because BJ already has the information.

However, (b) BJ will argue L can prepare her case by interviewing BJ employees about the restaurants serving BJ's food. L should not rely on a list created years ago and markings arbitrarily added by BJ's attorney. (a) L also has no

---

127. *Hickman v. Taylor*, 329 U.S. 495, 508–512 (1947).
128. *Id.* at 510.
129. *Id.* at 508–512.

substantial need for the list because the lawsuit involves BJ's restaurant and not other locations. L should investigate what happened to the food she ate. Thus, because the markings are not trustworthy, the markings will be redacted and only the list will be provided to L.

(4) Burger Joint's Manager and Attorney's Conversation
Scope of Discovery

See rule above. (Information About Chemicals: Motion to Compel). Here, L will argue the conversation is within the scope of discovery because it helps L narrow down the list of restaurants that possibly experienced food poisoning from BJ's produce. However, the conversation might be privileged.

Attorney-Client Privilege

Information protected by the attorney-client privilege is not discoverable. The attorney-client privilege attaches to communication if (a) the person who asserts the privilege is the client; (b) the communication is to an attorney or a subordinate acting under the direction of the attorney; (c) the communication is made in private with no third party present; and (d) the communication is made for the purpose of seeking legal service.[130] The privilege can be waived, but only by the client.[131]

Here, (a) BJ is asserting the privilege because BJ refused to produce the recording. (b) The communication was between BJ's attorney and BJ's manager. (c) The communication was made in the presence of the attorney's legal assistant, but the assistant was taking notes under the direction of the attorney. Thus, the assistant's presence will not destroy the confidentiality of the communication. (d) BJ's manager was discussing potential witnesses with the attorney, which is asking for legal advice; the manager will likely defer to the attorney's expertise on the selection of witnesses. Thus, the attorney-client privilege applies.

A few additional requirements are necessary for the privilege to apply because BJ is a corporation. The attorney-corporation privilege requires the communication to be (e) within the scope of the employee's corporate duties; (f) necessary to supply a basis for legal advice; and (g) treated as confidential within the corporation.[132]

130. *Colton v. U.S.*, 306 F.2d 633, 637 (2d Cir. 1962).
131. *Hickman v. Taylor*, supra note 127.
132. *Upjohn Co. v. U.S.*, 449 U.S. 383, 394-95 (1981).

Here, (e) BJ's manager is likely responsible for meeting with attorneys about pending litigation because the manager holds a supervisory role. However, L might argue that litigation is usually handled by higher positions, such as the Chief Executive Officer, or the legal department. More facts are necessary, but it is likely BJ's manager was acting within the scope of his duties. (f) BJ's manager needed to meet with the attorney to put together BJ's litigation plan. (g) BJ is keeping its litigation strategy confidential because BJ refused to give the information to L and only the legal assistant and attorney were present at the meeting. In conclusion, L's motion will not be granted because the conversation is privileged.

Answer 7

(1) Motion for Summary Judgment (MSJ)

The court shall grant a MSJ if there is no genuine dispute as to any material fact.[133] A material fact impacts the outcome of the case.[134] A genuine issue means a reasonable jury could differ on the conclusions regarding the material fact.[135] When reviewing a MSJ, the court must draw reasonable inferences in the light most favorable to the non-moving party unless the record blatantly contradicts the inferences.[136] The material facts at issue are whether Ariel (A) was the original creator of the story, and whether Bruce (B) copied her story or independently developed the themes, characters, and scenes in his book.

Here, B will argue an essential element of A's claim is negated because A's manuscript was only accessible to her staff. B had no access to her story because B was not A's staff member. B also stated he did not remember A's ideas from the convention. B's argument is reasonable because people have fickle memories and do not always recall information from years ago. Moreover, the theme of animals on a journey to save the world from a villain is a common storyline used by writers and not unique. It is possible B developed the book on his own.

However, A will argue reasonable people could differ on whether B copied A's story because B had access to A's idea at the convention. A will argue B's themes, scenes, and characters were similar to A's manuscript, which means B likely copied her story.

The court must draw reasonable inferences in A's favor, such as B had access to her story, because B is the moving party. Based on the evidence presented, reasonable jury members could differ on whether B copied A's story. Thus, the court was correct in denying B's MSJ because the judge is not allowed to access the credibility of witnesses and the final outcome will depend on the credibility of each party's testimony.[137]

---

133. Fed. R. Civ. P. 56.
134. *Scott v. Harris*, 550 U.S. 372, 380 (2007).
135. *Id.*
136. *Id.*
137. *Id.*

(2) Judgment as a Matter of Law (JML)

A motion for a JML can be made after the party presents its own evidence at trial or after the nonmoving party presents its evidence, but must be made before the case is submitted to the jury.[138] The standard of review for a JML is the same as a MSJ. The court must view the motion in the light most favorable to the non-moving party.[139] The court may grant a JML if there is no legally sufficient evidentiary basis for a reasonable jury to find for a party on certain issues.[140] Sufficient evidence requires proof that is beyond mere speculation.[141]

Here, the analysis is the same as above (Motion for Summary Judgment), but the facts revealed at trial suggest B had access to A's manuscript. A will argue that B's friend was A's staff member, which means B's friend could have leaked A's manuscript to B. Although B claims he never spoke to his friend about the manuscript, it is possible B's friend gave B access.

However, because A is the moving party, the court must look at the case in the light most favorable to B. Without concrete evidence that B and B's friend discussed A's manuscript, A's accusations are mere speculation and not enough to satisfy the burden of proof. Thus, because reasonable jury members could differ on B's access to A's story, there is still a genuine dispute of material fact. The judge correctly allowed the jury to decide the issue by denying A's motion for a JML.

(3) Judgment Non-Withstanding the Jury Verdict (JNOV)

A court can grant a motion for JNOV to reverse or amend the jury's verdict if the judge determines that no reasonable jury could have reached the jury's decision.[142] JNOV was created to avoid extremely unreasonably jury decisions that are not supported by the evidence, but is rarely granted. When a judge grants a motion for JNOV, the judge can order a new trial or make a judgment as a matter of law.[143] If the case involves testimony by parties whose credibility must be assessed, then the judge is more likely to grant a new trial because judges cannot assess credibility.

---

138. Fed. R. Civ. P. 50.
139. *Galloway v. United States*, 319 U.S. 372, 395-396 (1943).
140. Fed. R. Civ. P. 50.
141. *Galloway v. United States*, supra note 139.
142. Fed. R. Civ. P. 50.
143. Fed. R. Civ. P. 59.

New Trial

The court can grant a new trial if the decision was based on evidence that was false, there was clear weight of the evidence against the verdict, there were errors in the trial process that impacted the verdict, or the lack of a new trial will result in a miscarriage of justice.[144] Here, B will argue A merely made blanket accusations that B was copying her work without providing concrete proof that B had access to her manuscript. Thus, no reasonable jury could conclude B was at fault.

However, A has a stronger argument because there is no clear evidence against the jury's decision. The facts also showed B had access to the manuscript through his friend, B's story had several similarities to A's manuscript, and B attended the conference where A shared her storyline. The evidence presented supports both sides, which means a reasonable jury could have determined B copied A's work. Thus, when examining the merits of the case, the judge should not have granted B's motion for JNOV because the jury's verdict was supported by evidence.

Remittitur

However, when examining the damages awarded to A, the judge correctly ordered a new trial. If the judge believes the damages awarded are too high, then the judge can offer the plaintiff the option to accept a lower amount or go through a new trial. If the plaintiff agrees, then the defendant's request for a new trial is denied.[145] Here, the damages were unreasonable because the jury awarded A 90% of B's royalties. Although B may have copied A's storyline, B still needed to write the book and secure a publishing deal. Thus, allowing A to take nearly all of B's proceeds is extreme. The judge correctly asked A to accept a lower judgement and granted a new trial to determine reasonable damages when A refused.

---

144. *Id.*

145. *Dimick v. Schiedt*, 293 U.S. 474, 486-87 (1935). See also *Hetzel v. Prince William Cnty., Va.*, 523 U.S. 208, 209 (1998).

Answer 8

(1) Appellate Review

A court of appeals has jurisdiction over appeals from all final decisions of districts courts of the United States, except if directly reviewed by the Supreme Court.[146]

Final Judgment

A final judgment is a finding of fact by the jury that leaves nothing more for the court to do except execute the judgment.[147] The judgment must be on the merits of the underlying substantive claim and not dismissed for procedural or jurisdictional reasons. Here, the jury ruled in favor of Wanda (W) on her racial discrimination claim against Theme Park (TP). The court's only remaining action is to pay W damages. Thus, there is a final judgment on the merits and TP can request an appeal.

Court's Discretion

There is no constitutional right to an appeal.[148] The appeals court has the discretion to hear the case to correct mistakes, resolve questions of law to ensure trial judges interpret the law uniformly and correctly, and vary the interpretations of the law if the law is evolving.[149]

Here, no facts indicate there was an error during trial or that the trial courts are interpreting the laws differently. But based on TP's petition for review, there are varying interpretations of §42. The jury believes §42 requires employers to select minority applicants over White applicants if the applicants are equally qualified whereas TP believes racial discrimination under §42 only occurs when an unqualified White applicant is selected over a more qualified minority candidate. Thus, the court should grant review to clarify §42's vague standard. However, if the lower courts are applying the law uniformly or there is no change in the political environment to suggest TP's interpretation is more appropriate, then the appeals court should deny the appeal.

---

146. 28 U.S.C. § 1291 (2012). See also *Firestone Tire & Rubber Co. v. Risjord*, 449 U.S. 368, 373 (1981).

147. *Id.*

148. *McKane v. Durston*, 153 U.S. 684 (1894). See also *Highmark Inc. v. Allcare Health Management System, Inc.*, 134 S.Ct. 1744, 1748 (2014).

149. *Id.*

(2) Vu's (V) Claim

Claim Preclusion

Res judicata prevents one party from relitigating a claim that was already decided.[150] Res judicata applies when there is (a) a final judgment on the merits, (b) the second lawsuit involves the same parties, and (c) the claim is the same as the first lawsuit.[151]

(a) <u>Final Judgment</u>: See rule and analysis above. (Appellate Review: Final Judgment).

(b) <u>Same Claim</u>: The second claim must arise from the same common nucleus of operative fact as the first claim, which means the facts are related in time, space, and origin, and the evidence used to prove both claims is essentially the same.[152] Claims that arise from the same factual situation should be litigated together and joined as compulsory claims or they are barred.

Here, V will argue the claims originated from the same common nucleus of operative fact because the discrimination V experienced was identical to W. V applied to be a manager, but a White candidate was promoted. Thus, even though this occurred in the food and beverage (F&B) department and not the retail department, the defendant in both claims was a minority and the hiring events were nearly identical. Moreover, the jury is likely to look at the same evidence to analyze TP's liability, such as there is only one minority manager out of 30 at TP even though 80% of the leads and associates are people of color. The jury will likely draw the conclusion that the lack of minority managers at TP is caused by discriminatory hiring practices in all departments.

However, TP will argue the first action must have actually litigated the issues related to the second action's claims. Issues from V's claim were never addressed because the F&B department may examine different qualifications and implement different hiring procedures. TP will also argue that no facts suggest V and the White candidate were equally qualified like W and her competition. Thus, racial discrimination in retail against W is not the same claim as discrimination in F&B against V.

---

150. *Migra v. Warren City Sch. Dist. Bd. of Educ.*, 465 U.S. 75, 77 n.1 (1984).
151. *Mathews v. New York Racing Ass'n, Inc.*, 193 F. Supp. 293, 294 (S.D.N.Y. 1961).
152. *Interoceanica Corp. v. Sound Pilots, Inc.*, 107 F.3d 86, 90 (2d Cir. 1997).

(c) <u>Same Parties</u>: The parties are not the same because the original claim was between W and TP. V was never a party to the original claim.

In conclusion, res judicata does not apply.

Issue Preclusion

Collateral estoppel prevents parties from relitigating issues that were previously decided in a prior case. V will use collateral estoppel to prevent TP from relitigating the issue that TP's hiring and promotion practices are not discriminatory. For collateral estoppel to apply, (a) the issue in the second claim must be the same as the issue in the first claim, (b) the issue must have been actually litigated and decided in the first claim, and (c) the issue must be necessary to the court's final judgment in the first claim.[153]

(a) <u>Same Issue</u>: See rule and analysis above. (Vu's Claims: Claim Preclusion: Same Claim). If V, W, and the White candidates were equally qualified, then the jury would use the same facts to determine if TP's hiring practices were racially discriminatory. If V and the White candidate were not equally qualified, then the issues are different and collateral estoppel will not apply.

(b) <u>Actually Litigated</u>: If the first decision was vague, overinclusive, or too speculative to constitute a decision over the second claim, then collateral estoppel will not apply.[154] Here, the validity of TP's hiring practices was actually litigated in the first claim because W's lawsuit examined whether TP promoted White candidates over minority candidates. Thus, TP cannot relitigate the issue if the hiring policies in the retail department are the same as the F&B department.

(c) <u>Necessarily Determined</u>: The issue must have been outcome determinative, which means the result of the case would be different if the decision on this issue was different.[155] Collateral estoppel does not bar litigation on an issue if there was uncertainty over what issues the jury decided during the first lawsuit.[156] Here, the issue was necessarily determined because if the jury determined that TP's hiring practices did not discriminate against minorities, then the result of the W's claim would have been different; W would have lost.

---

153. *S. Pac. R. Co. v. United States*, 168 U.S. 1, 48-49 (1897). See also *Interoceanica Corp. v. Sound Pilots, Inc.*, supra note 152.

154. *Cromwell v. Cnty. of Sac*, 94 U.S. 351, 353 (1876).

155. *Russell v. Place*, 94 U.S. 606, 608-09 (1876).

156. *Id.*

Different Parties

Unlike res judicata, collateral estoppel focuses on the issues and not the people in the lawsuit.[157] Thus, the parties from the first claim do not need to be the same as the second claim.[158] Defensive collateral estoppel is a shield for the defendant because it prevents the plaintiff from relitigated issues by simply switching adversaries.[159] Offensive collateral estoppel is a sword for the plaintiff because it allows the plaintiff to prevent the defendant from relitigating issues decided against the defendant in the previous lawsuit.[160] Offensive collateral estoppel is only applicable if the defendant litigated and lost the issue against the first plaintiff.[161] If the defendant won the issue against the first plaintiff, then offensive collateral estoppel does not apply because the defendant cannot stop the new plaintiff from relitigating the same issue.[162]

Here, V is using collateral estoppel offensively to prevent the same defendant, TP, from denying its racial discrimination in hiring by stating that a jury already determined TP's practices were illegal in W's lawsuit. Before granting V's request to use collateral estoppel, the court will balance the following factors: (a) if there was a full and fair opportunity to litigate the issue in the previous suit; (b) if allowing collateral estoppel will encourage parties to wait and see on the issue rather than joining the first suit; (c) the court's interest in preventing multiple lawsuits for judicial efficiency; (d) if it is unfair to give conclusive effect to any ruling because the prior rulings are inconsistent; and (e) if the defendant failed to put its resources into litigating the first case because there was no incentive; the defendant can relitigate the issue if the first case was a side show.[163]

Here, (a) (c) (d) no facts suggest W's case was a side show, or that rulings were inconsistent, or that TP did not have a chance to fairly litigate the issue of racially discriminatory hiring during the first lawsuit. (b) However, the first lawsuit did encourage V to wait and see. V only brought a lawsuit against TP after V learned that W was successful. The court does not want to encourage V and other leads to delay bringing their lawsuits against TP.

---

157. *Bernhard v. Bank of Am. Nat. Trust & Sav. Ass'n*, 19 Cal. 2d 807, 812-13 (1942).
158. *Id.*
159. *Blonder-Tongue Labs., Inc. v. Univ. of Illinois Found.*, 402 U.S. 313, 328-29 (1971).
160. *Id.*
161. *Parklane Hosiery Co. v. Shore*, 439 U.S. 322, 329-30 (1979).
162. *Id.* at 326-327.
163. *Id.* at 326-327 n.5.

In conclusion, if the issues were the same and actually litigated, then V can assert offensive collateral estoppel against TP unless the court determines judicial efficiency is hindered by encouraging employees to delay bringing claims against TP under §42.

(3) Wanda's (W) Claim

Claim Preclusion

See rules above. (Vu's Claim: Claim Preclusion).

(a) <u>Final Judgment</u>: See rule and analysis above. (Appellate Review: Final Judgment).

(b) <u>Same Claim</u>: See rule above. (Vu's Claim: Same Claim). Here, TP will argue W is relitigating the same issue of racial discrimination in promotion and advancement opportunities under the same law, §42. However, W will argue her claims are not the same because her second lawsuit relates to TP's training program for managers and not TP's hiring process. W's argument is stronger because hiring practices and training programs are different company functions.

(c) <u>Same Parties</u>: The parties are the same because the original claim was between W and TP.

In conclusion, TP cannot use res judicata to prevent W from litigating her new claim.

Constitutional Law Answers

Answer 1

(1) Federal Court's Power

Judicial Review

Article III of the U.S. Constitution states that courts have the right to review all cases and controversies that arise under the Constitution, Laws of the U.S., and Treaties.[164] *Marbury v. Madison* established that the U.S. Supreme Court and any inferior courts created by Congress have the right to interpret the rules and how they should be applied.[165] Here, Congress created the federal district court as an inferior court, which means there is judicial review.

Political Questions

The judiciary hesitates to review issues that are impossible to resolve without making a policy determination or textually committed to another branch of the government.[166] Here, State Z will argue that decisions about pollution-control techniques are reserved for state and federal legislatures. The courts are not equipped to make policy determinations because judges are not elected officials and the legislative branch has more resources to research the environmental needs of communities. However, the court has jurisdiction to determine if State Z's laws conflict with the federal laws, which is not a legislative decision. Thus, State Z's argument will fail.

---

164. U.S. Const. art. III, § 2, cl. 1.
165. *Marbury v. Madison*, 5 U.S. 137, 173-174, 177 (1803).
166. *Al-Aulaqi v. Obama*, 727 F. Supp. 2d 1, 14 (D.D.C. 2010).

(2) Erin's (E) Standing

Standing

To satisfy Article III's case or controversy requirement, at least one party must have standing. Standing requires (a) an actual or imminent injury, (b) causation, and (c) that the injury will be remedied by a favorable decision.[167]

(a) Actual Injury

The injury cannot be a generalized grievance that is widespread, abstract, and indefinite,[168] or raise third-party rights; the injury must affect the plaintiff in a personal way.[169] Here, E will argue that she suffered an actual injury because she was deprived of observing the animals thrive in their natural habitats. E was distraught, which suggests that she experienced some emotional distress when the animal sightings decreased.

State Z will argue that E's stress is a general injury suffered by many others in the community. Courts previously determined that the loss of enjoyment of observing animals is not an imminent injury if the plaintiff has no immediate intent to observe the animals.[170] Although E will argue she regularly visits State Z to view the animals and plans to return soon, if E cannot prove her intent, then she has no standing unless she is validly asserting the rights of AA.

Third-Party Standing

The prohibition on third-party standing does not apply if the plaintiff and third-party's interests are significantly close, or the third-party is hindered from asserting its legal rights.[171] Here, E will argue her interests are identical to AA's interests because they both want AA to receive funding to protect the environment and animals. AA's duties increased after State Z adopted relaxed pollution standards because more animals were injured. AA needs money to rehabilitate the injured animals. Similarly, E wants to observe the animals, which cannot occur unless pollution is reduced and AA receives more resources to treat the animals. However, E's interest relates to animal observations while AA's interest is to get funding. Thus, the interests are distinct and AA will need to bring its own claim unless E can prove AA is unlikely to bring a claim against

---

167. *Lujan v. Defenders of Wildlife*, 504 U.S. 555 (1992).
168. *Id.*
169. *Allen v. Wright*, 468 U.S. 737 (1984).
170. *Lujan v. Defenders of Wildlife*, supra note 167.
171. *Al-Aulaqi v. Obama*, supra note 166.

State Z because AA wants to preserve its relationship with the state to avoid being shutdown.

Ripeness and Mootness

A case cannot be brought too early or too late. A case is not ripe for review if the case relies on future events that may cause harm.[172] A case is moot if the events that occur after the filing of the case resolved the dispute.[173] Here, E will argue her claim is ripe because she regularly travels to State Z, which suggests she will return soon to observe the animals. State Z will argue E's injury is speculative because she has no trip planned. State Z will also argue E's case is moot because State Z gave AA 15% additional funding, which resolved the resource-shortage problem. However, a case should not be dismissed as moot if the wrong is capable of repetition, but evading review,[174] or there is voluntary cessation with the possibility of the harm returning.[175] State Z could easily retract the extra money granted to AA after the case is dismissed. Thus, because the harm might return, E likely does have a claim ripe for adjudication.

(b) Causation

The injury must be traceable to the unlawful conduct of the actor being sued.[176] Here, the number of injured animals and pollution increased after State Z adopted relaxed pollution standards, which suggests there is a correlation between State Z's legislation and the environmental harm. State Z will argue that several other factors, such as migration patterns and natural disasters, may have impacted the animals and environment, but State Z's argument is weak. The causation element is met.

(c) Remedy

The concrete injury must be redressed by a favorable decision.[177] Here, if the courts determine State Z's pollution requirements are too relaxed, then State Z will need stricter standards. If State Z adopts stricter standards, then agencies will reduce their pollution, fewer animals will be injured, and more animals will return to their habitats.

---

172. *Poe v. Ullman*, 367 U.S. 497 (1961).
173. *Id.*
174. *Roe v. Wade*, 410 U.S. 113 (1973).
175. *Los Angeles County v. Davis*, 440 U.S. 625, 631 (1979).
176. *Massachusetts v. E.P.A.*, 549 U.S. 497 (2007).
177. *Id.*

Conclusion

E does not have standing if her interest is distinct from AA's and AA can defend itself in court.

(3) Spending Power and the 10th Amendment

Article I Powers

Congress can enact laws that are necessary and proper to carry out its enumerated powers as long as the law does not violate other parts of the Constitution.[178] Article I specifically states Congress has the power to lay and collect taxes and pay debts to provide for the general welfare of the United States, but its action must be uniform throughout the nation.[179] Here, Congress validly used its spending power to promote the general welfare because the Pollution Prevent Act (PPA) was passed to create a cleaner and safer environment for all residents by reducing pollution. The act uniformly applies to every federal agency and allows all states to receive additional funding by adopting the PPA's pollution standards. Congress did not discriminate based on the agency or state's size, demographics, or location.

10th Amendment

The 10th Amendment states "the powers not delegated to the United States by the Constitution, nor prohibited by it to the States, are reserved to the States respectively, or to the people."[180] State Z will argue the environment is an area of local concern, which means the federal government cannot pass laws regulating the state's actions.[181] However, State Z's argument will fail because the federal law imposes no requirements on the states and merely gives states the option to adopt the PPA. Even though regulating health and safety is primarily a local concern, the federal government can set uniform national standards.[182]

State Z will argue the PPA indirectly requires states to apply federal standards[183] because the additional 10% in federal funding for adopting the PPA removes the opt-in choice; an extra 10% can dramatically impact a state's

---

178. U.S. Const. art. I, § 8, cl. 18.
179. U.S. Const. art. I, § 8, cl. 1.
180. U.S. Const. amend. X.
181. *United States v. Butler*, 297 U.S. 1 (1936).
182. *Gonzales v. Oregon*, 546 U.S. 243 (2006).
183. *New York v. United States*, 505 U.S. 144 (1992).

budget. However, this argument fails because State Z did not adopt the PPA and still functions without any extreme difficulties, which suggests the 10% in bonus funding for environmental programs was not essential to State Z's operations.

Moreover, the PPA passes the *S. Dakota v. Dole* test that requires conditions on federal spending to be (1) for the general welfare, (2) unambiguous, (3) related to the federal interest, and (4) not unconstitutional under another provision.[184]

Here, (1) the PPA serves the general welfare because the act establishes the best pollution-prevention techniques and provides states with additional funding to improve environmental programs. (2) The act is unambiguous because it explicitly conditions the additional 10% in federal funding on the adoption of the PPA. The act is not vague about the conduct it encourages. (3) The additional funding promotes the federal government's interest in lowering pollution because the money specifically helps the state's environmental programs. (4) As stated above, the act does not violate the 10th Amendment. Thus, the PPA is constitutional and State Z's argument will fail.

---

184. *S. Dakota v. Dole*, 483 U.S. 203 (1987).

Answer 2

(1) Article I Powers

Taxing Power

Congress can enact laws that are necessary and proper to carry out its enumerated powers as long as the law does not violate other parts of the Constitution.[185] Article I specifically states Congress has the power to lay and collect taxes as long as it is for the general welfare of the United States and there is a rational relationship between the tax and the purpose.[186] The purpose can include reasons beyond raising revenue, such as moral motives, but must be reasonable.[187]

Here, the Cancer Kills Act (CKA) promotes the general welfare because it raises money to research a cure for cancer, a disease killing many Americans. The tax is rationally related to promoting healthy habits and decreasing mortality rates because a well-known research study revealed that lung cancer was the leading cause of deaths in the U.S., and that tobacco caused lung cancer. The CKA attempts to eliminate a source of lung cancer by discouraging the sale of tobacco cigarettes through an 8% tax on the revenue of cigarettes and imposing operational obstacles on sellers. If cigarettes are less accessible to customers, then people might be less likely to smoke and get lung cancer. If less people get lung cancer, then there will be fewer deaths in the country. Thus, the 8% tax is constitutional.

State B will argue that the additional 1% tax imposed on stores near middle and high schools is not rationally related because no facts suggest lung cancer is more prominent in teenagers or that teenagers are more likely to purchase cigarettes. However, the federal government will argue that locked containers behind the counter discourage theft among the youth who idolize smoking. To win this argument, Congress needs more evidence to show a correlation between lung cancer, cigarettes, and teenagers. If Congress cannot show a relationship, then the 1% tax and closed-container requirement is unconstitutional.

---

185. U.S. Const. art. I, § 8, cl. 18.
186. *United States v. Kahriger*, 345 U.S. 22 (1953).
187. *United States v. Doremus*, 249 U.S. 86 (1919).

Taxes as a Penalty

Congress can impose taxes to raise revenue,[188] but if the motive behind the tax is to coerce the state to act as Congress wishes, then the tax is unconstitutional.[189] If a tax raises minimal revenue, then it is more likely a penalty and Congress has exceeded its powers.[190]

Here, the federal government will argue the 8% tax on cigarette sales is to raise revenue for cancer research and is not a penalty. Although the derivative effects of the tax discourage the sale of cigarettes, the 8% tax is near the average sales tax in the U.S. (8.45%). Thus, the 8% tax is constitutional.

However, the 1% tax is more likely a penalty because it raises minimal money and the motive behind the tax is to discourage stores near middle and high schools from selling cigarettes; the CKA penalizes stores that fail to lock their cigarettes behind the counter. Thus, the 1% tax is unconstitutional.

Conditions on Spending

S. Dakota v. Dole requires conditions on federal spending to be (1) for the general welfare, (2) unambiguous, (3) related to the federal interest, and (4) not unconstitutional under another provision.[191] Here, (1) CKA promotes the general welfare because it encourages healthy habits and raises money for cancer research. (2) The CKA is unambiguous because it explicitly cuts 50% of the state's federal cancer research funding if the state fails to reasonably regulate CKA's provisions. (3) Although CKA's goals are to decrease the sale of cigarettes and discourage smoking, conditioning half the cancer research funds on proper enforcement of the CKA is not related to the federal interest of curing cancer. If the federal government wants to find a cure, then reducing the state's cancer-research funds impairs the state's research. (4) The CKA also likely violates the 10th Amendment.

10th Amendment

The 10th Amendment states "the powers not delegated to the United States by the Constitution, nor prohibited by it to the States, are reserved to the States respectively, or to the people."[192] Here, states have sovereignty over traditional

188. *Bailey v. Drexel Furniture Co.*, 259 U.S. 20, 38 (1922).
189. *Id.*
190. *Id.*
191. *S. Dakota v. Dole*, supra note 184.
192. U.S. Const. amend. X.

government functions, such as protecting state residents from lung cancer and monitoring the sale of goods within state borders.[193] However, the federal government can set uniform national standards, such as the CKA, that apply equally to everyone.[194] Thus, the CKA is valid unless the regulation directly orders a state government to enact a particular legislation or federal program.[195]

Here, the CKA explicitly requires state governments to use any reasonable means to ensure stores comply with the federal act. The CKA also penalizes state governments that refused or failed to properly monitor and promote the act. Thus, the CKA violates state sovereignty because it does not give state governments the choice to adopt the federal program or enact local regulations related to the sale of cigarettes. States are coerced to comply because losing 50% of their cancer-research funding would be an extreme penalty.

(2) Greg's (G) Rights

Delegation

Congress can delegate certain rule-making authority to other branches if the delegation is within the appropriate duties of that branch,[196] and the delegation gives sufficient direction on how to carry out the delegated power.[197] Although there are few limitations on Congress's authority to delegate, Congress may not delegate its inherent law-making authority.[198] In *A.L.A. Schechter Poultry Corp. v. United States*, the court held that authorizing trade associations to write codes of "fair competition" was too vague to be a valid delegation.[199] In *Amalgamated Meat Cutters v. Connally*, the court allowed the president to impose wage and price controls because the delegation was temporary and required the president to create standards that would limit his discretion.[200]

Here, the CKA supplied state governments with the standard of "any reasonable means" to regulate the federal government's program. G will argue the delegation is too vague because, similar to "fair competition," the phrase "reasonable means" is not specific. If Congress does not give more guidance on what

---

193. *Nat'l League of Cities v. Usery*, 426 U.S. 833 (1976).

194. *Gonzales v. Oregon*, supra note 182.

195. *New York v. United States*, supra note 183; *Printz v. United States*, 521 U.S. 898 (1997).

196. *City of New York v. Clinton*, 985 F.Supp. 168, (D.D.C. 1998).

197. *Panama Ref. Co. v. Ryan*, 293 U.S. 388 (1935).

198. U.S. Const. art. I, § 1.

199. *A.L.A. Schechter Poultry Corp. v. United States*, 295 U.S. 495 (1935).

200. *Amalgamated Meat Cutters and Butcher Workmen of North America, AFL-CIO v. Connally*, 337 F.Supp. 737, 748 (D.D.C. 1971).

conduct is expected, then the governor has unfettered discretion to enforce the CKA.

However, the government will argue "reasonable means" is a valid objective standard. *Connally* suggests the delegation of Congress's power is broad and likely to be upheld if some standard exists for courts to determine if the governor's actions exceeded the scope of the delegation. Here, the governor cannot subjectively impose penalties on stores that violate CKA, but must reasonably regulate the federal program. The issue is not if Congress correctly delegated its power, but whether the governor established reasonable regulations. Thus, if fining G $1200 and prohibiting G from selling cigarettes was a reasonable method to induce compliance with the CKA, then G will need to pay the fine and stop selling cigarettes.

Answer 3

(1) Bonnie's (B) Claims

(a) 11th Amendment

Courts can determine if a state is in compliance with the Constitution or federal law,[201] but a court's judicial review power does not extend to suits in law or equity against a state by its own citizens,[202] citizens of another state, or citizens of any foreign state.[203] Here, the governor will argue B cannot bring a lawsuit against a representative of the state because State A has sovereign immunity. However, a citizen can sue a state official for injunctive or declaratory relief if the citizen shows the official had some degree of fault.[204]

B will argue the governor negligently deported B because he did not check B's U.S. citizenship. The governor will argue he reasonably assumed B was a citizen of a foreign state because B was not a citizen of State X, but the governor's argument is weak. The governor could have easily checked B's dual citizenship status. Thus, B can sue the governor for injunctive relief to reverse her deportation.

Here, the governor will argue B's claim for pain and suffering is invalid because it requests money damages. Citizens cannot sue state officials for money damages if the state official is indemnified by the state because the money damages would come from the State Treasury.[205] The governor is likely indemnified by the state because the governor was acting within the scope of his municipal duties; the president's treaty required states to deport foreigners from Country A, B, and C to their home country for prosecution.

However, B will argue Congress can abrogate state sovereign immunity to enforce civil rights under the 14th Amendment.[206] B is a U.S. citizen, which means B's 14th Amendment procedural due process rights were violated when she was deported. B was entitled to a fair hearing before being deprived of her liberty. In conclusion, the court can review B's claims because the 11th Amendment is unlikely to apply.

---

201. *Marbury v. Madison*, supra note 165.
202. *Hans v. Louisiana*, 134 U.S. 1 (1890).
203. *U.S. Const. amend. XI.*
204. *Ex Parte Young*, 209 U.S. 123 (1908); 42 U.S.C.A. § 1983 (West).
205. *Id.*
206. *Fitzpatrick v. Bitzer*, 427 U.S. 445 (1976).

(b) Foreign Powers of the President

The president is the Nation's Chief Executive and Commander in Chief of the Armed Forces.[207] Article II implicitly grants the president the broad power to conduct foreign policy[208] because it allows the president to ensure the nation's laws are faithfully executed and to protect national security.[209] Here, the president was acting within the scope of her foreign duties because the treaty was an international agreement between the U.S. and Country A, B, and C. The president has the discretion to enter treaties that she believes will keep the country safe. The president likely believed that working closely with other countries to stop terrorism and prosecute terrorists would make the U.S. safer.

Treaty Ratification

Although the president has the exclusive authority to negotiate treaties in the international world, a treaty is not self-executing.[210] Congress must explicitly ratify the treaty before the treaty is enforceable.[211] Here, Congress never ratified the treaty because it was silent. Thus, State X's governor has no power to deport B to Country A. Even if the treaty was ratified, because B is a U.S. citizen, the treaty cannot override B's right to a jury trial.[212]

In *Hamdi v. Rumsfeld*, the court determined that an American citizen, held in the U.S. as an enemy combatant, must be given a meaningful opportunity to contest the factual basis for that detention before a neutral decision maker.[213] Although the Authorization of Use of Military Force (AUMF) allows the president to use any necessary and appropriate force against persons associated with the September 11, 2011 terrorist attacks, the president's AUMF power only applies during wartime.[214] Here, the facts do not suggest there is an ongoing war. Thus, the treaty is unconstitutional because it deprives U.S. citizens of their right to a fair trial.

---

207. U.S. Const. art. I, §§ 1,8 , art. 2.

208. *United States v. Curtiss-Wright Exp. Corp.*, 299 U.S. 304 (1936).

209. U.S. Const. art. 2, § 3; *Youngstown Sheet & Tube Co. v. Sawyer*, 343 U.S. 579, 598 (1952).

210. *Medellin v. Texas*, 552 U.S. 491 (2008).

211. *Id.*

212. *Reid v. Covert*, 354 U.S. 1, 21 (1957).

213. *Hamdi v. Rumsfeld*, 542 U.S. 507 (2004).

214. *Id.*

(2) Digital's Claims

Domestic Powers of the President

Article II allows the president to ensure the nation's laws are faithfully executed and to promote national security.[215] Here, the president wanted access to information to help her identify threats and protect citizens. Thus, her actions were valid if they did not conflict with other rules and acts of Congress.[216] Presidential powers are not fixed, but fluctuate, depending upon their disjunction or conjunction with those of Congress. There are three assertions of power: (1) expressed or implied authority, (2) acts in the twilight zone, and (3) acts that contradict the will of Congress.[217]

Expressed or Implied Authority

The president acts with the greatest authority if Congress passed a law that gave or implied the president had certain powers.[218] Here, Congress was silent about the president's order, which means Congress did not give the president any authority to act.

Twilight Zone

The president acts with less authority if Congress is silent about the president's act.[219] In some cases, Congress's silence is acquiescence to the president's act, but each act is analyzed on a case-by-case basis.[220] In *Dames & Moore v. Regan,* the president issued an executive order blocking all transfers of property to Iran and suspended all claims in U.S. Courts.[221] Congress had passed an act that authorized the president to block all transfers of property, but was silent on whether the president could suspend claims. The court held the president's acts were constitutional.[222]

Here, similar to *Regan,* the president will argue she was acting within her power because Congress's silence about her order suggested Congress agreed NATC should be able to access metadata from internet and phone companies. However, Digital will argue the present case is different because the president's

---

215. U.S. Const. art. 2, § 3; *Youngstown Sheet & Tube Co. v. Sawyer,* supra note 209.
216. *Id.*
217. *Youngstown Sheet & Tube Co. v. Sawyer,* supra note 209.
218. *Id.*
219. *Id.*
220. *Dames & Moore v. Regan,* 453 U.S. 654 (1981).
221. *Id.*
222. *Id.*

Executive Order was nearly identical to the bill recently rejected by Congress. Thus, unlike *Regan*, silence cannot automatically be interpreted as consent.

Contradicts Acts of Congress

The president acts with the lowest authority if Congress spoke on the topic and the president contradicted Congress's actions.[223] Here, Digital will argue the president's bill was identical to the president's Executive Order; both gave NATC unfettered discretion to seize all internet and phone metadata. Congress is unlikely to approve an Executive Order with the same terms as the bill it recently rejected. Thus, it is unlikely the president was acting within the scope of her power and the Executive Order is invalid.

---

223. *Youngstown Sheet & Tube Co. v. Sawyer*, supra note 209.

Answer 4

(1) Dangerous Firearms Act (DFA)

Commerce Clause

Article I allows Congress to regulate commerce with foreign nations, among the several states, and with the Indian Tribes,[224] which includes channels and instrumentalities of interstate commerce as well as economic activities that substantially affect interstate commerce.[225]

Channels and Instrumentalities

Channels include the use of roads, railways, and waterways,[226] and instrumentalities include goods and persons.[227] Here, the DFA impacts both channels and instrumentalities of interstate commerce. Guns are instrumentalities of interstate commerce because they can travel across state lines, and the transportation of guns between states usually involves roads, waterways, or railways.

However, State Z will argue the DFA is unconstitutional because customers do not always transport guns from one state to another, and some companies only manufacture and sell guns within state borders. Thus, requiring the sale of hard cases goes beyond Congress's power to regulate interstate commerce because some activities, such as State Z's rifle business, are fully intrastate.

Substantial Effect on Interstate Commerce

If the court determines the sale of hard cases is fully intrastate, then Congress cannot regulate the activity unless the activity substantially affects interstate commerce.[228] Regulation of an intrastate activity is more likely to be upheld if it is an economic activity.[229] Courts are skeptical about the affect of non-economic activities on interstate commerce because the link between non-economic activities and commerce is too far removed; conceptually, any activity could impact interstate commerce.[230]

---

224. U.S. Const. art. I, § 8, cl. 3.
225. *U.S. v. Lopez*, 514 U.S. 549, 558–59 (1995).
226. *Gibbons v. Ogden*, 22 U.S. 1 (1824).
227. *Hammer v. Dagenhart*, 247 U.S. 251, 271–72 (1918).
228. *Gibbons v. Ogden*, supra note 226.
229. *U.S. v. Lopez*, supra 225.
230. *Id.*

Here, manufacturing and selling rifles and hard cases is an economic activity because it involves the exchange of money between parties. The activity likely substantially affects interstate commerce because customers who purchased rifles without hard cases in State Z can transport the guns across state lines. State Z's case is similar to *Wickard v. Filburn* where Congress was allowed to regulate wheat grown for home consumption because it would impact the prices of wheat;[231] and *Katzenbach v. McClung* where Congress could regulate restaurants that discriminated, even though the restaurant's goods were only sold intrastate, because the restaurant purchased supplies in state and out of state.[232]

Similar to *Katzenbach,* State Z's rifles are sold intrastate, but the customers can take the goods interstate. Moreover, similar to *Wickard,* if State Z is not required to sell hard cases, then the market price of rifles could be affected because State Z could sell rifles at a cheaper price than other retailers who must sell rifles with a hard case. Thus, State Z's claim will fail because the sale of hard cases is an activity that substantially affects interstate commerce. Congress constitutionally used its Commerce Clause power when it passed the DFA.

(2) Section 2 of the Hunter's Act

Dormant Commerce Clause

Interstate commerce that is not regulated by Congress or national in character can be regulated by the states if the state's laws do not place an undue burden on interstate commerce.[233]

Facially Discriminatory or Facially Neutral

A state's regulation on interstate commerce is per se invalid if it facially discriminates against out-of-state interests.[234] Here, Section 2 does not facially discriminate against any out-of-state interests because the act focuses on the type of safety feature rather than where the gun was originally manufactured or sold. Under the Hunter's Act, another state could sell guns with a trigger-identification system and the buyer could easily bring the gun into State X's

---

231. *Wickard v. Filburn*, 317 U.S. 111 (1942).
232. *Katzenbach v. McClung*, 379 U.S. 294 (1964).
233. *S. Carolina State Highway Dep't v. Barnwell Bros.*, 303 U.S. 177 (1938).
234. *City of Philadelphia v. New Jersey*, 437 U.S. 617 (1978).

borders. The act is not facially discriminatory, but discriminatory intent can be inferred from the discriminatory impact.[235]

Here, although the law does not explicitly discriminate against other states, State X sells rifles that include a trigger-identification system that is rarely used by other competitors. Thus, Chester (C) will argue State X likely passed the Hunter's Act to ensure consumers only purchased State X's trigger-identification guns. The Hunters Act's creates barriers for other sellers to enter the State X gun market.

In *Hunt v. Washington State Apple Adver. Comm'n*, the court held a Washington law that required all boxes with apples to have a USDA grade label was unconstitutional.[236] Even though it was evenly applied to in-state and out-of-state products, other states could only comply by altering their containers, which burdened interstate sales.[237] Here, like in *Hunt*, C has a strong argument that State X's trigger-identification requirement burdens interstate sales because it requires other states to alter how they manufacture guns. Thus, Section 2 is unconstitutional if it doesn't pass the appropriate standard of review.

Standard of Review

If the law exclusively limits out-of-state interests, then the state has the heavy burden of proving that the law is certain to achieve its legitimate purpose and that the purpose cannot be served by less discriminatory means.[238] If the restriction mostly, but not exclusively, limits out-of-state interests, then the state is only required to show the law is likely to achieve its legitimate purpose and the challenger must rebut the state's justification that the purpose cannot be served by nondiscriminatory alternatives.[239] Here, the latter standard applies because the Hunter's Act also requires manufacturers, sellers, and consumers within State X to sell and use guns with the trigger-identification system.

Legitimate Purpose

The law must be passed for a reason other than out-of-state status, such as a legitimate public welfare concern, health, or safety.[240] Here, C will argue

---

235. *Hunt v. Washington State Apple Advertising Com'n*, 432 U.S. 333, 352 (1977).
236. *Id.*
237. *Id.*
238. *City of Philadelphia v. New Jersey*, supra note 234.
239. *Hunt v. Washington State Apple Advertising Com'n*, supra note 235.
240. *City of Philadelphia v. New Jersey*, supra note 234.

State X restricted the sale and possession of guns to increase the sale of its products. However, State X will argue the trigger-identification requirement was passed to increase safety within State X's borders. Hunting is common in State X, which means citizens regularly use guns. The trigger-identification system prevents gun from being fired by anyone other than the authorized user, which makes it difficult to discharge a stolen gun or for children to accidentally set off a gun. State X has a legitimate interest in protecting people from theft and personal injury.

Least Restrictive Means

If a legitimate local purpose is found, then the question becomes one of degree.[241] If the affects on interstate commerce are only incidental, then the law will be upheld.[242] But if the burden on interstate commerce clearly outweighs the local interests and benefits, then the statute is unconstitutional, even if it regulates evenhandedly.[243]

Here, C will argue the burden on interstate commerce is high because the law essentially excludes out-of-state sellers from State X's rifle market. Other manufacturers rarely use the trigger-identification system. If sellers want to access State X's market, then sellers must manufacture guns similar to the guns created in State X. The law also burdens State X residents who cannot afford the trigger-identification guns or would rather purchase a different type of gun. Hunting is a common way to obtain food in State X, which means the sale of rifles is especially important to State X residents.

State X will argue that safety is more important than accessibility to different types of guns. However, State X can achieve its safety goals in less restrictive ways. The gun market includes other safety features, such as safety catches that prevent accidental discharge. State X's trigger-identification system prevents theft and children from discharging the guns, but it does not prevent the authorized user from accidentally shooting his or her rifle. Thus, safer features may exist in other rifle models. Unless an exception applies, C has a strong argument that State X violated the Dormant Commerce Clause because State X could amend the Hunter's Act to exclude rifles without reasonable safety features from its borders.

---

241. *Pike v. Bruce Church, Inc.*, 397 U.S. 137, 142 (1970).
242. *Maine v. Taylor*, 477 U.S. 131 (1986).
243. *Id.*

Market Participant Exception

A state can discriminate against out-of-state competitors if the state makes money as a participant in the market.[244] The Commerce Clause was intended to require independent justification for a market regulator's action, but not a market participant acting in the free market.[245] Here, State X sells hunting rifles. Thus, even though Section 2 of the Hunters Act technically violates the Dormant Commerce Clause, the act is constitutional because State X is a market participant and can discriminate against out-of-state residents.

(3) Hunter's Act

Section 1 of the Hunter's Act

The laws of the United States are the supreme law of the land,[246] which means state laws are invalid when a federal authority totally occupies the field.[247] Under the Supremacy Clause, federal law preempts state law in three forms: (1) express preemption, (2) field preemption, and (3) implied conflict preemption.[248]

Express Preemption

Express preemption is when Congress clearly expresses its intent to preempt all state laws and regulation of that field.[249] Here, State X's law is likely preempted because it directly conflicts with the DFA. Under the DFA, it is illegal for civilians to use any type of firearm without a license. But the Hunter's Act allows State X residents to freely sell, buy, own, and use hunting rifles without a license within State X's borders.

Field Preemption

Field preemption occurs when the breadth and scheme of the federal regulations makes it clear that the federal government intends to be the sole voice because it left no room for state regulation.[250] Here, State Y will argue that

---

244. *Reeves, Inc. v. Stake,* 447 U.S. 429, 436 (1980).
245. *Id.*
246. U.S. Const. art. VI, cl. 2.
247. *Gibbons v. Ogden,* supra note 226.
248. *Holk v. Snapple Beverage Corp,* 575 F.3d 329, 334 (3d Cir. 2009).
249. *Id.*
250. *Id.*

field preemption applies because Congress specifically required a license for all firearms and left no area for state governments to regulate.

Implied Conflict Preemption

Conflict preemption occurs when compliance with both federal and state law is impossible.[251] Here, a resident of State X cannot buy a gun without a license under the Hunter's Act and simultaneously comply with the DFA's requirement to obtain a license. State Y's argument will succeed because DFA will preempt Section 1 of the Hunter's Act.

Section 2 of the Hunter's Act

See preemption rules above (Section 1 of Hunter's Act).

Express Preemption

Here, State X will argue no express preemption exists because the DFA requires a hard case to transport guns while Section 2 regulates the types of guns that can be sold and possessed within state borders. The DFA has not explicitly preempted Section 2 of the Hunter's Act because both acts work in unison to make gun usage safer.

Field Preemption

Here, State X will argue the DFA only included two laws related to firearms. If the federal government intended to prevent states from passing additional laws related to firearm safety, then the federal government would have enacted more regulations.

State Y will argue the DFA preempted State X's regulation because it began legislating in the gun-safety area. This is a weak argument because states have different demographics and economics. Federalism specifically split the U.S. government into two systems, the federal system and state system, to resolve problems related to governing a large geographic area with diverse local needs. Federalism gives people the choice to move from one area to another based on the types of government policies they prefer. State X residents might prefer trigger-identification systems to State Y's state-of-the-art safety features. If a State X resident prefers State Y guns, then the resident could move to State Y. Thus, the federal government likely left room for the states to set their own firearm-safety standards.

---

251. *Id.*

Conflict Preemption

Here, people can comply with both the DFA and Hunter's Act because they can register their trigger-identification gun and put it in a hard case. Thus, Section 2 of the Hunter's Act is not preempted and State Y's argument will fail.

Answer 5

(1) State Action

The Supreme Court declared the 14th Amendment applied to state and local government actions, but not private conduct.[252] Here, Greenwood Authority (GA) is an agency run by State Z, which means GA is a state actor. However, Victoria (V), a private actor, is actually running the restaurant and discriminating against non-vegans. Thus, unless the restaurant serves a public function or the government's actions are entwined, there is no state action.

Public Function

If a property serves a public function, then it is treated as a public institution, even if managed by a private entity.[253] In *Evans v. Newton*, the park owned by a private party was considered a public institution because it served the public. Terry (T) will argue V's restaurant is similar to *Evans* because it is the only restaurant in State Z that serves vegan food. V's restaurant is valuable to the public because it is the sole location for vegan residents to eat their choice of protein. However, unlike a park, a restaurant is not something open to the public for free. A restaurant is a commercial service that requires consumers to pay money. Moreover 97% of State Z's population is omnivorous, which diminishes the public service of V's vegan restaurant.

Entwinement

If the government maintains and manages the property, or regulates the activities on the property, then there is likely state action,[254] and the private party's behavior will be treated as the behavior of the state itself; entwinement is not the same as encouragement.[255] In *Brentwood Acad. v. Tennessee Secondary Sch. Athletic Ass'n,* there was state action because the private entity was composed of public schools that received most of their funds from the government and conducted many meetings on government property.[256] In *Burton v. Wilmington Parking Auth.*, the state leased a space to a private restaurant that denied service to black people.[257] The court held the government's

---

252. *United States v. Stanley*, 483 U.S. 669 (1987).
253. *Evans v. Newton*, 382 U.S. 296 (1966).
254. *Id.*
255. *Brentwood Acad. v. Tennessee Secondary Sch. Athletic Ass'n*, 531 U.S. 288 (2001).
256. *Id.*
257. *Burton v. Wilmington Parking Auth.*, 365 U.S. 715 (1961).

licensing and regulation was sufficient for state action because it created a symbolic relationship where the government placed itself behind the discrimination, maintained the building, and benefited from the revenue of the restaurant.[258]

Here, T will argue GA's actions were similar to the duties of the government in *Burton* because GA leased the building to V and made annual inspections for wear and tear. However, GA will argue it was not managing the building because V was responsible for damages caused by the tenant and natural disasters. Unlike *Brentwood*, GA provided no funding to V. GA also never interfered with the daily management of her restaurant. GA had nothing to do with V's decision to hire vegans over non-vegans. GA merely provided a space for V to run her private restaurant and never endorsed V's discrimination. But GA's arguments will fail because GA benefited from the revenue of the restaurant lease, annually inspected the property, and allowed the discrimination to take place on government property. The court should deny GA's motion to dismiss because state action exists through entwinement.

(2) Local Employment Act (LEA)

Privileges and Immunities Clause (P&I) of Article IV

The citizens of each State shall be entitled to all the privileges and immunities of citizens in the several States.[259] Here, the LEA discriminates against out-of-state citizens by making it harder for them to obtain jobs because it specifically requires businesses in State Z to ensure 50% of their employees are State Z citizens.

Standard of Review

If a state discriminates against out-of-state citizens, then the state must have a reason beyond the mere fact that they not citizens,[260] and there must be a substantial relationship between the state's discriminatory action and its objective.[261]

In *Toomer v. Witsell*, the court held a law conserving natural resources violated the P&I clause because it discriminated against out-of-state fishermen by creating a monopoly for its residents.[262] In *Vicinity v. Mayor & Council*

---

258. *Id.*
259. U.S. Const. art. IV, § 2, cl. 1.
260. *Toomer v. Witsell*, 334 U.S. 385 (1948).
261. *Vicinity v. Mayor & Council of City of Camden*, 465 U.S. 208 (1984); *Supreme Court of New Hampshire v. Piper*, 470 U.S. 274 (1985).
262. *Toomer v. Witsell*, supra note 260.

of City of Camden, the court held a city was allowed to pressure private employers to hire city residents by requiring at least 40% of contractors and sub-contractors working on city constructions projects to be Camden residents.[263]

Here, T will argue LEA is unconstitutional because it requires 50% of the workforce of businesses within State Z to be State Z employees. The law creates unequal employment opportunities for State Z citizens and non-citizens.

However, State Z will argue the law is constitutional because, unlike *Toomer*, LEA does not create a monopoly for state citizens. LEA creates equal hiring opportunities for State Z citizens and nonresidents because it only requires 50% of the workforce to be State Z citizens and not 100% of the employees. Moreover, LEA is nearly identical to *Camden* because it only encourages employers to hire state citizens and does not discourage the hiring of non-citizens. Thus, State Z's interest in creating more employment opportunities for its residents is likely a substantial reason beyond mere discrimination against non-citizens.

Substantial Relationship

In *Hicklin v. Orbeck*, the court held that preferential hiring of residents over non-residents violated the constitution because discrimination against non-citizens of a state is only allowed when those non-citizens are the source of evil at which the statute is aimed; and there was no evidence that non-residents were the major cause of state unemployment.[264] Here, State Z's citizens have low employment rates, but no facts suggest non-residents caused the unemployment of State Z citizens. Under *Hicklin*, LEA is likely unconstitutional because there is no relationship between limiting employment of nonresidents and raising employment rates of State Z residents. The right to earn a living is a fundamental right that is essential to the survival of nonresidents in the state, unlike recreational activities, such as hunting.[265]

Privileges and Immunities Clause (P&I) of the 14th Amendment

No State shall make or enforce any law which shall abridge the privileges or immunities of citizens of the United States.[266] Here, T is not a citizen of the United States, but an international visiting student. Thus, it is unlikely T's rights were violated under the P&I clause.

---

263. *Vicinity v. Mayor & Council of City of Camden*, supra note 261.
264. *Hicklin v. Orbeck*, 437 U.S. 518 (1978).
265. *Baldwin v. Fish & Game Comm'n of Montana*, 436 U.S. 371 (1978).
266. U.S. Const. amend. XIV.

Answer 6

State Action

The Supreme Court declared the 14th Amendment applied to state and local government actions, but not private conduct.[267] Here, there is state action because State D passed the Asian Immigrant Act (AIA).

Section A

Substantive Due Process (Right to Marry)

Fundamental rights include liberties that are deeply rooted in the nation's history and tradition.[268] The right to marry is a fundamental right.[269] Here, Section A directly and substantially interferes with a citizen's marriage decisions because it limits the right of citizens to marry Asian immigrants. If a regulation directly interferes with a fundamental right, then it must be necessary to achieve a compelling government interest.[270]

Compelling Government Interest

Here, the government will argue that increasing access to higher education for U.S. citizens is a compelling government interest because it is difficult to earn a living without a college degree in America. Thus, the U.S. government has a compelling interest to protect its citizens by limiting immigration. If more people immigrate to America, then the competition to attend college increases because each university has a limited number of admission slots.

Necessary

The government must use the least restrictive means to achieve its purpose.[271] Here, the government specifically limited a citizen's right to marry Asian immigrants because when the number of Asians immigrating increased, the percentage of Americans attending college decreased. Thus, Section A was necessary to control the immigrant population. The government targeted marriage rights because it assumed the practice of mail-order brides caused

---

267. *United States v. Stanley,* supra note 252.
268. *Moore v. City of E. Cleveland, Ohio,* 431 U.S. 494, 503 (1977).
269. *Loving v. Virginia,* 388 U.S. 1, 12 (1967).
270. *Id.*
271. *Gonzales v. O Centro Espirita Beneficente Uniao do Vegetal,* 546 U.S. 418, 418 (2006).

the increased Asian immigration. The government will argue Section A is the least restrictive means because the law does not place a complete ban on all marriages. Section A created an exception for immigrants who already had a college degree or lived in American for three years because the extended residency and diploma indicated the immigrant was not marrying for the sole purpose of accessing education in America.

However, Ron (R) and Lian (L) will argue that no statistically significant research connects mail-order bride marriages to the increase in immigration, the increased competition in education, or to Asian immigrants. The unemployment rates are a national problem and not specific to State D. More facts are necessary to understand the impact on State D, but it is likely AIA was based on a hunch and stereotypical beliefs, which are not enough to overcome strict scrutiny. Moreover, there are less restrictive means available. For example, rather than completely banning marriage to Asian immigrants, the government can create more agencies focused on identifying fraudulent marriages. Thus, the AIA will fail the strict scrutiny test because the government did not show the restriction on marriage was necessary to make education more available to U.S. citizens.

Equal Protection

The 14th Amendment commands that states cannot deny any person within its jurisdiction the equal protection of the laws,[272] which essentially requires that similarly situated individuals obtain the same benefits.[273] If a law facially discriminates against a class of persons, then the law must pass the appropriate level of scrutiny.[274]

Gender (Facially Neutral)

A facially neutral law raises equal protection issues if the law was enacted with a discriminatory purpose and has a discriminatory impact on a certain class of persons.[275] To prove a discriminatory purpose exists, the plaintiff must show the decision maker selected or reaffirmed a particular course of action because of the adverse effects upon an identifiable group.[276]

---

272. U.S. Const. amend. XIV.
273. *City of Cleburne, Tex. v. Cleburne Living Center*, 473 U.S. 432, 439 (1985).
274. *Washington v. Davis*, 426 U.S. 229 (1976).
275. *Id.*
276. *McCleskey v. Kemp*, 481 U.S. 279 (1987).

Here, the law is facially neutral because it does not reference a specific gender. But Section A likely discriminates against women because it was passed under the assumption that U.S. citizens were using mail-order brides services. Although Section A says "Asian immigrants," its underlying goal is to prevent Asian women from marrying American men to gain citizenship.

However, no facts suggest the law disproportionately impacts Asian females. *Palmer v. Thompson* held that a discriminatory purpose alone is insufficient to prove that a facially neutral law constitutes a race or national origin classification.[277] The court held that closing swimming pools to all citizens in the community rather than desegregating them did not violate the Equal Protection Clause.[278] It is possible that all Asians, regardless of gender, are experiencing the same obstacles created by the AIA. Thus, because the law was applied equally to all Asian immigrants and there is no evidence to show a disparate impact on women, Section A does not violate the Equal Protection Clause under a gender classification standard.

Race

If the law discriminates against a suspect class, which is a class of persons that was historically subject to discriminatory treatment due to lack of political power or an unpopular trait, then strict scrutiny is required.[279] Here, Section A facially discriminates against a certain race because the text explicitly refers to Asian immigrants. Asians are a suspect class because, historically, Asians experienced discriminatory treatment in America. For example, during World War II, all individuals of Japanese descent were sent to internment camps regardless of their citizenship status. Thus, to survive strict scrutiny, the law must be narrowly tailored to achieve a compelling government interest.[280]

Compelling Government Interest

See analysis above. (Section A: Substantive Due Process (Right to Marry)).

Narrowly Tailored

Here, the government targeted Asian immigrants because citizens believed Asian immigrants were responsible for increasing the competition in higher education. The government will argue Section A is narrowly tailored because

---

277. *Palmer v. Thompson*, 403 U.S. 217 (1971).
278. *Id.*
279. *Grutter v. Bollinger*, 539 U.S. 306 (2003).
280. *Id.*

the law only limits the immigration of one race, Asians, and does not restrict the immigration of all minorities.

However, R and L will argue no statistically significant research connects Asian immigrants to the decrease in college acceptance rates of Americans. Moreover, the government assumes that mail-order bride services only apply to Asians and not other races. The lower college-acceptance rates could be caused by other domestic and international factors, such as a general increase in immigration or a recession.

In *Grutter v. Bollinger*, the court stated that narrow tailoring does not require the exhaustion of every conceivable race-neutral alternative, but the government must, in good faith, consider workable race-neutral alternatives.[281] The court held that putting different racial groups on separate admission tracks or using quotas for university admissions to insulate applicants from competing with certain groups was not allowed.[282] Section A is similar because it places Asians on a different track than any other race and does not consider other possible causes for the decrease in the college acceptance rates of Americans. The government also has reasonable race-neutral alternatives to achieve its goal, such as implementing a residency requirement before applying to college or requiring a student visa in addition to a marriage license. Thus, Section A cannot limit Asians from immigrating because it is not narrowly tailored.

Education

Section A treats immigrants without a college education differently because the exception allows American citizens to marry immigrants with college degrees. Discrimination based on educational accomplishments is analyzed under rational basis because the classification does not involve a suspect or quasi-suspect class.[283] To survive rational basis, the law must be rationally related to a legitimate government interest.[284]

Legitimate Government Interest

If there is a compelling government interest to ensure citizens have access to education, then there is definitely a legitimate government interest to help citizens obtain the skills necessary to earn a decent living. See analysis above. (Section A: Substantive Due Process (Right to Marry)).

---

281. *Id.*
282. *Id.*
283. *Romer v. Evans*, 517 U.S. 620 (1996).
284. *New York City Transit Auth. v. Beazer*, 440 U.S. 568 (1979).

Rationally Related

Here, the government will argue Section A is rationally related because fewer immigrants entering the country without a college education decreases the number of people interested in higher education, which decreases competition in college admissions and creates more slots at universities for American citizens.

R and L will argue that targeting immigrants without a college degree is over-inclusive because immigrants do not always enter the U.S. to obtain a college education. Many immigrants come for family or work. The law is also under-inclusive because immigrants with a college degree might want a second degree and apply to college. Thus, treating immigrants with a college degree differently does not achieve the purpose of creating more educational opportunities for American citizens.

However, under the rational basis test, the challenger bears a high burden of proving the law is not rationally related. In *New York City Transit Auth. v. Beazer*, the court allowed the NYTA to deny employment to anyone using methadone, even though half of the methadone users were employable.[285] The court held excluding methadone users from safety-sensitive positions based on satisfactory performance of a program was rationally related.[286] Here, Section A will be upheld under *New York City Transit Auth.* because there is a possible correlation between the increase in immigration and decrease in college admission rates of American citizens.

Age

Section A discriminates based on race because it only applies to immigrants between the ages of 18 and 30. Age is not a suspect or quasi-suspect classification, which means the law must pass the rational basis test.[287]

Legitimate Government Interest

See analysis above. (Section A: Education).

Rationally Related

Here, the government will argue that prohibiting individuals between the ages of 18 and 30 from immigrating to the U.S. creates more opportunities in

---

285. *Id.*
286. *Id.*
287. *Massachusetts Bd. of Ret. v. Murgia*, 427 U.S. 307 (1976).

higher education because most people attend college and get married in their 20s. Section A refers to a specific age group to ensure the law is not over-inclusive. However, R and L will argue Section A's age restriction will not resolve the problem because people get married and go to college at various points in their life. In *Massachusetts Bd. of Ret. v. Murgia*, the court held a law requiring police officers to retire at age 50 was rationally related because a career in law enforcement requires physical strength and physical ability declines with age.[288] In this case, there is no rational relationship between the age and the government's purpose because there is no statistically significant research that individuals between 18 and 30 years old decreased the college acceptance rates of Americans. Thus, Section A cannot constitutionally limit a specific age group from marrying American citizens.

Alienage

Resident aliens are a suspect class because they are politically powerless and a discrete and insular minority, which means courts must apply strict scrutiny.[289] However, rational basis is the appropriate test because Section A discriminates against immigrants outside the country and not resident aliens. See analysis above (Section A: Age). Section A is not rationally related because there is no statistically significant research connecting immigration to college acceptance rates.

Conclusion

Even though the government has a compelling interest to increase the number of Americans attending college, Section A is unconstitutional because the means used to achieve the purpose violate the Equal Protection Clause.

Section B

Substantive Due Process (Parental Rights)

See rule above. (Section A: Substantive Due Process). A parent's right to make decisions concerning care, custody, and control of his or her children is a fundamental right.[290] Here, L's parental rights are inhibited because Section B prohibits her from teaching her two-year old daughter Chinese. Thus, Section B must be narrowly tailored to achieve a compelling government interest.[291]

---

288. *Id.*
289. *Graham v. Richardson*, 403 U.S. 365 (1971).
290. *Troxel v. Granville*, 530 U.S. 57 (2000).
291. *Grutter v. Bollinger*, supra note 279.

Compelling Government Interest

Here, the facts are silent about why the government wants to limit a child's ability to speak multiple languages, but the government's best argument is Section B protects children from confusion. The main language in the U.S. is English and speaking more than one language might hurt the child's linguistic skills and assimilation. However, this is a weak argument because promoting diversity is a compelling interest in America and discouraging children from bilingualism discourages diversity.

Narrowly Tailored

Even if the interest was compelling, it is unlikely a blanket limitation on teaching multiple languages to children will resolve issues related to assimilation or development of linguistic skills. In *Meyer v. Nebraska*, the court held a Nebraska law that outlawed the teaching of foreign languages to students who had not completed the eight grade violated the 14th Amendment.[292] Section B is exactly the same as *Meyer* and is unconstitutional.

Section C

Substantive Due Process (Keeping the Family Together)

See rule above. (Section A: Substantive Due Process). Families, even extended ones, have a fundamental right to live together.[293] In *Moore v. City of E. Cleveland*, the court held that a law prohibiting a grandmother from living with her grandchild was an intrusive regulation of the family and unconstitutional.[294] Here, Section C is similar to *Moore* because it restricts an American's right to live with his or her extended family members by imposing a restriction related to immigration and sponsorship. Thus, Section C must be narrowly tailored to achieve a compelling government interest.[295]

Compelling Government Interest

Here, no facts state the government's interest, but Section C was likely passed to discourage excessive immigration to America. The government assumed increased immigration lead to the decrease in college acceptance rates of Americans. Thus, there might be a compelling government interest to protect a

---

292. *Meyer v. Nebraska*, 262 U.S. 390 (1923).
293. *Moore v. City of E. Cleveland, Ohio*, 431 U.S. 494 (1977).
294. *Id.*
295. *Grutter v. Bollinger*, supra note 279.

citizen's right to earn a living. See analysis above. (Section A: Substantive Due Process (Right to Marry)).

Narrowly Tailored

The government will argue Section C is narrowly tailored because it creates an exception for immediate family members, such as the citizen's spouse and child. However, this is a weak argument because no statistically significant research connects immigration to the decrease in the college acceptance rates of Americans. Thus, Section C is unconstitutional.

Answer 7

State B's Abortion Rules

State Action

The Supreme Court declared the 14th Amendment applied to state and local government actions, but not private conduct.[296] Here, state action is present because State B imposed the additional obstacles to abortion.

Substantive Due Process (Abortion)

Fundamental rights include liberties that are deeply rooted in this Nation's history and tradition.[297] The right to decide whether to bear a child is a fundamental right, but the right is not absolute.[298] States cannot place an undue burden on a woman seeking to exercise her right to an abortion before fetal viability.[299] Courts define undue burden as a substantial obstacle to getting an abortion.[300]

Spousal Consent

Here, State B will argue the government has a compelling government interest to ensure men can voice their concerns about aborting their children. However, bearing a child is a greater limitation on the mother's liberty than the father's liberty because women carry the child in their uterus for nine months. In *Planned Parenthood of Se. Pennsylvania v. Casey*, the court held that laws requiring informed consent, a 24-hour waiting period between consent and the time of abortion, a licensed physician, or parental consent did not create an undue burden on a woman's right to abortion.[301] However, *Casey* also held that requiring a woman to sign a statement that she notified her spouse about the abortion is an undue burden because a man does not have dominion over his wife.[302] Thus, State B's spousal consent requirement is unconstitutional.

Reflection

Here, Melinda (M) will argue a mandatory reflection is a substantial obstacle to abortion because women with busy lives do not have time to write

---

296. *United States v. Stanley*, supra note 252.
297. *Moore v. City of E. Cleveland, Ohio*, supra note 268.
298. *Planned Parenthood of Se. Pennsylvania v. Casey*, 505 U.S. 833 (1992).
299. *Id.*
300. *Id.*
301. *Id.*
302. *Id.*

reflections. A reflection requirement is extremely paternalistic and assumes women are not adults. *Casey* allows parental consent and consent from a judge for minors, but M is not a minor and should be allowed to make decisions without submitting a one-page paper.

However, State B will argue a woman should seriously consider all possibilities before killing the fetus. State B wants the mother to analyze her feelings to ensure she will not regret her decision. The one-page reflection is similar to the 24-hour waiting period in *Casey* because it allows the woman to make an informed decision rather than acting impulsively. Thus, because no health risk is involved in requiring a reflection, and the reflection is short and not a 10-page paper, State B's reflection requirement will likely be upheld.

Equal Protection

The 14th Amendment commands that states cannot deny any person within its jurisdiction the equal protection of the laws,[303] which essentially requires that similarly situated individuals obtain the same benefits.[304] If a law facially discriminates against a class of persons, then the law must pass the appropriate level of scrutiny.[305]

Wealth (Facially Neutral)

A facially neutral law raises Equal Protection issues if the law was enacted with a discriminatory purpose and has a discriminatory impact on a certain class of persons.[306] To show a discriminatory purpose exists, the plaintiff must show the decision maker selected or reaffirmed a particular course of action because of the adverse effects upon an identifiable group.[307]

Here, State B requires an extremely expensive fee to hire a state-licensed physician. The fee does not explicitly mention poor people, but the high fee adds a greater obstacle for individuals with less money. Thus, a disproportional impact on low-income communities exists because poor people have limited access to safe abortions. Although State B's purpose is unknown, M will argue State B made the fee expensive to discourage abortion because State B is pro-life. Thus, there is discriminatory impact and likely a discriminatory purpose.

---

303. U.S. Const. amend. XIV.
304. *City of Cleburne, Tex. v. Cleburne Living Center*, supra note 273.
305. *Washington v. Davis*, supra note 274.
306. *Id.*
307. *McCleskey v. Kemp*, supra note 276.

Level of Scrutiny

Under the Equal Protection Clause, the appropriate standard of review for classifications based on wealth is rational basis. However, wealth or lack thereof triggers heightened scrutiny when the classification affects a fundamental right.[308] Here, M's fundamental right to decide whether to bear a child is affected by the expensive fees. Thus, a heightened scrutiny applies.

Heightened Scrutiny: Undue Burden

In *Boddie v. Connecticut,* the court held that requiring an individual to pay court fees to sue for a divorce was unconstitutional because people should be able to dissolve a marriage without state approval and fees; the right to marriage is a fundamental right.[309] Similarly, in *Griffin v. Illinois,* the court held a state must furnish an indigent criminal defendant with a free trial transcript if the transcript is necessary for adequate and effective appellant review.[310] The court emphasized that equal protection of criminal trials requires no distinction between a group's ability to pay because wealth does not bear on a person's guilt or innocence.[311] In both cases, the court held mandatory fees were unconstitutional if it limited the individual's fundamental rights and required the fees to be waived or eliminated.

Here, M will argue her case is identical to *Boddie* and *Griffin*. State B's fees are likely an undue burden on a woman's right to decide whether to bear a child because, even with a full-time salary, M cannot afford the licensed physician. Primary school teachers are paid a humble wage, but usually earn enough to live decently. Thus, State B likely established an excessively high fee to make the service unavailable to more individuals.

State B will argue the government is merely promoting the interests of its citizens who support pro-life campaigns. Moreover, there are alternatives, such as unlicensed doctors, for individuals with less wealth. However, this is a weak argument because the cheaper option creates a high possibility of damage to the uterus. Thus, the expensive fee is unconstitutional.

Rational Basis Review

If the court determines the appropriate level of scrutiny is rational basis, then State B must show the law is rationally related to a legitimate government

---

308. *San Antonio Indep. Sch. Dist. v. Rodriguez,* 411 U.S. 1 (1973).
309. *Boddie v. Connecticut,* 401 U.S. 371 (1971).
310. *Id.*
311. *Griffin v. Illinois,* 351 U.S. 12, 15 (1956).

interest.[312] Under rational basis, State B has a stronger argument because states have the autonomy to regulate markets within their borders to satisfy local concerns. Thus, as a pro-life state, State B has an interest to charge higher abortion fees. If M wanted a cheaper abortion, then she could go to another state.

Hope Elementary's (H) Rule

State Action

See rules above. (State B's Abortion Rules). Here, state action exists because H is a public school, which means it is run by the state.

Equal Protection

See rules above. (State B's Abortion Rules). Here, H will argue its rule is facially neutral because it does not explicitly use the word "women." However, the rule applies to teachers who become "pregnant" before marriage and not any teacher who "has a child." The word "pregnant" only includes women. Thus, H's rule is likely facially discriminatory.

If H's rule was not discriminatory on its face, discriminatory impact and discriminatory purpose are both present. H's rule has a disparate impact on women because it imposes stricter standards on female teachers compared to male teachers; only women become pregnant. H also had a discriminatory purpose because H specifically passed the rule to protect children from "promiscuous" messages. The word "promiscuous" is more commonly associated with women. Thus, H's rule includes a gender classification and may violate the Equal Protection Clause.

Gender

The appropriate scrutiny for a law that treats one gender differently is intermediate scrutiny; the law must be substantially related to achieve an important government interest.[313]

Important Government Interest

Here, H will argue that regulating the actions of teachers is an important interest because teachers influence the development of children. If elementary schools allow teachers to become pregnant without being married, then the school sends a message to young girls that children out of wedlock are

---

312. *New York City Transit Auth. v. Beazer*, supra note 284.
313. *Craig v. Boren*, 429 U.S. 190 (1976).

socially acceptable. M will argue that not everyone shares H's pro-marriage and paternalistic views. In today's society, families are diverse and include children with unwed parents. Thus, banning the interaction between pregnant, unwed mothers and children teaches children to embrace prejudicial beliefs. H's rule does not serve an important government interest because it discourages diversity.

Substantially Related

Here, M will argue that requiring pregnant women to resign or be terminated does not prevent children from being distracted by "promiscuous" messages. If State B truly wanted to terminate bad role models, then State B would create a rule that applied to unwed men, unwed women, divorced parents, and any other characteristic that might be socially unacceptable. State B's decision to only prevent pregnant women from working at the school is underinclusive. Moreover, less restrictive means are available, such as sex education classes or allowing the teacher to take extended leave until the baby is born. A complete ban is too extreme.

However, H will argue the rule is substantially related because teachers are role models and children will naturally believe the teacher's behavior is exemplary. Thus, allowing pregnant teachers to interact with children creates awkward situations where children may ask about a non-existent father as the woman's pregnancy advances. The rule doesn't include men because children will never notice whether a man has a child unless the man voluntarily shares the information.

In *United States v. Virginia*, the court held that a complete bar against women attending a school because the cadets lived in barracks with surveillance and no privacy was unconstitutional.[314] In *Geduldig v. Aiello*, the court held the exclusion of certain pregnancy-related conditions from the disability insurance system was constitutional because the insurance system also excluded other conditions that affected both men and women.[315] Here, similar to *Virginia*, H banned unwed, pregnant woman from working at the school based on a biological factor. M's case is also different from *Geduldig* because the conditions in the rule do not affect both men and women; they only apply

---

314. *United States v. Virginia*, 518 U.S. 515 (1996).
315. *Geduldig v. Aiello*, 417 U.S. 484 (1974).

to pregnant women. Thus, women are unfairly targeted without an important government interest to justify the discrimination and H's rule will fail under the 14th Amendment.

Procedural Due Process

The 14th Amendment states that no state shall deprive any person of life, liberty, or property, without due process of the law.[316] In *Perry v. Sindermann*, the court determined that a professor who held his position at a state college for many years was entitled to a hearing that informed him of the grounds for non-retention and the opportunity to challenge their sufficiency.[317] Similarly, M will argue she is entitled to a hearing to challenge her termination because she worked at Hope Elementary, a state school, for many years, and she had exemplary reviews and was well liked by students and parents. In addition, M likely has a property right because she lives in a government-owned, rent-controlled apartment.

H will argue M has no right to a hearing because *Cleveland Bd. of Educ. v. Loudermill* held a public employee who can only be discharged for cause is entitled to a pre-termination hearing whereas an employee who can be terminated without cause has no right to a hearing.[318] H never stated M could only be discharged for cause, which means M has no right to a hearing. H clearly explained that if M violated the rule, then she would be terminated immediately or must resign. However, some type of process is likely required before M's job and property can be deprived.

Required Process

To determine the amount of process due, the court should weigh three factors: (1) the interests of the individual and the injury threatened by the official action; (2) the risk of error through the procedures used and probable value, if any, of additional or substitute procedural safeguards; and (3) the costs and administrative burden of the additional process, and the interests of the government in efficient adjudication.[319]

(1) Here, M's interest in retaining her job is high because her job provides income and a rent-control apartment. If she lost her job and paid an

---

316. U.S. Const. amend. XIV.

317. *Perry v. Sindermann*, 408 U.S. 593 (1972).

318. *Cleveland Bd. of Educ. v. Loudermill*, 470 U.S. 532 (1985).

319. *Mathews v. Eldridge*, 424 U.S. 319 (1976).

additional $200 in monthly rent, then M may struggle to pay her bills and maintain her current lifestyle. M's financial status is important if she decides to keep the baby because raising children and medical treatments for pregnancies are expensive.

(2) The risk of error is high because no procedures are used at the school and M's termination was based on rumors about M's pregnancy. No facts suggest H investigated or confirmed if M was actually pregnant. H assumed facts and denied M's request for a hearing to contest her termination. M is likely entitled a meeting or review of the situation to challenge how the pregnancy would impact the children.

(3) The costs and administrative burden of additional process would likely be low for the school because, at minimum, H must review M's performance or give her time to comply with the rule. Resolving the situation may take a few meetings, but can be accomplished quickly if the person reviewing the employee's claims is efficient.

In conclusion, H must, at least, have a meeting or a small hearing to analyze the options, confirm the rumors are true, and review M's file before terminating her because M's pregnancy may not impact her performance as a teacher and she was deprived her rent-control benefits.

Answer 8

(1) Section C

Free Exercise Clause

The government may not compel affirmation of religious beliefs, punish the expression of religious doctrines, or lend its power to one side in controversies over religious authority.[320] If a law burdens a religious practice, and is not neutral or generally applicable, then the law must be narrowly tailored to meet a compelling government interest.[321] Here, Risky Studios (R) will argue State Z lent its power to certain religions because it gave funding to the Church of Religions (COR). The government indirectly promoted some religions over others because COR's diversity event unlikely featured every religion. COR only promotes commonly-practiced religions.

However, State Z will argue Section C is constitutional because it is neutral. The law is generally applicable to all situations related to diversity because all races, genders, and religions are eligible for funding. State Z provides the same treatment to any film promoting diversity. For example, if R passed Section A and B, then R's film, even if it had nothing to do with religion, would receive funding for promoting diversity. State Z's argument is stronger.

Compelling Government Interest

If Section C promoted religion, then the law must be narrowly tailored to achieve a compelling government interest.[322] Here, promoting diversity in the entertainment industry is a compelling government interest because there is an extreme lack of diversity in film. America's population is diverse and films play a vital role in educating people about different cultures.

Narrowly Tailored

Here, State Z will argue that funding to promote diversity is the least restrictive means because it encourages good behavior without being coercive. Film companies are not required to hold an event, but merely have the option. A film company can deny the money if it does not want the additional responsibility.

---

320. *Employment Div., Dep't of Human Res. of Oregon v. Smith*, 494 U.S. 872, 877 (1990).
321. *Church of the Lukumi Babalu Aye, Inc. v. City of Hialeah*, 508 U.S. 520, 531–532 (1993).
322. *Id.*

R will argue that State Z can promote diversity in many other ways, such as making its own film, creating an agency that hosts events, or designing promotional materials advocating for diversity. Thus, because the government must show the means are narrowly tailored, the government likely failed to prove the least restrictive means were used because the funding program promotes religion. However, Section C is constitutional because it is generally applicable.

Establishment Clause

If the government's relationship involves excessive entanglement with religion, then the law is unconstitutional. To be valid, the statute must have (1) a secular legislative purpose, (2) must not advance or inhibit religion, and (3) must not excessively entangle the church and state.[323]

(1) Here, the secular purpose is to promote diversity and not to support a particular religion. Section C uses the film industry to increase awareness of diversity in various areas, such as race, gender, and religion. (2) R will argue the law indirectly advances religion because it promotes some religions over others. COR's event is unlikely to feature all religions. However, State Z will argue Section C does not advance any religion because any identify-based group can obtain the funding. (3) State Z will also argue Section C does not excessively entangle the government with the church because funding is available to all groups. Although COR's diversity event is about religions and uses government funds, the event is a one-time event. State Z is not involved in COR's daily operations.

In conclusion, if financing an event is enough to show the government endorsed some religions over others, then Section C is unconstitutional.

(2) Section B

Overbroad

A statute is overbroad if it punishes a substantial amount of speech.[324] Here, State Z will argue Section B is not overbroad because it only restricts 60% of the casting notices. Writers, directors, and producers can still freely express themselves through the storyline and remaining 40% of casting notices. Section B also only applies to companies filming within State Z's borders. A film company that does not pass Section B can still film in other states.

---

323. *Lemon v. Kurtzman*, 403 U.S. 602 (1971).
324. *Virginia v. Hicks*, 539 U.S. 113, 118–19 (2003).

R will argue Section B limits more speech than necessary because it requires casting notices to promote diversity, which impacts characters on the screen. By restricting casting notices, State Z is indirectly influencing the film creator's message. However, Section B is unlikely overbroad because it restricts a small portion of the film and allows companies with non-diverse casts to film elsewhere.

Vague

A law is unconstitutionally vague if men of common intelligence must guess at its meaning and do not know what type of conduct or speech is prohibited.[325] Here, although Section C includes a concrete percentage of casting notices that must pass the DFA's review, R will argue there is no comprehensible normative standard. Section B says casting notices must "promote diversity." The words "promote diversity" are vague because reasonable people differ on the definition. For example, some people might believe printing the words "promote diversity" on the casting notices is enough to pass Section B while others believe 60% of the casting notices must request a variety of races, genders, and religions or be neutral. Section B is likely vague because companies do not know what conduct is required to pass the DFA's review.

Content-Based Restrictions

Any law restricting the content of protected speech, which is the communication of specific ideas, must be narrowly tailored to meet a compelling government interest.[326] R will argue Section B regulates content because the casting decisions impact the message of the film; characters reflect the film creator's ideas. However, State Z will argue R's speech is unprotected obscene speech.

Obscene Speech

Speech that appeals to (1) the prurient interest from a community standard, and (2) lacks serious literary, artistic, political, or scientific value, and is (3) patently offensive to the community is not protected by the First Amendment.[327]

(1) Here, R will argue the casting notices do not encourage or send any prurient messages. The notices are job postings. However, State Z will argue R's

325. *Coates v. City of Cincinnati*, 402 U.S. 611 (1971).
326. *Reed v. Town of Gilbert, Ariz.*, 135 S.Ct. 2218, 2226 (2015).
327. *Miller v. California*, 413 U.S. 15, 24 (1973).

films appeal to the prurient interest because they involve graphic sexual scenes and only include actors and actresses with sex appeal. Thus, the casting notices indirectly send a message that being sexy is valuable. The court will likely agree with State Z, which means R must prove the notices have some value. (2) R will argue casting notices have artistic value because casting notices impact the actors and actresses who audition for the film. The talent hired ultimately influences the film's message. All films, even those that appeal to the prurient interest, have artistic value because they are a mode of expression. In some cases, films also have political significance, such as releasing a film with graphic sexual scenes to protest the conservative status quo. (3) Whether R's casting notices or films are patently offensive will depend on the community. For example, Hollywood is liberal and rarely offended by sexual casting notices whereas other communities without a robust artistic community might find R's actions offensive.

In conclusion, R's casting calls are protected speech because they impact the characters in the film; strict scrutiny will apply.

Strict Scrutiny

Section B must be narrowly tailored to achieve a compelling government interest.[328]

Compelling Government Interest

State Z has a compelling government interest to promote diversity in films. See analysis above. (Section A: Compelling Government Interest).

Narrowly Tailored

Here, R will argue Section B is not narrowly tailored because State Z is indirectly controlling the entire film by regulating casting notices. The actors and actresses selected for the films are vital to the message of the film. State Z also has less restrictive means available than denying filming permissions within state borders. State Z could provide the company with an opportunity to fix the notices, or allow filming within state borders, but deny the company's request to show the film in State Z theatres.

State Z will argue Section B uses the least restrictive means because the scope of the filming prohibition is limited to State Z and only regulates 60% of the film's casting notices. The film's creator has the freedom to control all other aspects of the film, such as the 40% remaining casting notices,

---

328. *Reed v. Town of Gilbert, Ariz.,* supra note 326.

behind-the-scenes employees, and storyline. The company can also recruit people through their own personal networks, hire a non-diverse cast, or film in a different location. Section B does not restrict the companies recruitment and casting decisions. Section B likely passes strict scrutiny because it promotes diversity and leaves other options open for companies.

(3) Section A

Content-Neutral

Here, Section A regulates conduct because it requires casting notices to be posted on the Labor & Workforce website. Section A is content neutral because the casting notices can say anything as long as they are available to the general public. The government can regulate any conduct related to speech, such as the time, place, and manner, if the law passes the appropriate level of scrutiny.[329]

Level of Scrutiny

If the speech takes place in a public or designated forum, which is an area that has historically been open to speech-related activities, then the regulation must be (1) content-neutral, (2) narrowly tailored to serve and important government interest, and (3) leave alternative channels of communication open.[330] If the forum is a limited forum, which is a closed forum that is only open to certain groups, or a non-public forum that is closed to speech and regulated by the government, then the regulation must be (a) viewpoint neutral, and (b) reasonably related to a legitimate government purpose.[331] Here, the forum is likely a limited or non-public forum because the Labor & Workforce website is owned and managed by State Z. The website is not a public space where people can share their views on various issues, but closed to speech that is not government-approved.

Viewpoint Neutral

Although the government can regulate what topics are allowed in limited and non-public forums, the government cannot hinder public debate and must allow both sides of the controversy to express their views.[332] Here, Section A is viewpoint neutral because it does not restrict any views about diversity or other content-based topics.

---

329. *Clark v. Community for Creative Non-Violence*, 468 U.S. 293, 293 (1984).
330. *Id.*
331. *Rosenberger v. Rector and Visitors of University of Virginia*, 515 U.S. 819, 829–30 (1995).
332. *Id.* at 894.

Legitimate Government Purpose

State Z has a compelling government interest to promote diversity in films, which means it has a legitimate government purpose. See analysis above. (Section A: Compelling Government Interest). State Z also has an interest to promote access to equal employment opportunities for its citizens. The entertainment industry is dominated by Whites and insular, which means the hiring is often based on personal connections. If State Z requires casting notices to be posted in a public space, then Section A creates opportunities for minorities and other groups to audition. Section A includes groups that are normally excluded from the hiring process. Section A also encourages film companies to explore new talent when creating films.

Reasonably Related

R will argue that revoking permission to film within State Z's borders is not rationally related because the location of filming does not impact who is cast in the films or the hiring process. However, State Z will argue Section A prevents companies from using government lands for discriminatory purposes. Section A also creates opportunities for State Z citizens to earn a living within its borders and promotes opening additions to talented minorities. Thus, because rational basis review places the burden on the challenger and allows any conceivable connection between the means and end, Section A is constitutional.[333]

---

333. *New York City Transit Auth. v. Beazer*, supra note 284 at 602.

Contracts Answers

Answer 1

(1) Buyer's (B) Defenses

Governing Law

The Uniform Commercial Code (UCC) governs the sale of goods, which are tangible moveable objects,[334] while common law governs all other contracts.[335] For hybrid contracts, if the predominate purpose of the transaction is to sell goods, then the UCC applies.[336] If not, then common law applies. Here, although the transaction included the Farmer's (F) land and farming equipment, the sale was predominately for 500 acres of land. F hired a real estate agent because F likely cared more about selling the land than selling the farming equipment. Thus, common law governs the contract.

Duress

A contract is voidable if: (a) an improper threat is made to the promisor, (b) the threat induced the promise, and (c) the inducement is reasonable.[337] A threat is improper if what is threatened is a crime or tort, or the threat is a breach of the duty of good faith and fair dealing.[338]

Here, (a) Agent's (A) threat was improper because A's statement, "you'll be sorry," suggested A intended to harm B. Physically hurting someone or damaging their property is a crime and a tort. A's threat also breached the duty of good faith and fair dealing because A used his authority to coerce B into the contract. (b) A's threat induced B's promise to purchase F's land because B only signed the contract after A showed up to her home, threatened her, and shoved

---

334. Unif.Commercial Code § 2-105.
335. *Ritz-Craft Corp. v. Stanford Management Group*, 800 F. Supp. 1312, 1317 (D. Md. 1992).
336. *Kirkendall v. Harbor Insurance Co.*, 887 F.2d 857 (8th Cir. 1989).
337. Restatement (Second) of Contracts § 175 (1981).
338. Restatement (Second) of Contracts § 176 (1981).

the contract in her face. B was scared. (c) B's inducement was reasonable because A did not threaten B over the phone. A was physically in B's space. A will argue B could have closed the door or walked away, but this is a weak argument. B was a teenager and a teenager would be afraid if an adult showed up at her doorstep and threatened her. Thus, B can void the contract because she entered it under duress.

Incapacity

If a minor enters a contract, then the minor can disaffirm the contract anytime during minority or for a reasonable time after the minor turns 18 years old.[339] Here, B was 17 years old when she entered the contract to buy F's land. B was still 17 years old when she told F she did not want to purchase the land. Thus, B had the right to disaffirm the contract as a minor.

A will argue B is bound to the sale because minors cannot void contracts for necessities.[340] A home is a necessity because it provides shelter. However, A's argument is weak because A went to B's home, which suggests B already lived in a house and probably did not need another one. Thus, B can void the contract.

(2) Farmer's (F) Defenses

Governing Law

See rule above. (Buyer's Defenses: Governing Law). Here, common law applies because the contract was for A's services. F hired A to sell 500 acres of land and farm equipment.

Unconscionability

If a contract or term is unconscionable at the time the contract was created, then the court may refuse to enforce the contract or may enforce the contract without the unconscionable term.[341] For a contract or term to be invalid there must be both (a) procedural unconscionability and (b) substantive unconscionability. Courts use a sliding-scale approach that allows for a greater degree of one type of unconscionability and a lesser degree of the other.[342]

---

339. Restatement (Second) of Contracts §§ 12, 14 (1981).
340. *Shumate v. Twin Tier Hospitality, LLC,* 655 F.Supp.2d 521, 531 (M.D. Pa. 2009).
341. R.2d of Contracts § 208 (1981).
342. *Quilloin v. Tenet HealthSystem Philadelphia, Inc.,* 673 F.3d 221, 230 (3d Cir. 2012).

Procedural Unconscionability (PU)

PU exists when there is a gross inequality of bargaining power; a mere disparity is not enough.[343] Here, F will argue he had no bargaining power because A presented a standard form agreement that F could not read. F had limited literacy, which means F could not understand or change the terms of A's adhesion contract. However, A will argue F could have refused to sign the contract or waited for someone to read the terms to him. A's argument is weak because F asked A to explain the contract, but A refused. Instead, A told F not to worry about the terms. Reasonable people in F's position would trust a professional real estate agent and sign the contract.

Substantive Unconscionability (SU)

SU exists when the contract terms are unreasonably favorable to one party; imbalance in values is not enough.[344] Here, F will argue the terms are unreasonably favorable to A because A had no experience, but charged twice the normal commission rate of an entry-level real estate agent. A should have charged F the regular market rate of an entry-level agent or a lower rate because A never sold a single property, was unlicensed, and learned about real estate through online videos. In conclusion, the contract is likely void because PU and SU are both present.

Fraud

A contract is voidable if: (a) the manifestation of assent was induced (b) by a fraudulent or material misrepresentation, and (c) the recipient was justified in relying on the material misrepresentation.[345]

(a) A misrepresentation induces a party's assent if it substantially contributes to the party's decision to enter the contract.[346] Although F's subjective thoughts are unknown, F will argue he wanted a qualified agent to sell his farmland and only signed the agreement because A claimed to be an expert in real estate.

(b) A misrepresentation is fraudulent if the maker knows the assertion is not in accord with the facts or does not have the confidence that he states the truth.[347] Here, F will argue A knowingly misrepresented his experience level

---

343. R.2d of Contracts § 208, supra note 341.
344. *Id.*
345. Restatement (Second) of Contracts § 164 (1981).
346. Restatement (Second) of Contracts § 167 (1981).
347. Restatement (Second) of Contracts § 162 (1981).

because A never sold a single property and was unlicensed. A knew he did not qualify as an expert, but lied to obtain F's business. However, A will argue he was confident in his abilities because watching online videos is similar to attending class. A's argument is weak because reasonable people know that online videos cannot replace actual experiences.

(c) A recipient's fault in not discovering the facts before making the contract does not make his reliance unjustified unless it amounts to a failure to act in good faith or is outside the scope of reasonable standards of fair dealings.[348] Here, A will argue F's reliance was unjustified because A should have conducted a background check before signing the contract, such as verifying A's real estate license. F did nothing and relied solely on A's sales pitch. However, F will argue that a reasonable person would trust a professional to accurately represent his qualifications. F's reliance is likely justified because the court has a strong interest to protect consumers from fraud, especially when a fiduciary relationship is involved. In conclusion, F can void the contract because A misrepresented his expertise.

Mutual Mistake

A contract is voidable if, at the time of formation, the parties were mistaken about a basic assumption on which the contract was made and that assumption had a material effect on the agreed upon terms.[349] If neither party knew or had reason to know the meaning attached by the other, then there is no mutual assent.[350] Here, F and A had no idea that the other attached a different meaning to the term "Agent's duties are complete after the deal is closed." Both parties' interpretations are reasonable because "deal is closed" could be interpreted to mean after the contract was signed or after the money was received. Moreover, neither party bore the risk of mistake. There was no language about mistake in the contract and the court did not allocate the risk to either party.[351] Thus, F can void the contract because the parties were mistaken about the meaning of a material term.

---

348. Restatement (Second) of Contracts § 172 (1981).
349. Restatement (Second) of Contracts § 152 (1981).
350. Restatement (Second) of Contracts § 20 (1981).
351. Restatement (Second) of Contracts § 154 (1981).

Answer 2

(1) Customer (C) v. Tim's Estate

Governing Law

The Uniform Commercial Code (UCC) governs the sale of goods, which are tangible moveable objects,[352] while common law governs all other contracts.[353] Here, the UCC applies because the contract is for watches.

Formation

An enforceable contract requires mutual assent and consideration.[354] Courts evaluate the existence of mutual assent by analyzing the presence of offer and acceptance.[355]

Offer

Under the UCC, a valid offer invites acceptance in any reasonable manner and medium sufficient to show an agreement.[356] The UCC is generally liberal on indefiniteness.[357] Advertisements are not offers, but invitations to deal, unless the advertisement is clear, definite, and explicitly leaves nothing open for negotiation.[358] Here, Tim's (T) newspaper advertisement offered to sell Meko watches in exchange for antique watches. T's advertisement was definite because it specifically told consumers the performance required to get the 50% discount. Thus, T's newspaper advertisement was likely a valid offer.

Unilateral versus Bilateral Offer

A unilateral contract invites acceptance by full performance.[359] A bilateral contract invites acceptance by performance or promise.[360] Here, T's offer appeared to invite acceptance by full performance because T asked patrons to physically trade the antique watches. T did not ask patrons for promises to trade watches at a later date. However, C will argue that T intended to make a bilateral contract because T agreed that C could deliver the 1926 antique

---

352. UCC § 2-105, supra note 334.
353. *Ritz-Craft Corp. v. Stanford Management Group*, supra note 335.
354. Restatement (Second) of Contracts §§ 17, 22(1) (1981).
355. *Kolodziej v. Mason*, 774 F.3d 736, 741 (11th Cir. 2014).
356. Unif.Commercial Code § 2-206.
357. Unif.Commercial Code § 2-204.
358. *Lefkowitz v. Great Minneapolis Surplus Store*, 251 Minn. 188, 86 N.W.2d 689 (1957).
359. Restatement (Second) of Contracts § 45 (1981).
360. Restatement (Second) of Contracts §§ 50, 56 (1981).

watch next Friday. If T intended to create a bilateral contract, then a contract was formed when C promised to deliver the watch. If T intended to create a unilateral contract, then no contract was formed, but T's right to revoke the offer was limited because T created an option contract.[361]

Option Contract and Revocation

An offeree's power of acceptance is terminated by revocation.[362] However, if the offeror invites acceptance by full performance, then the offeror loses the unilateral power to revoke the offer once performance begins because the promisor needs a reasonable amount of time to complete performance.[363] Here, C agreed to deliver the watch to T by next Friday. Thus, performance began when C left the store and T cannot revoke his offer until next Friday. But if T created a firm offer, then T could not revoke his offer for two weeks.

Firm Offer

A merchant cannot revoke his offer to buy or sell goods if he explicitly agrees, in a signed writing, to keep the offer open.[364] The merchant's offer is irrevocable for the time stated in the writing, or if no time is stated, then for a reasonable amount of time.[365] There is a 3-month limit on irrevocability.[366] Here, T is a merchant because, as an owner of a watch shop, T regularly deals in the watch industry and holds himself out as having a particular knowledge about watches.[367] T explicitly agreed to hold the 50% off Meko watch for two weeks while C retrieved the 1926 antique watch from his parent's house. If T's written note was signed, then T cannot revoke his agreement to keep his offer open for two weeks.

Termination of the Power of Acceptance by Death

An offeree's power of acceptance is terminated by the death of the offeror.[368] Here, T's estate will argue that the offer was terminated when T died in a car accident. However, death does not terminate an offeree's power of acceptance

---

361. Restatement (Second) of Contracts § 25 (1981).
362. Restatement (Second) of Contracts § 36 (1981).
363. R. 2d of Contracts § 45, supra note 359.
364. Unif.Commercial Code § 2-205.
365. *Id.*
366. *Id.*
367. Unif.Commercial Code § 2-104.
368. R. 2d of Contracts § 36, supra note 362.

under an option contract.[369] Thus, because T created a valid option contract, C still had the power to accept T's offer by trading in the 1926 antique watch by Friday.

Acceptance

Notification of performance is not required for a unilateral offer.[370] But notice is required for a bilateral contract.[371] Here, if T created a unilateral contract, then C fully performed when he arrived on Friday with the 1926 antique watch. If T formed a bilateral contract, then C validly accepted because T had notice that C would deliver the watch on Friday.

Conclusion

A valid contract exists between C and T. Thus, T's estate must pay C monetary damages.

(2) WatchWorks (W) v. Tim's Estate

Governing Law and Formation

See rules above. (Consumer v. Tim's Estate: Governing Law and Formation). Here, the UCC applies because the contract was for watches.

Offer

See rules above. (Consumer v. Tim's Estate: Offer). If one or more terms of the proposed bargain were left open, then there was likely no intent to create a contract.[372] Although the UCC is liberal on indefiniteness, T will argue his email was an invitation to deal because the email did not specify the quantity or price of the watches. T left important terms open for negotiation.

However, W has a stronger argument that T's email was a valid offer because T stated he would purchase "every Meko watch produced by the manufacturer over the next six months." Under the UCC, parties can accept contracts, even if the prices are not settled, because courts can fill the missing gaps with the reasonable price at the time of delivery.[373] Courts held that output contracts are definite because the requirement of good faith and fair dealing ensures the

---

369. Restatement (Second) of Contracts § 37 (1981).
370. Restatement (Second) of Contracts § 54 (1981).
371. Restatement (Second) of Contracts §§ 56, 62 (1981).
372. UCC § 2-204, supra note 357.
373. Unif. Commercial Code § 2-305.

quantity represents a foreseeable figure.[374] Thus, T's open price term can be resolved using gap fillers and T's offer to purchase "every" watch qualifies as an offer to enter an output contract.

Counter-Offer and Conditional Acceptance

A counter-offer terminates the offeree's power of acceptance.[375] A reply to an offer that purports to accept it, but is conditional on the offeror's assent to additional or different terms, is not an acceptance, but a counter-offer.[376] Here, T will argue W did not accept T's offer because W changed the notice terms. T requested notice on the 1st of the month, but W agreed to provide notice on the 14th of the month.

However, W will argue its email reply never made its acceptance conditional on T's agreement to notice on the 14th. Under the UCC, a definite expression of acceptance constitutes an acceptance even if it states terms additional to or different from those offered unless acceptance is expressly made conditional on assent to the additional or different terms.[377] W explicitly stated, "We accept your offer," provided the price, and suggested a different notice date. Thus, W's acceptance was likely valid.

If W did not accept T's offer, then W will argue T's subsequent email agreeing to W's notice date was a valid acceptance. However, this argument will fail because T conditioned his acceptance on W's agreement to deliver the watches on the 28th of each month to Z street. The words "only if" made T's email a conditional acceptance.

Lapse of Time

An offer expires after a reasonable amount of time or after the time period fixed by the offer.[378] Here, W will argue it accepted T's terms when it shipped the watches. However, T's argument is stronger because W never explicitly accepted T's new terms or gave T notice about the quantity of watches produced that month. Thus, T's counter-offer expired on the 14th because a reasonable person would assume W rejected the offer by not responding.

---

374. Unif.Commercial Code § 2-306.
375. R. 2d of Contracts § 36, supra note 362.
376. Restatement (Second) of Contracts §§ 50, 39 (1981).
377. Unif.Commercial Code § 2-207.
378. Restatement (Second) of Contracts § 41 (1981).

Silence as Acceptance

If the offer was still open after the 14th, then W will argue silence can serve as acceptance if: (a) the offeree took the benefits of the services offered with a reasonable opportunity to reject them, (b) the parties agreed beforehand that silence was acceptance, or (c) acceptance by silence was part of the course of dealings.[379]

Here, although W never replied to T's counter-offer, W will argue that shipping goods without notice is a normal course of dealings in the watch industry.[380] But, without more facts, this is a weak argument because T's son rejected W's goods when they arrived on the 28th. T's son never accepted W's watches and the parties never agreed beforehand that silence would constitute acceptance. Thus, T reasonably assumed W's silence was a rejection and not acceptance of his terms.

Conclusion

If W's email response was a valid acceptance, then there is a contract. If not, then no contract exists because W never validly accepted T's additional terms before the counter-offer expired.

---

379. Restatement (Second) of Contracts § 69 (1981).
380. UCC § 2-206, supra note 356.

Answer 3

(1) Marcie (M) v. Pet Shop (P)

Governing Law

The Uniform Commercial Code (UCC) governs the sale of goods, which are tangible moveable objects,[381] while common law governs all other contracts.[382] For hybrid contracts, if the predominate purpose of the transaction is to sell goods, then the UCC applies.[383] If not, then common law applies. Here, the contract was predominately M's foster care services. However, P agreed to give M a cat tree in exchange for her services. Thus, the governing law could be either UCC or common law. The court might apply the minority rule, the gravamen test, and examine whether the underlying action was brought because of defective goods or because of the services rendered.[384] Under gravamen, although P's defense focuses on M's poor foster care services, M's action is mainly to recover goods.

Formation Under Common Law

An enforceable contract requires mutual assent and consideration.[385] Courts evaluate the existence of mutual assent by analyzing the presence of offer and acceptance.[386]

Offer and Counter-Offers

An offer is a manifestation of the willingness to enter into a bargain that would cause a reasonable person to believe his assent to the offeror's terms would form a contract.[387] Under common law, an offeree's response operates as acceptance only if it is the precise mirror image of the offer.[388] If the response conflicts with the existing terms or adds new terms, then it is a counter-offer.[389] A counter-offer terminates the power of acceptance.[390]

---

381. UCC § 2-105, supra note 334.
382. *Ritz-Craft Corp. v. Stanford Management Group*, supra note 335.
383. *Kirkendall v. Harbor Insurance Co.,* supra note 336.
384. *In re Trailer and Plumbing Supplies,* 133 N.H. 432, 436 (1990).
385. R.2d of Contracts §§ 17, 22(1), supra note 354.
386. *Kolodziej v. Mason*, supra note 355.
387. Restatement (Second) of Contracts § 24 (1981).
388. Restatement (Second) of Contracts §§ 38-39 (1981).
389. *Id.*
390. R. 2d of Contracts § 36, supra note 362.

Here, a reasonable person would believe P's request for foster care services was an offer because P specifically asked M to care for Jumper (J) and left no material terms open. Although M agreed to care for J, M's response was not a valid acceptance because it changed the original offer terms. M stated P must give her a free cat tree in exchange for fostering J. Thus, there was unlikely a contract at this point in the negotiations.

M will argue that P's email was a valid acceptance because P agreed to give M the cat tree. However, this argument will fail because P added a term that required M to keep J in healthy condition. M's subsequent response also added a term that required P to give her cat toys if J had no medical problems. Under common law, all correspondence before M's email was preliminary negotiations that left P with the power to accept M's proposed terms.

Acceptance

Here, although P never responded to M's email, P allowed M to pick up J from the store. If P did not assent to the terms, then P would have prevented M from removing J from the premises and continued negotiating the payment for foster care services. In conclusion, under common law, there is a valid contract for the cat tree and toys in exchange for M caring for J until he is adopted.

Formation Under UCC

A valid offer invites acceptance in any reasonable manner and medium sufficient to show an agreement.[391] Here, M and P's email exchange shows they intended to create a contract that included the cat tree for foster care services. Thus, because the UCC encourages contracts, there is a valid contract. The issue is if the terms about J's medical condition and M's cat toys are included.

Battle of the Forms

Under the UCC, a definite expression of acceptance constitutes an acceptance even if it states terms additional to or different from those agreed upon.[392] Under the last-shot doctrine, the additional terms become part of the contract unless (a) the offer expressly limits acceptance to the terms of the offer, (b) the terms materially alter the contract, or (c) the party objects to

---

391. UCC § 2-206, supra note 356.
392. UCC § 2-207, supra note 377.

the new or different terms within a reasonable time after notice of the terms was received.[393]

Here, neither party limited acceptance to the terms of their counter-offers, but P will argue the cat toys are not included because M's last email materially changed the terms of their agreement. M's new terms required P to provide additional cat toys for the same foster care services. However, M will argue P had a reasonable amount of time to object to M's terms because M fostered J for over a month and P never rejected M's contract. Moreover, M likely added the cat toys because P unilaterally decided M must keep J in healthy condition. Instead of opposing P's counter-offer, M increased her compensation to match the increased duties. Thus, the contract included M's additional terms because the contract was not materially altered.

Conclusion

Under the UCC and common law, there was a valid contract for the cat tree and toys. M will recover damages if the court determines she fully performed her foster care services.

(2) Bella (B) v. Marcie (M)

Governing Law and Formation

See rule above. (Marcie v. Pet Shop: Governing Law and Formation Under Common Law). Here, common law applies because the contract includes services to find J.

Offer

Rewards are unilateral contracts because they invite acceptance by full performance.[394] Any person who learns of the reward offer has the power to accept by rendering the specified performance.[395] Here, M's reward posters were valid offers because a reasonable person would believe M would pay $200 for the safe return of J. M's posters were on every street corner in town and M's contact information was provided. M's actions indicate she was desperate to find J. The issue is whether M revoked her offer before B accepted.

---

393. *Id.*

394. R. 2d of Contracts § 54, supra note 370.

395. *McGuigan v. Conte*, 629 F.Supp.2d 76, 81 (D. Mass. 2009). See also Restatement (Second) of Contracts §§ 23, 29 (1981).

Mailbox Rule

Revocation is effective upon receipt[396] while acceptance is valid upon proper dispatch.[397] The method of acceptance is set by the offeror, but if no method is set, then proper dispatch requires appropriate care and a reasonable medium of communication.[398]

Here, B will argue she accepted M's offer before M revoked because B sent a letter to M on Wednesday morning and M did not revoke her reward offer until Thursday. However, M will argue B's letter was not the appropriate medium of communication because M provided a phone number on the poster, which suggested M wanted a phone call and not a physical letter. B will argue that her letter was reasonable under the circumstances because M was not home. But M, as the offeror, can set the method of acceptance. Thus, B's letter was not a valid acceptance.

Unilateral Contract

B will argue she accepted M's offer when she delivered J to M's house on Friday because M could not revoke her offer. An offeree's power of acceptance is terminated by revocation.[399] However, if the offeror invites acceptance by full performance, then the offeror loses the unilateral power to revoke the offer once performance begins because the promisor needs a reasonable amount of time to complete performance.[400]

Here, B will argue she started performance after she saw the posters. B also gave M notice of her performance when she delivered the letter to M on Wednesday. Thus, M could not revoke her offer until B had the opportunity to return J on Friday. However, M will argue she could revoke her offer at anytime because the reward signs were posted for two weeks without any success. The jury would need to decide whether two weeks is a reasonable amount of time to find a lost cat. If two weeks is enough time, then M could revoke her offer.

---

396. Restatement (Second) of Contracts § 42 (1981).
397. Restatement (Second) of Contracts § 63 (1981).
398. Restatement (Second) of Contracts § 35 (1981).
399. R. 2d of Contracts § 36, supra note 362.
400. R. 2d of Contracts § 45, supra note 359.

Indirect Revocation

Revocation terminates the power of acceptance.[401] Revocation is valid, even if not communicated directly, if the offeree knows something happened to revoke the offer.[402] Here, B will argue M did not clearly revoke her offer because M did not post new flyers to clarify the $200 reward was no longer available. A reasonable person in B's position would assume M removed the posters on Thursday because M received B's letter that B found J on Wednesday.

However, M will argue she properly revoked her reward offer because she removed all the signage. An offer made to the public must be revoked in the same medium to inform people the offer is no longer open.[403] B should have realized that the absence of the posters meant the reward was no longer available.

Conclusion

If an option contract was not created, then no contract existed because M validly revoked her offer on Thursday before B accepted on Friday.

---

401. Restatement (Second) of Contracts § 43 (1981).
402. *Id.*
403. Restatement (Second) of Contracts § 46 (1981).

Answer 4

(1) Phil (P) vs. Sharon (S): Consideration

Governing Law

The Uniform Commercial Code (UCC) governs the sale of goods, which are tangible moveable objects,[404] while common law governs all other contracts.[405] For hybrid contracts, if the predominate purpose of the transaction is to sell goods, then the UCC applies.[406] If not, then common law applies. Here, although the contract involves goods and services, the UCC applies because the transaction was predominately related to S's promise to give P a car.

Consideration

Valid consideration requires the contract to be a bargained-for exchange in which there is a legal detriment to the promisee or a benefit to the promisor.[407]

Bargained-for Exchange

A bargained-for exchange occurs when the promise or performance provided by each party was sought out and exchanged for the promise or performance provided by the other party.[408] Here, P will argue an exchange existed because S agreed to give P a luxury car in exchange for his life-saving services. S explicitly stated the car was payment for his services. S never mentioned the car was a gift until P arrived at the dealership to claim his payment.

However, S will argue the exchange was not bargained for because P saved S before he knew S owned a luxury car dealership. S will also argue that gratuitous promises are unenforceable gifts.[409] S agreed to give P a luxury car as a thank you for rescuing her and not as a formal transaction. Thus, no consideration exists because P's actions were not induced by S's promise to give him a car.

---

404. UCC § 2-105, supra note 334.
405. *Ritz-Craft Corp. v. Stanford Management Group*, supra note 335.
406. *Kirkendall v. Harbor Insurance Co.*, supra note 336.
407. *Neuhoff v. Marvin Lumber and Cedar Co.*, 370 F.3d 197, 201 (1st Cir. 2004).
408. Restatement (Second) of Contracts § 71 (1981).
409. *Kirksey v. Kirksey*, 8 Ala. 131, 133 (1845).

Legal Benefit and Detriment

Under the traditional rule, courts determined that some right, interest, or benefit provided to one party in exchange for some forbearance, detriment, or responsibility given by the other party is enough to show consideration.[410] P will argue that valuable consideration was present because P, the promisee, incurred a legal detriment when he provided his lifeguard services to S, and S, the promisor, obtained the benefit of not drowning. Thus, under the *Hamer v. Sidway* standard, consideration is met even though there was no bargained-for exchange.

Adequacy of Consideration

S will argue a luxury car, worth more than $800,000, is excessive payment for lifeguard services, but P will argue S cannot put a price on her life. Courts usually do not look into the adequacy of consideration[411] because courts believe parties are in the best position to determine the terms.[412] Thus, $800,000 is a fair term and not nominal consideration.

Pre-Existing Duty

S will argue that consideration is not present under both the traditional and modern standards because P had a pre-existing duty to save S's life. Performance of a legal duty already owed to a promisor is not consideration;[413] similar performance is only valid consideration if it differs from the original duty in a way that reflects more than a pretense of a bargain.[414] Here, P was obligated to save drowning patrons because he was the lifeguard on duty. P even recognized that he was "only doing his job." Thus, consideration is not present because P already had a duty to save people drowning at the community center.

Alternatives to Consideration

Courts created alternative courses of recovery for plaintiffs who were unable to prove the elements of consideration. The doctrines of material benefit and promissory estoppel allow parties to recover expectancy damages by showing reliance or unjust enrichment.

---

410. *Hamer v. Sidway*, 124 N.Y. 538, 545 [27 N.E. 256] (1891). See also R. 2d of Contracts § 71, supra note 408.

411. Restatement (Second) of Contracts § 79 (1981).

412. *Batsakis v. Demotsis*, 226 S.W. 2D 673 (Tex. 1949).

413. Restatement (Second) of Contracts § 73 (1981).

414. *Id.*

Promissory Estoppel

A promise is binding if: (a) the promisor reasonably expects to induce action or forbearance on the part of the promisee, (b) the promise does induce such action or forbearance, and (c) injustice can only be avoided by enforcement of the promise; the remedy may be limited as justice requires.[415]

(a) Here, P will argue that S should have expected him to rely on her promise because S had apparent authority to give him a free car; S was the owner of the luxury car business and not a low-level employee. S also insisted P take the car after he refused. A reasonable person would know that persisting to give someone a free car would make the recipient believe the intentions were true and not an exaggerated side comment. However, S will argue a reasonable person would not know the details of P's life because P was a stranger. S could not predict the free car would replace his bicycle or that P would quit his job. Most people wait until they receive a new car before selling their only mode of transportation. (b) S's promise did induce P's actions because he sold his bicycle and quit job in anticipation of receiving the free car. (c) P will argue that avoiding injustice requires S to give P a free car without taxes because P needs transportation to find a new job.

In conclusion, if S should have known P would rely on her promise, then S must give P the value of the luxury car or at least the value of a new bike.

Material Benefit Rule

Promises made in recognition of a benefit previously received are legally binding to the extent necessary to prevent injustice.[416] Here, P saved S's life before S promised to give P a luxury car. Thus, P's services were invalid past consideration. However, P will argue that S's promise was made in recognition of the benefit P previously conferred upon S because S explicitly stated the car was payment for P's life-saving services. The car is necessary to prevent injustice because P quit his job and sold his bike based on S's promise. P needs transportation to find a new job.

S will argue the material benefit rule does not apply when the promise was conferred as a gift.[417] The luxury car was a gift to thank P for his help and not payment for his services because P already received a wage as the lifeguard on

---

415. Restatement (Second) of Contracts § 90 (1981).
416. Restatement (Second) of Contracts § 86 (1981).
417. Id.

duty. P cannot recover under this theory because S stated the car, excluding taxes, was a gift from her.

(2) Phil (P) vs. Sharon (S): Specific Performance

Specific performance will be granted if (a) there is a valid contract, (b) there is an inadequate remedy at law, (c) the enforcement of the performance is feasible, and (d) no defenses apply.[418] Whether there is an inadequate remedy at law is the most important consideration.

Here, (a) there was a valid contract. (b) P will argue the luxury car is unique, which means it is one of a kind or very rare,[419] because few people can afford to buy cars over $800,000. P will also argue the car has personal significance to him because he desperately needs transportation to find a new job. However, S has a stronger argument because, although luxury cars are expensive, several individuals in upper-class society purchase luxury cars. S runs an entire business focused on selling cars over $800,000, which suggests there is high demand in the market. Moreover, P does not necessarily need a luxury car from S's business. Thus, S could pay P money damages to purchase any car or bicycle to resolve his transportation problem. (c) P has a stronger argument for feasibility of enforcement because the court can easily enforce a judgment against S. The transaction involves a one-time exchange and requires little oversight. (d) No defenses apply. In conclusion, specific performance is unlikely to be available because luxury cars are not unique.

---

418. Restatement (Second) of Contracts §§ 359, 362 (1981).
419. Unif.Commercial Code § 2-716.

Answer 5

(1) John (J) v. Rose (R)

Governing Law

The Uniform Commercial Code (UCC) governs the sale of goods, which are tangible moveable objects,[420] while common law governs all other contracts.[421] For hybrid contracts, if the predominate purpose of the transaction is to sell goods, then the UCC applies.[422] If not, then common law applies. Here, the UCC governs because the transaction was for a mattress. The two-year warranty service was an incidental term that was not the basis of the bargain.

Formation

An enforceable contract requires mutual assent and consideration.[423] Courts evaluate the existence of mutual assent by analyzing the presence of offer and acceptance.[424]

Consideration

Valid consideration requires the contract to be a bargained-for exchange in which there is a legal detriment to the promisee or a benefit to the promisor.[425] A bargained-for exchange occurs when the promise or performance provided by each party was sought out and exchanged for the promise or performance provided by the other party.[426] Here, consideration is present because R agreed to pay J money for a mattress in exchange for J's delivery of the mattress.

Mutual Assent

Under the UCC, a valid offer invites acceptance in any reasonable manner and medium sufficient to show an agreement.[427] Here, R and J agreed she would pay him cash in exchange for the mattress. But R will argue the contract should fail for indefiniteness because they never agreed on a price. A contract with an open price term is valid if the parties intended to agree and there is a

---

420. UCC § 2-105, supra note 334.
421. *Ritz-Craft Corp. v. Stanford Management Group*, supra note 335.
422. *Kirkendall v. Harbor Insurance Co.*, supra note 336.
423. R.2d of Contracts §§ 17, 22(1), supra note 354.
424. *Kolodziej v. Mason*, supra note 355.
425. *Neuhoff v. Marvin Lumber and Cedar Co.*, supra note 407.
426. R. 2d of Contracts § 71, supra note 408.
427. UCC § 2-206, supra note 356.

reasonably certain basis for determining an appropriate remedy.[428] The UCC is generally liberal on indefiniteness. R and J's actions indicated they intended to be bound because J sent a confirmation memo, J delivered the mattress, and R paid J $600. Thus, mutual assent is present and the court can use gap fillers to determine a remedy.[429]

Statute of Frauds (SOF)

Contracts for the sale of goods valued at $500 or more, or contracts that cannot be performed within one year require a signed writing to be enforceable.[430] Here, R agreed to pay $600 or $1200 for the mattress and the mattress's market value was $2400. All three prices are over $500. J agreed to give R a two-year warranty on the mattress, which means Best Beds will take more than a year to fulfill its performance on the warranty. Thus, the contract is within the SOF and a signed writing is required.

Signed Writing

To satisfy the SOF, the writing must be signed by or on behalf of the party to be charged.[431] A valid signature can be any symbol made or adopted with an intention to authenticate the writing as that of the signer.[432] Here, the confirmation memo with Best Bed's company logo on the bottom satisfies the SOF. However, J wants to enforce the contract against R and R never signed the confirmation memo; R verbally agreed to the terms of the memo when J called her over the telephone. Thus, unless an exception applies, the contract is invalid.

Full Performance Exception

If the contract falls within the SOF, but there is no signed writing, then the contract is still enforceable if the goods were received and accepted.[433] Here, J's employee delivered the mattress. R did not ask the employee to return the mattress, but accepted the goods and told the employee that she would work out the price with J. The only performance remaining was R's payment and J's two-year warranty. Thus, J's lack of a signed writing will not preclude his recovery.

---

428. UCC § 2-204, supra note 357. See also UCC § 2-305, supra note 373.
429. UCC § 2-305, supra note 373.
430. Restatement (Second) of Contracts § 110 (1981). See also Unif.Commercial Code § 2-201.
431. Restatement (Second) of Contracts § 131 (1981).
432. Restatement (Second) of Contracts § 134 (1981).
433. Unif.Commercial Code § 2-606.

Public Policy Against Enforcing Illegal Contracts

R will argue the contract is void because J obtained the mattress illegally. Contracts may be declared void against public policy if the contract includes illegal subject matter or things obtained by illegal means.[434] Here, J obtained most of his inventory by burglarizing other mattress stores, which is a crime. R specifically purchased from J because she wanted to benefit from his illegal operation. J will argue the mattress R received was not stolen, but without more facts, this is mere speculation. Thus, a valid contract does not exist because the court wants to discourage parties from entering contracts that promote illegal sales and theft.

(2) John's (J) Remedies

Expectancy Damages

The goal of contract law is to give the non-breaching party the benefit of the bargain by putting the non-breaching party in the position he would have been if the contract had been performed.[435] Expectancy damages include (a) the loss in the value to the non-breaching party, plus (b) any other loss, including incidental or consequential loss, caused by the breach, less (c) any cost or other loss that the non-breaching party has avoided by not having to perform.[436] To provide J with the appropriate remedy, the court must first determine the terms of his agreement with R.

Modification

Under common law, valid modifications require new consideration.[437] Performance of a legal duty already owed to a promisor is not new consideration;[438] similar performance is only valid consideration if it differs from the pre-existing duty in a way that reflects more than a pretense of a bargain.[439] Under the UCC, modification is permitted without new consideration as long the modification was made in good faith.[440] The terms at issue include (a) the price of the two-year warranty and (b) the price of the mattress. R will argue common

---

434. Restatement (Second) of Contracts § 179 (1981).
435. Restatement (Second) of Contracts § 347 (1981).
436. Id.
437. R. 2d of Contracts § 73, supra note 413.
438. Id.
439. Id.
440. Unif.Commercial Code §2-209.

law applies because the warranty was a service and not a good. However, J has a stronger argument that the UCC applies because the predominate purpose of the contract was the sale of a mattress.

(a) Price of the Two-Year Warranty

If the contract is divisible, then common law will apply to the warranty term. R will argue the terms were not modified by R's subsequent telephone conversation with J because he had a pre-existing duty under the terms in the confirmatory memo. The original terms in the confirmatory memo already included a free two-year warranty. J's duties never changed when R agreed to pay an additional $10 a month for the warranty.

If the contract is not divisible, then the UCC applies because the warranty is incidental to the purchase of the mattress. J will argue the modification was made in good faith because he had unexpected costs and most companies charge consumers for warranties. J's request was not unreasonable. Moreover, R agreed to pay the extra $10 a month, which shows her assent to the modification.

In conclusion, if common law applies, then the modification is not valid and J cannot recover any payments from R. However, if the UCC applies, then J can recover $240 in warranty fees.

(b) Price of the Mattress

When a buyer fails to remit payment when it comes due, then the seller may recover the price of the goods accepted by buyer.[441] Here, J can recover the value of the mattress because R accepted the mattress. However, there are three different prices for the mattress: $600, $1200, and $2400.

If the parties did not agree upon a price, then the court will fill the open price with a reasonable price at the time of delivery.[442] $600 is likely an unreasonable price because it is 75% off the market value of the mattress. R will argue that $1200 is a reasonable price because J sells similar mattresses at his store for that price. J will argue the market price, $2400, is a more appropriate price. The court is more likely to agree with R because J usually sells his mattresses at a discounted rate. 50% is a reasonable discount between long-time friends. Thus, J can collect the remaining $600 from R because she already paid $600.

---

441. Unif.Commercial Code §2-709.
442. Unif.Commercial Code § 2-305.

Answer 6

Stephanie (S) v. Ronnie (R)

Governing Law

The Uniform Commercial Code (UCC) governs the sale of goods, which are tangible moveable objects,[443] while common law governs all other contracts.[444] For hybrid contracts, if the predominate purpose of the transaction is to sell goods, then the UCC applies.[445] If not, then common law applies. Here, common law governs because the contract concerns bodyguard services.

Formation

An enforceable contract requires mutual assent and consideration.[446] Courts evaluate the existence of mutual assent by analyzing the presence of offer and acceptance.[447]

Consideration

Valid consideration requires the contract to be a bargained-for exchange in which there is a legal detriment to the promisee or a benefit to the promisor.[448] Here, S sought out R's bodyguard services in exchange for paying him an annual salary of $80,000 and paying for his packing services. R was induced by her offer and agreed to move to the rainforest. Thus, consideration is met.

Offer and Acceptance

An offer is a manifestation of the willingness to enter into a bargain that would cause a reasonable person to believe his assent to the offeror's terms would form a contract.[449] An offeree's response operates as acceptance only if it is the precise mirror image of the offer.[450] A reply to an offer that purports to accept it, but is conditional on the offeror's assent to additional or different

---

443. UCC § 2-105, supra note 334.
444. *Ritz-Craft Corp. v. Stanford Management Group*, supra note 335.
445. *Kirkendall v. Harbor Insurance Co.*, supra note 336.
446. R.2d of Contracts §§ 17, 22(1), supra note 354.
447. *Kolodziej v. Mason*, supra note 355.
448. *Neuhoff v. Marvin Lumber and Cedar Co.*, supra note 407.
449. R. 2d of Contracts § 24, supra note 387.
450. R. 2d of Contracts §§ 38-39, supra note 388.

terms is not an acceptance, but a counter-offer.[451] A counter-offer terminates the offeree's power of acceptance.[452]

Here, S's offer included the wage and duration of employment, $80,000 per a year until S dies. A reasonable person would understand that agreeing to S's terms would conclude the bargain because the terms are specific. However, R's response was not a valid acceptance because R added a new term that conditioned his acceptance on S paying for his packing services. R's response was a counter-offer that shifted the power of acceptance to S. A valid contract was created when S stated, "it would not be a problem" for her to pay for R's packing expenses because S accepted the exact terms of R's counter-offer.

Statute of Frauds (SOF)

Contracts that cannot be performed within one year require a signed writing to be enforceable.[453] The SOF includes long-term contracts (a) that may be excused within a year or (b) where one party's performance cannot possibly occur within a year; indefinite-term contracts that might be performed or terminated within one year are not within the SOF.[454] Here, R agreed to care for S until she died. The contract is indefinite because the date of S's death is unknown. S could die within one day or live for several years. Thus, the contract is not within the SOF because R could complete his performance within a year.

Formation Conclusion

A valid contract exists because there is mutual assent, consideration, and a signed writing is not required. The prevailing party will depend on who breached the terms of the contract first.

Plain Meaning

A party seeking their interpretation bears the burden of demonstrating that their view is the correct one.[455] Under the four-corners approach, the court only looks at the document itself and the plain meaning of the term to determine if the term is unambiguous.[456] Under the contextualist approach, the court looks

---

451. R. 2d of Contracts §§ 50, 39, supra note 376.

452. R. 2d of Contracts § 36, supra note 362.

453. R. 2d of Contracts § 110, supra note 430. See also UCC § 2-201, supra note 430.

454. *McIntosh v. Murphy*, 52 Haw. 112, 36 (1970).

455. *Tamm, Inc. v. Pildis*, 249 N.W.2d 823, 832 (1976).

456. *Mitchill v. Lath*, 247 N.Y. 377, 378 (1928).

at the intent of the parties, extrinsic evidence, the document itself, and the plain meaning of the term to determine if the term is unambiguous.[457]

Here, S agreed to pay for R's packing expenses in exchange for his bodyguard services, and R agreed to pay Lucy (L) for her packing services by sponsoring her trip to the rainforest. The plain meaning of sponsor is to provide funds for a project or activity or the person carrying it out. R will argue that his packing expenses included L's airfare to the rainforest and S will argue that the packing expenses included L's room and board. Both interpretations of the word sponsor are reasonable under the four-corners and contextualist approaches. Thus, the term is ambiguous and extrinsic evidence will be admitted to determine the meaning of sponsor.

Parol Evidence Rule (PER)

Under the PER, extrinsic evidence, oral or written, made prior to or contemporaneously with the final written agreement is inadmissible to vary, modify, or contradict a completely integrated agreement.[458] Subsequent statements or agreements are not affected by the PER.[459]

Here, R will want to admit his conversation with L to prove L's airfare to the rainforest was payment for her packing services. S will try to exclude R's conversation with L, but she will fail because the conversation took place after R and L executed the valid written agreement. Moreover, extrinsic evidence is always allowed to help interpret ambiguous terms.[460] Thus, R's conversation with L is admissible to determine if sponsor included L's airfare.

Material Breach by Ronnie

Regardless of the interpretation of the word "sponsor," S will argue R breached the contract by quitting his job before she died. To determine whether a failure to render performance is a material breach, the court considers: (a) the extent to which the injured party will be deprived of the benefit he reasonably expected; (b) the extent to which the injured party can be adequately compensated for the benefit he was deprived; (c) the extent to which the party failing to perform will suffer forfeiture; (d) the likelihood that the party failing to perform will cure his failure, taking account of all the circumstances including any reasonable assurances; and (e) the extent to which the behavior of the

457. *Masterson v. Sine*, 68 Cal.2d 222, 227 (1968).

458. *Id.* at 225. See also Restatement (Second) of Contracts §§ 209-210, 213 (1981).

459. *Id.*

460. Restatement (Second) of Contracts § 214 (1981).

party failing to perform comports with standards of good faith and fair dealing.[461]

Here, (a) S reasonably expected R to be her bodyguard for the remainder of her life because she already paid R for bodyguard services and he agreed to the terms of her contract. S was deprived of this benefit because she only received a few months of R's services. (b) S might have trouble finding a replacement bodyguard, but S cannot force R to work for her because the U.S. Constitution prohibits involuntary servitude. Luckily, S can be adequately compensated if the court requires R to return the $80,000 and fund S's search for a new bodyguard. (c) R will not suffer forfeiture because he did not perform the majority of his contract. Thus, it is fair for R to return S's money for the months he did not work. (d) R never promised to cure his breach. R moved back to the U.S. without the intent to return to the rainforest. (e) R left without notice. R's actions were not made in good faith because nothing forced R to leave. In conclusion, the factors weigh in favor of finding R materially breached the contract.

Non-Occurrence of an Express Condition

R created an express condition because he specifically agreed to move "only if" S paid for all his packing expenses. A condition is an event that must occur for performance under a contract to become due.[462] If the condition does not occur, then performance is excused.[463] Here, if "sponsor" includes paying for L's airfare, then R will argue his performance was discharged because S failed to pay for his packing expenses when she refused to pay L's airfare. S has no excuse for not performing because R informed S of the alternative method of payment for L's packing services. R printed and sent copies of the agreement to S and S agreed to the terms.[464] Thus, S was bound to sponsor L's trip to the rainforest and her failure to pay for L's flight, room, or board was a non-occurrence of a condition. R will be excused from performing unless he waived the condition.

Waiver

If a condition is waived, then the non-occurrence of a condition will not discharge the duty of the party protected by the condition and the party will be

---

461. Restatement (Second) of Contracts § 241 (1981).
462. Restatement (Second) of Contracts §§ 224–225 (1981).
463. *Id.*
464. Restatement (Second) of Contracts § 226 (1981).

required to perform.[465] A waiver is often defined as the voluntarily and intentional relinquishment of a known right.[466] New consideration is not necessary,[467] but someone cannot waive an essential part of a bargain.[468] (a) Estoppel waiver happens after the condition was meant to occur and is immediately binding.[469] (b) Election waiver happens before the condition was meant to occur and requires some reliance.[470] Election waiver can be rescinded if there was no reliance.[471]

Here, S will argue that R waived the packing-services condition because he told S not to worry about L's flight, room, or board. R's waiver was estoppel waiver because it happened after the condition was meant to occur. R said he would only move if S paid for his packing expenses, but R's waiver occurred after R paid for and received packing services, moved to the rainforest, and started working as S's bodyguard. Thus, R's waiver was immediately binding and no reliance was necessary.

Condition v. Promise

R will argue that paying for his packing expenses was not a condition, but a promise. Thus, by not paying for his packing expenses, S breached first. When it doubt, the court finds a promise over a condition because courts loath enforcing express conditions that cause huge forfeitures by preventing the non-breaching party from collecting remedies if the condition does not occur.[472] Thus, to avoid either S or R suffering a forfeiture, the court will likely agree that paying for R's packing expenses in the form of a flight, room, or board was a promise rather than a condition.

Material Breach by Stephanie

See rule above. (Material Breach by Ronnie). Here, S's failure to pay for R's packing expenses is unlikely a material breach because the cost of packing expenses were minor compared to the $80,000 S would pay annually for R's bodyguard services. (a) However, R reasonably expected to receive compensation for his packing services because the parties agreed S would cover

---

465. Restatement (Second) of Contracts § 225 (1981).
466. *Clark v. West*, 193 N.Y. 349, 86 N.E. 1 (1908).
467. Restatement (Second) of Contracts § 84 (1981).
468. *Id.*
469. *Clark v. West*, supra note 466.
470. *Id.*
471. *Id.*
472. *Howard v. Federal Crop Ins. Corp.*, 540 F.2d 695 (4th Cir. 1976). See also Restatement (Second) of Contracts § 299 (1981).

these expenses. S deprived him of this benefit by not paying for L's flight, room, or board. (b) R can easily be compensated because S can reimburse R the money he paid. (c) S's forfeiture is unlikely great because she gave R an $80,000 check, which suggests she is not struggling financially and can afford to pay L's airfare. (d) No facts state S was willing to cure her non-performance, but (e) S likely acted in good faith because S did not completely refuse to pay for L's sponsorship. S believed airfare was not included in the word "sponsor," but did offer to cover L's room and board. In conclusion, the factors suggest S's failure to pay for packing services was a minor breach and R's performance would not be discharged.[473]

Breach Conclusion

The packing-expenses term was likely a promise and not a condition. Whether the word sponsor included airfare or room and board is irrelevant to the breach analysis because S did not sponsor any portion of L's trip to the rainforest. However, S's failure to pay for the packing expenses was a minor breach, which means R was required to perform and materially breached first by quitting his job. If the packing-expenses term was a condition, then R likely waived the condition and materially breached first because he was still required to perform his duties under the contract.

Stephanie's Remedies

R was likely the breaching party. Thus, S is entitled to expectancy or restitution damages.

Specific Performance

Specific performance will be granted if: (a) there is a valid contract, (b) there is an inadequate remedy at law, (c) the enforcement of the performance is feasible, and (d) no defenses apply.[474] Whether there is an inadequate remedy at law is the most important consideration.

Here, (a) R will argue the contract was not certain because the court cannot determine S's lifespan. Thus, although R is paid $80,000 per a year, the number of service years remaining in R's contract is unknown. (b) S will argue there is an inadequate remedy at law because S wanted R's services and not a random bodyguard. R will argue an adequate remedy exists because he can

---

473. Restatement (Second) of Contracts § 242 (1981).
474. R. 2d of §§ 359, 362, supra note 418.

pay her money damages to hire an equivalent bodyguard. (c) R will argue enforcement is not feasible because the court would need to monitor R and S's employment relationship for the remainder of S's life, which could be many years. The court will likely agree with R and opt to award S monetary damages because the court cannot force R to work against his will.

Expectancy Damages

The goal of contract law is to give the non-breaching party the benefit of the bargain by putting the non-breaching party in the position he would have been if the contract had been performed.[475] Expectancy damages include (a) the loss in the value to the non-breaching party, plus (b) any other loss, including incidental or consequential loss, caused by the breach, less (c) any cost or other loss that he has avoided by not having to perform.[476]

Here, S's expectancy interest includes (a) the value of bodyguard services for the remainder of her life minus the cost of the packing expenses and minus $80,000 a year in wages. (b) S will also recover any expenses related to hiring a new bodyguard.

Certainty

S may not recover expectancy damages because the court cannot determine her lifespan and reasonable certainty is required to measure recoverable damages.[477] Thus, the number of years S would need to pay $80,000 for a bodyguard is unknown.

Restitution Damages

S's next best recovery theory is restitution damages, which includes disgorging R of the benefit she reasonably conferred upon him.[478] She will only recover restitution damages if allowing R to retain the benefits would result in unjust enrichment.[479] Here, R was paid $80,000 for the first year of bodyguard services, but only performed for a few months. Thus, allowing R to retain more than a few months of pay is unjust. R must return S's money, but the court might deduct the expenses R incurred from paying L's airfare, room, and board.

---

475. R. 2d of Contracts § 347, supra note 435.
476. Id.
477. Restatement (Second) of Contracts § 352 (1981).
478. Restatement (Second) of Contracts § 370 (1981).
479. Id.

Mitigation

Regardless of the remedy, the non-breaching party cannot continue performance and unreasonably increase damages after the breaching party repudiates or breaches the contract.[480] Here, S is required to hire a new bodyguard within a reasonable amount of time to avoid incurring more damages as a result of R's breach. S should be able to find another bodyguard because she lives in a village with people who are likely experienced with the rainforest environment.

---

480. Restatement (Second) of Contracts § 350 (1981).

Answer 7

(1) Samantha (S) v. Hiro (H)

Governing Law

The Uniform Commercial Code (UCC) governs the sale of goods, which are tangible moveable objects,[481] while common law governs all other contracts.[482] Here, the UCC applies because the contract was for stereos.

Formation

An enforceable contract requires mutual assent and consideration.[483] Courts evaluate the existence of mutual assent by analyzing the presence of offer and acceptance.[484] Consideration requires the contract to be a bargained-for exchange in which there is a legal detriment to the promisee or a benefit to the promisor.[485] Here, a valid contract exists because H convinced S to purchase A2 stereos in exchange for money. They both agreed to the terms and set up a delivery for Saturday. S fully performed her duties by paying for the stereos. Thus, the issue is whether H breached by shipping non-conforming goods or violating the contract's warranties.

Express Warranty

A seller's affirmation of fact or promise to a buyer that relates to the goods becomes the basis of the bargain and creates an express warranty that the goods shall conform to the affirmation or promise.[486] The seller does not need to use the words "warranty" or "guarantee," but mere statements about the value of the goods, seller's opinion, or praise for the goods will not create an express warranty.[487]

Here, S will argue H created an express warranty when he said, "You shouldn't have any problems. These stereos can do anything related to music." S told H that she needed the stereo to play all types of CDS. Thus, H's subsequent statement was equivalent to an affirmation that the stereos would play both MP3 and audio CDs. H will argue his statement was his opinion because he used

---

481. UCC § 2-105, supra note 334.
482. *Ritz-Craft Corp. v. Stanford Management Group*, supra note 335.
483. R.2d of Contracts §§ 17, 22(1), supra note 354.
484. *Kolodziej v. Mason*, supra note 355.
485. *Neuhoff v. Marvin Lumber and Cedar Co.*, supra note 407.
486. Unif.Commercial Code § 2-313.
487. *Id.*

the word "anything." A reasonable consumer would understand that H's vague word choice meant he was exaggerating the capabilities of the stereo. However, the court is more likely to agree with S because "anything" also includes playing MP3s. Thus, H should have disclosed the stereo's limited capabilities instead of promising that the stereo would provide S with great flexibility.

Implied Warranty of Merchantability

Every contract where the seller is a merchant includes an implied warranty that the goods are fit for the ordinary purpose for which the goods were created.[488] This implied warranty applies to the goods normally sold by the merchant.[489] Here, H is a merchant because he owns an electronic shop that sells stereos. Thus, any contract for electronic goods includes an implied warranty of merchantability.

S will argue H's A2 stereos were not fit for their ordinary purpose of playing music because the stereos could not play all music files. Many people download MP3 files and burn CDs. However, H's argument is stronger because no electronic shops in the city sold stereos that played MP3s. Thus, H probably did not breach the implied warranty of merchantability if he sold stereos that were similar to other stereos sold in the industry.

Implied Warranty of Fitness for a Particular Purpose

An implied warranty that the goods are fit for a particular purpose is created if the seller, at the time the contract was created, had reason to know of any particular purpose for which the goods were required, and the buyer relied on the seller's skill or judgment to furnish suitable goods.[490] Here, S specifically told H she needed stereos that would play all types of CDs and relied on H to select the best product for her needs. H should have realized S expected the stereos to play both audio CDs and MP3 CDs. H's statement, "You shouldn't have any problems. These stereos can do anything related to music," affirmed that the A2 stereos would meet S's needs by playing any type of CD. Thus, when the stereos failed to play the MP3 files, H breached the implied warranty of fitness for a particular purpose.

---

488. Unif.Commercial Code § 2-314.
489. *Id.*
490. Unif.Commercial Code § 2-315.

Perfect Tender

Under the UCC, the seller must make a perfect tender in quality, quantity, delivery, and any other terms agreed upon by the parties.[491] If H did not breach an express or implied warranty, then S will argue H breached his contract by shipping non-conforming goods. H delivered four stereos that did not play MP3 files and one defective stereo that would not turn on. Luckily for H, he delivered the stereos on Tuesday. Thus, because they agreed the delivery date was Saturday, H had four days to cure his breach.

Cure by Seller

If the buyer rejects any non-conforming goods and the time for performance has not yet expired, then the seller can notify the buyer of his intention to cure and make a conforming delivery within the contract time.[492] Here, when H learned about the defective stereo, H apologized and notified S that he would deliver the new stereo by Saturday. However, H never delivered a working stereo when the time of performance arrived. If the contract included stereos that played MP3s, then H also failed to cure the breach of this contract term.

Buyer's Revocation of Accepted Goods

H will argue that he did not need to cure his breach because S accepted the four stereos on Tuesday and did not reject the delivery. However, his argument is weak because if the seller does not make a perfect tender, then the buyer can (a) reject the whole and not pay for the goods, (b) accept the whole, or accept any units and reject the rest without waiving the right to sue for damages of the breach.[493] If the buyer already accepted the goods, then the buyer may return the goods to the seller if the buyer discovers the defect in the goods within a reasonable time before any substantial change in the condition of the goods and buyer notifies the seller.[494]

Here, S did not reject the four stereos on Tuesday because she took possession of the stereos. However, S notified H about the defective stereo on the same day of delivery, which is within a reasonable time after acceptance. H will argue S could not reject the four stereos after acceptance because she waited a couple

---

491. Unif.Commercial Code § 2-601.
492. Unif.Commercial Code § 2-508.
493. UCC § 2-601, supra note 491.
494. Unif.Commercial Code § 2-608.

days before contacting him about the stereos' failure to play MP3s. A reasonable person would check the delivered goods the same day of delivery. H's argument is weak because people do not always play music the same day they purchase a stereo.

In conclusion, H breached the contract unless his non-conforming delivery was excused.

Impracticability and Impossibility

A party's performance is discharged if: (a) an event, unexpected at the time of contracting, makes it impossible to perform, and (b) the risk of the unexpected occurrence was not allocated to either party by agreement or custom.[495] Impracticability applies when performance is still physically possible, but is subjectively very burdensome for the party to perform. Impossibility is examined from an objective point of view and applies when no one can physically perform the particular task. In general, a party is not excused from performance merely because it becomes more expensive or difficult.[496]

Here, H will argue S's request for stereos that played MP3s was impracticable because he did not sell any at his store. Thus, performing would be extremely burdensome for him because he would need to build the stereos or search for them outside the city. However, S will argue that no unexpected event occurred to justify H's failure to perform. S told H she needed stereos that played all types of CDs. H is a merchant who specializes in selling electronics and should have known the stereos might not conform to S's request. Thus, based on custom, H, as the seller, assumed the risk of the stereos not performing to S's standards.

If impracticability does not apply, then H will argue it was impossible for anyone to perform because S called all the electronic stores in the city and no one carried a stereo that played MP3s. The industry standard was to sell stereos that played audio CDs. If no one sells stereos that play MP3s, then H's performance will be excused. If not, then H breached the contract by delivering non-conforming goods.

---

495. Restatement (Second) of Contracts §§ 261, 271 (1981).
496. *Transatlantic Financing Corp. v. U.S.* 363 F.2d 312 (1966).

(2) Lupita (L) vs. Samantha (S)

Governing law

See rule above. (Samantha v. Hiro: Governing Law). Here, common law applies because the contract is for L's catering services.

Material Breach by Samantha

To determine whether a failure to render performance is a material breach, the court considers: (a) the extent to which the injured party will be deprived of the benefit he reasonably expected; (b) the extent to which the injured party can be adequately compensated for the benefit he was deprived; (c) the extent to which the party failing to perform will suffer forfeiture; (d) the likelihood that the party failing to perform will cure his failure, taking account of all the circumstances including any reasonable assurances; and (e) the extent to which the behavior of the party failing to perform comports with standards of good faith and fair dealing.[497]

Here, (a) L reasonably expected to be paid for her services because S hired her to cater the party and they executed a valid written agreement. L will be deprived of $2500 because S cancelled the party. (b) L can be adequately compensated because S can reimburse L for the cost of the food and labor related to the preparation. S can also pay L the $2500 they originally agreed upon or the liquidated damages amount. (c) L's loss includes the preparation materials, labor, and the payment for her services. (d) No facts suggest S intends to cure. (e) S cancelled the contract with L the day before the party. S did not give L any notice. S cancelled the party for an unreasonable reason because a party can still be enjoyable without music. Thus, S materially breached and must pay L damages unless her non-performance was excused.

Frustration of Purpose

A party's performance is excused if an unforeseen event undermines the party's principle purpose for entering into a contract, and both parties knew the principal purpose at the time the contract was made.[498] Frustration of purpose only applies if the risk of the unexpected occurrence was not allocated to either party by agreement or custom.[499]

---

497. R. 2d of Contracts § 241, supra note 461.
498. Restatement (Second) of Contracts § 265 (1981).
499. *Id.*

Here, S will argue the event was unforeseen because S could not predict H's stereos would not play her MP3 CDs. After S discovered she had no music, the principal purpose for hiring L to cater a dance party disappeared because if there was no music, then S's guests could not dance. Thus, S had to cancel her dance party. If S had no guests to feed at her party, then S did not need L's catering services.

However, L will argue the risk of the unforeseen event was allocated to S by custom. Caterers rarely know their client's plans or motives for a party. S never told L the party was a dance party. Thus, L should not be penalized for S's oversight or risks. If the court agrees with L, then S's duty to perform was not discharged.

(3) Lupita's (L) Remedies

Expectancy Damages

The goal of contract law is to give the non-breaching party the benefit of the bargain by putting the non-breaching party in the position he would have been if the contract had been performed.[500] Expectancy damages include (a) the loss in the value to the non-breaching party, plus (b) any other loss, including incidental or consequential loss, caused by the breach, less (c) any cost or other loss that he has avoided by not having to perform.[501]

Here, if S's performance was not excused, then L's recovery would include (a) $2500 for her services minus the costs she expected to incur, such as the cost of food and labor to prepare the food, less (c) any savings on the cost of labor required on the day of the actual party. If S's performance was excused, then L must rely on promissory estoppel to get reliance damages.

Promissory Estoppel

A promise is binding if: (a) the promisor reasonably expects to induce action or forbearance on the part of the promisee, (b) the promise does induce such action or forbearance, and (c) injustice can only be avoided by enforcement of the promise; the remedy may be limited as justice requires.[502]

Here, (a) S should have expected L to purchase the food earlier than the day before the party because a professional caterer would not wait until the last minute. However, S will argue she did not expect L to prepare food the day before

---

500. R. 2d of Contracts § 347, supra note 435.
501. *Id.*
502. Restatement (Second) of Contracts § 90 (1981).

the party because most caterers prepare food the day of the event. (b) L purchased and prepared the food based on S's promise to pay for her catering services on Saturday. (c) Injustice can only be avoided by paying L for the services she completed because L expended time and money on the materials and preparation. S will argue that L could use the food for another event, eat it, or return it. But this is a weak argument because food is perishable and the menu might be different for other parties. L has a strong case for promissory estoppel and can likely recover reliance damages.

Reliance Damages

As an alternative to expectancy damages, the injured party can recover reliance damages that place the party in the position he would have been had the contract never been made.[503] Reliance damages compensate parties for the expenditures made preparing to perform the contract.[504] Here, L's reliance damages include the cost of the food and the cost of labor to prepare the food. Reliance damages are L's most appropriate remedy unless the liquidated damages clause is valid.

Liquidated damages

Damages may be liquidated if a contract is breached, even if no loss is suffered, so long as it is a reasonable forecast of the injury resulting from the breach at the time of formation,[505] and potential damages are difficult to forecast.[506] A liquidated damages clause is unenforceable if it is inequitable and the amount would become a penalty.[507]

Here, L will argue that the liquidated damages clause is valid because the contract explicitly states the clause was "not a penalty." Although $5000 is twice the value of L's catering services, if L had breached the contract instead of S, then $5000 might be the appropriate value of a successful dance party. However, L's argument is weak because a reasonable forecast of the injury would be the actual costs of L's services or the cost to find a replacement caterer for S's party. Thus, the liquidated damage clause is not valid because double the cost of catering services functions more as a penalty than a remedy.

---

503. Restatement (Second) of Contracts § 349 (1981).

504. *Id.*

505. Restatement (Second) of Contracts § 356 (1981).

506. *Kelly v. Marx*, 44 Mass. App. Ct. 825 (1998).

507. *Dahlstrom Corp. v. State Highway Commission of State of Miss.,* 590 F.2d 614 (5th Cir. 1979).

Answer 8

(1) Contractor (C) v. Pablo (P)

Governing Law

The Uniform Commercial Code (UCC) governs the sale of goods, which are tangible moveable objects,[508] while common law governs all other contracts.[509] Here, common law applies because the contract is for services to build an in-law unit.

Formation

An enforceable contract requires mutual assent and consideration.[510] Courts evaluate the existence of mutual assent by analyzing the presence of offer and acceptance.[511] Consideration requires the contract to be a bargained-for exchange in which there is a legal detriment to the promisee or a benefit to the promisor.[512] Here, a valid contract exists because C and P executed a valid written agreement and exchanged money for services. The issue is who breached first, which depends on whether C was required to complete the construction by January 28th.

Parol Evidence Rule (PER)

Under the PER, extrinsic evidence made prior to or contemporaneously with the final written agreement is inadmissible to vary, modify, or contradict a completely integrated agreement.[513] A completely integrated agreement is a final expression of the contract that is adopted by the parties as a complete and exclusive statement of the terms of the agreement; all other agreements are partially integrated.[514] Here, C and P's contract is integrated because they memorialized the terms of their mutual assent in a valid written agreement.[515] The issue is whether the agreement is completely or partially integrated.

---

508. UCC § 2-105, supra note 334.

509. *Ritz-Craft Corp. v. Stanford Management Group*, supra note 335.

510. R.2d of Contracts §§ 17, 22(1), supra note 354.

511. *Kolodziej v. Mason*, supra note 355.

512. *Neuhoff v. Marvin Lumber and Cedar Co.*, supra note 407.

513. *Masterson v. Sine*, supra note 457. See also R. 2d of Contracts §§ 209–210, 213, supra note 458.

514. Restatement (Second) of Contracts § 210 (1981).

515. Restatement (Second) of Contracts § 209 (1981).

Traditional Rule

Under the four-corners approach, courts look at the face of the writing to determine if the parties intended to completely integrate their writing.[516] A merger clause is usually conclusive or near conclusive evidence of complete integration.[517]

Here, C will argue the agreement is completely integrated and did not include the January 28th deadline because the merger clause explicitly stated the agreement was a full statement of their agreement. Moreover, the essential terms were included in the writing, such as the cost of the labor and division of their duties. P will argue the agreement is partially integrated because the contract did not mention when C would be paid or when the construction should be completed, which are necessary terms to determine breach and a remedy. However, C's argument is stronger because the merger clause is conclusive evidence of complete integration.

Modern Rule

Under the contextualist approach, the court looks at the intent of the parties, extrinsic evidence, and the document itself to determine if the parties intended to completely integrate their agreement.[518] A merger clause is strong evidence of a complete integration, but not conclusive.[519]

See analysis above. (Contractor v. Pablo: Traditional Rule). Here, P will argue extrinsic evidence shows P and C explicitly negotiated the January 28th deadline. Thus, because the completion date was omitted from the contract, the agreement is partially integrated. Under the modern rule, although the merger clause presents strong evidence of integration, P's frantic actions to hire Joseph to complete the in-law unit by January 28th suggested the written agreement was missing an essential term.

Contract Terms

If the agreement is completely integrated, then no extrinsic evidence made prior to the final written contract is allowed.[520] Thus, P's conversation with C about the construction deadline would be barred. If the agreement is partially

---

516. *Mitchill v. Lath*, supra note 456.

517. *In re Martin*, 138 B.R. 508, 510–11(Bankr. E.D. Va. 1992).

518. *Masterson v. Sine*, supra note 457.

519. *Trans-Tec Asia v. M/V Harmony Container*, 435 F.Supp.2d 1015, 1030 (C.D. Cal. 2005).

520. Restatement (Second) of Contracts §213 (1981).

integrated, then extrinsic evidence of additional terms is admissible if those additional terms are consistent with the writing.[521] Contradictory terms are barred.[522] A consistent term is a term that might naturally be omitted from the writing or was agreed to for separate consideration.[523] Here, P will argue the date of completion, January 28th, does not contradict the terms in the writing because the agreement contains no terms about deadlines. P will also argue the term was naturally omitted because people do not always include a date of completion; construction is unpredictable. However, P's argument is weak because formal construction contracts usually include deadlines to ensure parties are held accountable for their performance and do not delay their work. Thus, this term would normally be included if it was negotiated by the parties.

Extrinsic Evidence After the Agreement

The PER does not exclude evidence made after the execution of the valid written agreement.[524] Thus, P can admit evidence that C expressed he might not be able to complete the in-law unit by January 28th due to heavy rains to show they agreed that time was of the essence.

Parole Evidence Overall Conclusion

The agreement is likely partially integrated because the contract is missing important terms. Thus, consistent evidence will be submitted to the jury to determine whether the in-law unit needed to be completed by January 28th.

Condition v. Promise

When it doubt, the court finds a promise over a condition because courts loath enforcing express conditions that cause huge forfeitures by preventing the non-breaching party from collecting remedies if the condition does not occur.[525] If the January 28th deadline is part of the contract, then P will argue his payment to C was conditioned upon C completing the unit by January 28th. Thus, P's non-performance was excused because the condition never occurred.

However, C will argue that P never used the words "only if" and never stated the payment would be conditioned upon completion by January 28th. P merely requested the unit to be completed by January 28th. Time did not

---

521. Restatement (Second) of Contracts §215 (1981).

522. *Id.*

523. Restatement (Second) of Contracts §216 (1981).

524. R. 2d of Contracts §§§ 209-210, 213, supra note 458.

525. *Howard v. Federal Crop Ins. Corp.*, supra note 472. See also R. 2d of Contracts § 299, supra note 472.

appear to be of the essence because P excluded this term from the written agreement. Thus, completing construction by the deadline was a promise and not a condition, and P's non-performance is only excused if C materially breached the contract first.

Anticipatory Repudiation

Anticipatory repudiation occurs if a party clearly and unequivocally states they will not perform, or a party makes statements indicating they will not perform unless a condition beyond the contract occurs, such as "I will not perform unless you pay me double."[526] Repudiation of the contract before the day performance is due is treated as material breach.[527] If a party repudiates the contract, then the non-breaching party must avoid damages and can (a) reasonably suspend performance, cancel the contract, and immediately sue, (b) wait for performance to be due or wait a reasonable time after repudiation and then sue, (c) sue sometime in between, or (d) ask for reassurance or urge performance.[528] The doctrine of repudiation only applies to contracts where both sides have not fully performed.[529]

Here, neither side fully performed because P paid $0 for C's services and C only completed 75% of the in-law unit. P will argue C's statement "I might not be able to complete the in-law unit by January 28th because the heavy rains in December delayed construction by a month" was a valid repudiation that allowed P to suspend his performance and hire another contractor to finish construction. However, C's argument is stronger because C used the word "might," which is not a clear and unequivocal statement that C would not perform. C did not demand an extension, but asked P for leniency on the deadline. Thus, P should have asked for reassurance or urged C to perform instead of canceling the contract.

Retraction and Assurances

Repudiation can be retracted before it has been accepted unless the non-breaching party (a) had knowledge that the repudiation was considered final, or (b) materially relied on the repudiation, or (c) gave the breaching party a reasonable time to retract and the deadline had passed.[530] C will argue he

---

526. Restatement (Second) of Contracts §250 (1981).
527. *Id.*
528. Restatement (Second) of Contracts §§ 251, 253 (1981).
529. R. 2d of Contracts § 250, supra note 530.
530. Restatement (Second) of Contracts §256 (1981).

retracted the statement within a reasonable time because he called P the following day to confirm the in-law unit would be completed by January 28th. P will argue he materially relied on C's repudiation because P hired another person, Joseph (J), to complete the job after C stated he might not complete the work on time. P paid J $100,000 in advance and could not breach the contract with J just because C changed his prediction. Thus, if C's statement was a valid reputation, then P was justified in relying on C's statement and C breached first.

Material Breach by Pablo

If C's statement was not a valid repudiation, then P likely breached first by canceling the contract and failing to pay C $200,000 for the labor. To determine whether a failure to render performance is a material breach, the court considers: (a) the extent to which the injured party will be deprived of the benefit he reasonably expected; (b) the extent to which the injured party can be adequately compensated for the benefit he was deprived; (c) the extent to which the party failing to perform will suffer forfeiture; (d) the likelihood that the party failing to perform will cure his failure, taking account of all the circumstances including any reasonable assurances; and (e) the extent to which the behavior of the party failing to perform comports with standards of good faith and fair dealing.[531]

Here, (a) C reasonably expected to be paid $200,000 for his labor because C and P executed a valid written contract. C was deprived of this benefit because he received no payments. (b) C can be adequately compensated in cash for his services. (c) P will suffer minimal forfeiture because P already received the benefit of an in-law unit that was 75% complete. (d) P is unlikely to perform because P told C not to worry about the in-law unit and hired someone else. (e) No facts suggest P acted in bad faith. P simply panicked after C shared his reservations about the completion deadline. However, P likely materially breached by cancelling the contract and hiring J because C was still willing and able to complete the last 25% of the in-law unit.

Agreement of Rescission

P will argue he did not breach because C agreed to rescind their original contract. Parties can agree to discharge the remaining duties of performance under the existing contract.[532] A party's manifestation of assent to discharge is

---

531. R. 2d of Contracts § 241, supra note 461.
532. Restatement (Second) of Contracts §283 (1981).

not effective unless it is made for consideration.[533] Here, P told C not to worry about completing the in-law unit and C stopped working without any protest. C's actions suggested he consented to cancelling the contract. Consideration was present because they created an implied contract that P would not pay C and C would not continue construction. However, P's argument is weak because C never explicitly agreed to discharge P's duty to pay. Thus, P is likely the breaching party and must pay C damages.

(2) Contractor's (C) Remedies

Expectancy Damages

The goal of contract law is to give the non-breaching party the benefit of the bargain by putting the non-breaching party in the position he would have been if the contract had been performed.[534] Expectancy damages include (a) the loss in the value to the non-breaching party, plus (b) any other loss, including incidental or consequential loss, caused by the breach, less (c) any cost or other loss that he has avoided by not having to perform.[535] Here, C's expectancy damages include (a) $200,000 for his services minus the $130,000 for the materials and labor he already spent, and (b) minus the costs C saved from not having to complete the remaining 25% of the in-law unit. P must also pay any incidental and consequential losses.

Reliance Damages

As an alternative to expectancy, the injured party can chose to recover reliance damages that place the party in the position he would have been had the contract never been made; this includes expenditures made preparing for the performance of the K.[536] Here, C can recover the $90,000 that he spent on the labor and materials he needed to complete 75% of P's in-law unit.

Restitution Damages

Another alternative to expectancy damages is restitution damages. Either party can disgorge the benefit the party conferred upon the other party if allowing the other party to retain the benefits would result in unjust enrichment.[537] Restitution damages require a reasonable expectation of being paid or getting

---

533. Restatement (Second) of Contracts §273 (1981).
534. R. 2d of Contracts § 347, supra note 435.
535. *Id.*
536. R. 2d of Contracts § 349, supra note 503.
537. R. 2d of Contracts § 370, supra note 478.

the return promise.[538] Here, C expected to be paid because P and C had a valid written contract. C will receive either (a) the value added to the property, which is the current value of the property, $150,000, minus the value of the land before C completed 75% of the in-law unit, or (b) the $90,000, which is the labor and materials C added to P's land.

(3) Pablo (P) v. Joseph (J)

Governing Law

See rule above. (Contractor v. Pablo: Governing Law). Here, common law applies because the contract is for the services to build an in-law unit on P's land.

Formation

See rule above. (Contractor v. Pablo: Formation). Here, a valid contract exists because J agreed to complete construction by January 28th and P paid J $100,000 for his services.

Material Breach by Joseph

See rule above. (Contractor v. Pablo: Material Breach). Here, (a) P reasonably expected J to complete the unit by January 28th because he already paid J for the services. P was deprived of this benefit because J never worked on the in-law unit. (b) P can be adequately compensated because J can reimburse P for the costs of his parents' lodging and the storage unit, cost to complete the building, and cost to litigate the lawsuit with C. (c) J will suffer minimal forfeiture because J was already paid to complete the job, and no facts state J had a valid excuse. (d) No facts suggest J intended to cure his breach because more than two months have passed since January 28th and the in-law unit is still incomplete. (e) J is likely acting in bad faith because J requested payment in advance and never showed up to start performance. Thus, J materially breached the contract and must pay damages to P.

(4) Pablo's (P) Remedies

Expectancy Damages: Cost of Performance vs. Diminution in Value

See rule above. (Contractor's Remedies: Expectancy Damages). Here, P expected to receive a completed in-law unit. To measure P's damages, the court

---

538. *Id.*

must apply the cost of performance or diminution in value standard.[539] In *Peevyhouse v. Garland & Mining Co.,* the court awarded the diminution in value because the cost of performance would cause economic waste.[540] The court reasoned that awarding the cost of performance would be grossly disproportionate because the breaching party already completed performance and the cost to perform to the standards of the non-breaching party was approximately $29,000 while the diminution in value of the completed performance was only $300.[541]

Here, the cost to complete the remaining 25% of the in law unit is $40,000. The diminution in value is $100,000, which is the value of the completed in-law unit, $250,000, minus the in-law unit's current value, $150,000. Unlike *Peevyhouse,* J never completed construction on the in-law unit and the diminution in value of P's land was not minimal compared to the cost of completion. The difference between the cost of completing the in-law unit and diminution in value is $60,000. Thus, the court is likely to award P $40,000 to complete the performance because it would be unfair for J to pay the diminution in value when the cost of completion is less than half the diminution in value.

Consequential Damages

Here, P will also recover the two months of hotel bills for his parents and the storage costs for his parents' furniture because these expenses were incurred as a result of J failing to complete the in-law unit by January 28th, unless a limitation applies.

Mitigation

The non-breaching party cannot continue to unreasonably increase damages after breach.[542] Here, J will argue that he is not responsible for the hotel and storage unit costs because P had the opportunity to mitigate his damages. On January 2nd, J agreed to work on the in-law unit, but never began construction. On January 3rd, C told P he could finish the work by January 28th. P never contacted J to inquire about his non-performance and never called C to ask C to complete the unit after P realized J was not going to perform. P should have mitigated his damages by hiring someone to complete the work or sending his parents to his sister's home earlier in the process rather than

---

539. Restatement (Second) of Contracts §348 (1981).
540. *Peevyhouse v. Garland Coal & Mining Co.*, 382 P.2d 109 (Okla. 1962).
541. *Id.*
542. R. 2d of Contracts § 350, supra note 480.

assuming J would perform and accruing months of hotel and storage bills. Thus, J will argue he is only responsible for the cost to complete the in-law unit.

Foreseeability

The non-breaching party can only recover damages that are a foreseeable result of breach at the time the contract was created.[543] A loss is foreseeable if it results from the ordinary course of events or is a result of special circumstances that the defendant had reason to know about at the time of the contract.[544] Here, J will argue P's hotel and storage bills were not foreseeable because P never told J that his parents were moving into the unit on January 28th. However, J's argument is weak because P explicitly told J to complete the work by January 28th. The reason P needed the in-law unit completed by January 28th is irrelevant because, at the time the contract was created, J knew that time was of the essence. Thus, P will likely recover consequential damages, if the mitigation limitation doesn't apply, because the damages were foreseeable.

Restitution Damages

See rule above. (Contractor's Remedies: Restitution Damages). Here, P's best remedy is likely restitution because P paid J $100,000 in advance and received no services. J would be unjustly enriched if P was awarded expectancy damages because it only costs $40,000 to complete the in-law unit. As a result, J would retain $60,000 as a windfall and benefit from his breach. Thus, the court is likely to award P restitution damages that P can use to hire another construction company to complete the unit.

543. Restatement (Second) of Contracts §351 (1981).
544. Id.

Criminal Law Answers

Answer 1

Before analyzing the defendant's guilt, the court must use intrinsic and extrinsic sources to determine the meaning of the ambiguous words in the statute. Intrinsic sources include the text and extrinsic sources include legislative history and public policy.[546] In *United States v. Dauray*, the court considered the plain language of the statute, applied the traditional canons of statutory construction, looked at legislative history, and canvassed relevant case law.[547] As a final resort, the court used the rule of lenity to resolve the ambiguity.[548]

(1) Desmond's (D) Crimes

Plain Meaning

A court must consider the ordinary, common sense meaning of the words in the statute, such as the dictionary definition.[549] The plain meaning of "doctor" is a person skilled in the science of medicine, or a person who is trained and licensed to treat sick people.

Here, D will argue he is a doctor because he was the village physician for years and received training from the previous physician, which means he is skilled in medicine and experienced in treating sick people. However, the prosecution will argue D is not a doctor because D never attended medical school or passed a license exam. D did not receive the required training and cannot legally treat patients.

The plain meaning of doctor supports both arguments so the court must look at other statutory interpretation rules to determine the meaning of doctor.

---

546. *Phillips v. AWH Corp.*, 415 F.3d 1303, 1320 (Fed. Cir. 2005).
547. *United States v. Dauray*, 215 F.3d 257, 264 (2d Cir. 2000).
548. *Id.* at 260.
549. *Id.*

Avoiding Absurdity

A statute should be interpreted in a way that avoids absurd results.[550] Here, both interpretations are reasonable. Many reasonable people believe that a doctor must attend medical school and obtain a license, but D's village, which is also full of reasonable people, believed D's training with the previous physician made D skilled in medicine.

Legislative History

If a word is ambiguous, then the court considers Congress's intended meaning of the word.[551] Here, the law was passed to discourage fraudulent medical practices. D will argue that his actions were not fraudulent because he had many years of training and experience, and he was qualified to diagnose patients. D will argue the law's objective is to prevent people with no medical background from treating patients for money. The statute did not apply to D because he was a doctor in his village.

However, the prosecution will argue that diagnosing patients without medical school training or a license is fraudulent. D's decision to treat Blair (B) with psilocybin mushrooms (P-mushrooms) suggests D is not a doctor because he failed to share the side effects and the mushrooms are a controlled substance. If license physicians do not commonly prescribe P-mushrooms, then the law likely discourages D's actions.

Rule of Lenity

After applying the statutory cannons of construction, if there is still reasonable doubt about a statute's intended scope, then the ambiguity must be resolved in the defendant's favor.[552] Due process requires fair warning of what conduct is considered criminal.[553] Here, if both interpretations are reasonable, then the court will agree with D's interpretation that a doctor does not need formal medical school training or a license. A doctor can become skilled in medicine through apprenticeships and experience.

---

550. *Id. at* 264.
551. *Id.*
552. *Id.*
553. *Id.*

Actus Reus: Impersonating a Doctor

To satisfy the actus reus element in Section 100, the defendant must voluntarily[554] impersonate a doctor. Here, D acted voluntarily because no one forced him to start his medical practice or treat B's depression. If D is not a doctor, then D impersonated a doctor by opening a medical practice, diagnosing patients, and prescribing medicine. If D is a doctor, then the actus reus element is not met.

Mens Rea: Purposefully

Under common law, the mens rea element is general or specific intent. Specific intent requires the defendant to (1) intentionally commit an act to achieve some further consequence, or (2) be aware of the statutory attendant circumstances.[555] General intent only requires the intent to complete the actus reus.[556]

Here, Section 100 is a specific intent crime because it includes the word purposefully. The prosecution will argue that D is not a doctor, which means he acted with the intent to impersonate a doctor when he started a medical practice. D wanted people to believe he was qualified to provide medical services. However, D will argue he never intended to impersonate a doctor because he is a real doctor who could treat patients. If D genuinely believed he was a doctor, then the mens rea element is not met.

Causation and Concurrence

The causation and concurrence elements are implicit in all crimes. Actual cause requires the defendant's act to be the cause of the prohibited result.[557] Proximate cause requires the act to be the direct cause of the social harm.[558] Concurrence requires the actus reus be completed with the appropriate mens rea; they must occur simultaneously.[559] Here, actual cause and proximate cause are met because there are no intervening causes. D's medical practice and treatment of B were the direct cause of B believing D was a doctor.

---

554. Model Penal Code § 2.01 (Am. Law Inst., Proposed Official Draft 1962).

555. *United States v. Bailey*, 444 U.S. 394, 403 (1980).

556. *Id.*

557. Model Penal Code § 2.03 (Am. Law Inst., Proposed Official Draft 1962).

558. *Id.*

559. *Morissette v. United States*, 342 U.S. 246, 251-52 (1952).

Conclusion

In conclusion, D is guilty of violating Section 100 if he was not a doctor and purposefully impersonated a doctor. If D is considered a doctor, then D did not have the required mens rea and will be acquitted.

(2) Blair's (B) Crimes

Canons of Construction

Noscitur a sociis states the meaning of an ambiguous word or phrase can be determined by the other words or phrases in the statute.[560] *Ejusdem generis* states that general words following a specific enumeration of persons or things are interpreted to encompass only persons or things similar to those specifically enumerated.[561]

Here, although Section 200 explicitly states "any other dangerous substance," the prosecution will argue the statute implicitly includes controlled substances, like P-mushrooms, because the examples listed are also controlled substances that dangerously impact a person's senses, such as marijuana, cocaine, and ecstasy. However, B will argue P-mushrooms are not dangerous because D commonly prescribed P-mushrooms as medicine. The P-mushrooms were used to cure B and not for illegal recreation purposes like cocaine or ecstasy. B's argument will likely fail because marijuana and morphine are used for medical purposes, but included in Section 200. Thus, using P-mushrooms for medical reasons will not exclude it from the catchall phrase "any other dangerous substances."

Legislative History

See rule above (D's crimes: Legislative History). Here, the prosecution will argue P-mushrooms are a dangerous substance because P-mushrooms often caused hallucinations and Section 200 was passed to discourage the sale of drugs that impact the senses. However, B will argue no facts suggest P-mushrooms are addictive, like cocaine; P-mushrooms were not the type of drug the law was intended to prevent. Moreover, B received P-mushrooms as a prescription. Section 200 was likely enacted to prevent the sale of drugs on the black market. Thus, B's use of P-mushrooms as medicine is unlikely the behavior Congress was trying to prevent.

---

560. *Ali v. Federal Bureau of Prisons*, 552 U.S. 214, 226 (2008).
561. *Id.* at 231.

In conclusion, P-mushrooms are likely a dangerous substance because, similar to the other drugs listed in the statute, P-mushrooms impair the senses and are a controlled substance.

Actus Reus: Possession of a Dangerous Substance

To satisfy the actus reus element in Section 200, the defendant must voluntarily[562] possess marijuana, cocaine, ecstasy, morphine, or any other dangerous substance. Here, if P-mushrooms are a dangerous substance, then B acted voluntarily by accepting the drugs and using them at home. No one forced her to accept D's prescription.

Mens Rea: Strict Liability

The court must consider the following six factors to determine if Section 200 is a strict liability crime: whether (a) there is a mens rea specified in the statute, (b) the crime is a public welfare offense, (c) the statute is aimed at punishing neglect, (d) the punishment includes light penalties, (e) the crime generates stigma that indicates moral wrongdoing, and (f) the statute creates a new crime.[563]

Here, the prosecution will argue Section 200 is a strict liability crime because (a) the statute does not include a mens rea and only prohibits conduct. However, B will argue (b) Section 200 is not a public welfare offense, such as violating building codes and health laws, because the crime requires the defendant to know the substance she possesses is dangerous. B will also argue (c) Section 200 is aimed at punishing affirmative action and not the failure to act, and (f) Section 200 is a newly created crime to discourage the sale of dangerous substances.

Elements (d) and (e) can be interpreted to support both sides because (d) reasonable minds differ on whether financial punishment is harsh. The facts do not include the extent of the fines, but if someone values money or has limited funds, then fines can be an extreme burden. If the punishment required the defendant to pay a small sum of money, then the punishment would likely be a light penalty, especially compared to jail time. (e) Reasonable minds also differ about the stigma associated with drug possession. Some communities commonly use controlled substances for medical purposes whereas other communities believe the use of any controlled substance is dangerous.

---

562. MPC § 2.01, supra note 554.
563. *Morissette v. United States*, supra note 559 at 254-55.

In conclusion, Section 200 is likely not a strict liability crime because more factors favor some type of mens rea to be found guilty.

Mens Rea: General Intent

See rules above (D's crimes: Mens Rea). Section 200 is likely a general intent crime because it punishes the act of possession rather than the intent to do something further with the dangerous substance. Here, B intended to commit the act because she willingly accepted the P-mushrooms, took them home, and ate them before bed.

Mistake of Fact and Willful Blindness

If a defendant is ignorant of a fact that negates the required mental state for the crime, then the defendant cannot be guilty of the crime.[564] For a specific intent crime, the mistake of fact must be honest and can be unreasonable.[565] For general intent crimes, such as Section 200, the mistake must be honest and reasonable. Reasonableness is measured from an objective viewpoint whereas an honest mistake requires the defendant to subjectively believe the facts in question were true.

Here, B will argue she honestly believed the P-mushrooms were not a dangerous substance because D never told her about the side effects, such as hallucinations. However, the prosecution will argue B's mistake was not reasonable because ordinary people know P-mushrooms are a controlled substance that can impair the senses. Even if B did not know D prescribed P-mushrooms, she should have known most medications have risks and side effects.

B should have asked D for more information before taking the medicine. If a defendant takes deliberate action to avoid confirming a fact, then the lack of the mens rea cannot shield the defendant from liability.[566] Here, B did not ask D any questions about the medicine or verify that D was a licensed physician. Thus, B's mistake will not negate the mens rea.

Causation and Concurrence

See rule above (D's crimes: Causation and Concurrence). Here, actual cause and proximate cause are met because there were no intervening causes. B voluntarily accepted the drugs from D and intended to take the drugs when she was in possession of the P-mushrooms.

---

564. Model Penal Code § 2.04 (Am. Law Inst., Proposed Official Draft 1962).
565. *Id.*
566. *Global-Tech Appliances, Inc. v. SEB S.A.,* 563 U.S. 754 (2011).

In conclusion, all elements are met and B is guilty of violating Section 200.

Section 300

Actus Reus: Harming Someone's Pet

To satisfy the actus reus element in Section 300, the defendant must voluntarily[567] cause harm to someone's pet. Here, if a ferret is a pet, then B harmed her brother's pet because the ferret was in poor condition after she locked it in the shed. No one forced B to take the P-mushrooms or kidnap the ferret. Thus, the actus reus element is met.

Mens Rea: Recklessly

A defendant acts recklessly if he acts with awareness of a substantial and unjustifiable risk and disregards that risk.[568] Here, the prosecution will argue that locking a ferret in a shed for a couple days without food and water is considered a substantial and unjustifiable risk because the ferret could die or suffer injuries. B's actions were unnecessary because no facts suggest the ferret intended to harm B.

However, B has a stronger argument that she was unaware of the risk because she was sleep walking when she kidnapped the ferret. Thus, she could not have consciously disregarded the risk. The mens rea is not met and B is not guilty of violating Section 300.

---

567. MPC § 2.01, supra note 554.
568. Model Penal Code § 2.02(2)(c) (Am. Law Inst., Proposed Official Draft 1962).

Answer 2

(1) Jared (J) and Greg's (G) Crimes

Battery

Battery is the unlawful application of force or offensive touching to the person of another.[569] Battery is a general intent crime, which means the intent to apply force is enough.[570] Here, G unlawfully applied force because he stabbed the boy in the stomach. G's statement, "You better tell me the information or I'm going to kill you," before the stabbing suggests G intended to use physical force to extract information from the boy. G is guilty of battery.

J committed an offensive touching because he grabbed the boy, put him in the trunk, and locked him in the warehouse. No reasonable person wants to be kidnapped. J intended to apply force because he agreed with G to kidnap the boy. J is also guilty of battery.

Assault

Assault is an attempt to commit a battery or an intentional creation of reasonable apprehension of imminent bodily harm in the mind of the victim;[571] mere words are not enough.[572] Here, assault is the lesser-included offense of battery because all the elements of assault are included in the greater crime of battery.[573] Double jeopardy forbids excessive prosecutions and cumulative punishments for greater and lesser-included offenses.[574] Thus, J and G cannot be guilty of assault because assault will merge with battery. However, if the prosecution charged G with assault with a dangerous weapon, then battery and assault would not merge because assault with a dangerous weapon includes an element not required in battery.[575]

Kidnapping

A person is guilty of kidnapping if he unlawfully moves another person a substantial distance from where he is found, or if he unlawfully confines another

569. *United States v. Delis*, 558 F.3d 177, 180 (2d Cir. 2009).
570. *Id.*
571. Model Penal Code § 211.1 (Am. Law Inst., Proposed Official Draft 1962).
572. *Allen v. United States*, 164 U.S. 492, 497 (1896).
573. *Claggett v. State*, 108 Md.App. 32 (Md. Ct. Spec. App. 1996).
574. *Brown v. Ohio*, 432 U.S. 161 (1977).
575. *U.S. v. Cantrell*, 92 F.3d 1194 (9th Cir. 1996).

for a substantial period in a place of isolation.[576] The extent of the movement is not material and generally secrecy is not required; kidnapping focuses on the confinement.[577]

Here, J and G moved the boy from his original location, the mall, because they put him in the van and drove him to the warehouse. J and G also confined the boy in a location of isolation because the warehouse was abandoned, which means people probably did not visit the area. The boy was also confined in the room for a week, which was long enough for the news to mention the boy in a missing persons report; news stations usually do not feature disappearances unless the person was missing for a substantial amount of time.

In most jurisdictions, kidnapping is a general intent crime,[578] which means J and G only needed intent to complete the actus reus.[579] Here, G and J actually wanted to kidnap and hold the boy for ransom. Thus, they intended the acts and are guilty of kidnapping.

(2) Greg's (G) Crimes

Homicide

Homicide is the killing of a human being.[580] Here, the actus reus is met because the boy died from loss of blood. The issue is whether the appropriate mens rea for murder was met.

Mens Rea

Murder is an unlawful killing with malice aforethought.[581] There are four types of common law murder: (a) intent to kill, (b) intent to inflict great bodily harm, (c) depraved heart murder, and (d) felony murder.[582] Intent to kill is a form of express malice and the remaining murders are forms of implied malice.[583]

---

576. Model Penal Code § 212.1 (Am. Law Inst., Proposed Official Draft 1962).

577. *People v. Jaffray*, 519 N.W.2d 108, 118 (Mich. 1994).

578. *U.S. v. Jackson*, 248 F.3d 1028, 1029 (10th Cir. 2001).

579. *United States v. Bailey*, supra note 555.

580. Model Penal Code § 210.1 (Am. Law Inst., Proposed Official Draft 1962).

581. *U.S. v. Pearson*, 159 F.3d 480, 486 (10th Cir. 1998).

582. *Id.*

583. *Gutierrez Marquez v. Gunn*, 29 F.3d 632 (9th Cir. 1994).

(a) Intent to Kill

The use of a deadly weapon authorizes a permissive inference of intent to kill.[584] A deadly weapon is any instrument used in a manner likely to produce death or serious bodily injury.[585] Here, the prosecution will argue G intended to kill because G said, "I am going to kill you" before he stabbed the boy in the stomach with a knife. G's actions and words are strong circumstantial evidence of his intent to kill.

G will argue he did not want to kill the boy. G wanted to compel the boy to share his contact information, which is why G did not stab the boy in a vital body part, such as the head or heart. G called 911 after leaving the boy at the mall because he wanted the boy to get medical attention and not die at the warehouse. Even though G felt subsequent regret, G's argument will likely fail because evidence suggests G intended to kill at the time he stabbed the boy.

(b) Intent to Cause Serious Bodily Injury

Here, G will argue he used a pocketknife instead of a large knife or gun because he only wanted to scare the boy and not cause serious bodily injury. However, this is a weak argument because G could have punched the boy. G intended to cause serious bodily injury because he used a dangerous weapon.

(c) Depraved Heart

A defendant is guilty of murder if the defendant shows an indifference to an unjustifiably high risk to human life.[586] Here, G knew his actions caused a high risk of death because G said the boy would die if the boy did not receive medical attention, and it is common knowledge that stabbing can cause death. G showed an indifference to the boy's life by leaving the boy at the mall instead of taking him to the hospital. G's actions were not justified risks because the boy did nothing to threaten or harm G. Thus, G is guilty of depraved heart murder.

(d) Felony Murder

For felony murder to apply the defendant must commit or attempt to commit the underlying felony.[587] Here, because the underlying felony requirement

---

584. *Perez v. Rozum*, 488 Fed.Appx. 656, 657 (3d Cir. 2012).
585. Model Penal Code § 210.0(4) (Am. Law Inst., Proposed Official Draft 1962).
586. *U.S. v. Pineda-Doval*, 692 F.3d 942, 944–45(9th Cir. 2012).
587. *Montoya v. U.S. Parole Comm'n*, 908 F.2d 635, 642 (10th Cir. 1990).

is met, G is guilty of kidnapping. See analysis above (Jared and Greg's Crimes: Kidnapping). The scope of liability under the felony murder rule is broad, but there are limitations.[588]

Res Gestae

The killing must be during the commission of a felony, which means the felons have not reached a place of temporary safety.[589] G will argue the boy died after the felony was completed because he died in the hospital, which was after G and J reached a point of safety. They left the boy in the parking structure and no facts suggest the police pursued them. However, this is a weak argument because the stabbing occurred during the kidnapping in the warehouse. Thus, because the stabbing caused the boy's death and the death occurred shortly after the stabbing, this limitation does not apply.

Merger

The felony must be independent of the killing, which means manslaughter or aggravated battery cannot qualify as the underlying felony.[590] Here, although battery and assault cannot be used as the underlying felony, the merger limitation will not apply because G is guilty of kidnapping. See analysis above. (Jared and Greg's Crimes: Kidnapping).

Agency

Under the majority view, a defendant is not liable for a co-felon's death.[591] Here, the boy was not a co-felon. Thus, the agency limitation does not apply.

Foreseeability

The death must be a foreseeable result of the felony.[592] Here, the boy's death was foreseeable because victims of kidnapping are likely to resist or refuse to cooperate, which could agitate a co-felon and create a struggle that results in death.

Conclusion

G is guilty of felony murder because the boy died during the commission of the kidnapping. G is also guilty under the other three types of common law

---

588. *Id.*
589. *People v. Bodely*, 32 Cal. App. 4th 311, 314 (1995).
590. *State v. Campos*, 921 P.2d 1266, 1269-71 (N.M. 1996).
591. *State v. Canola*, 374 A.2d 20, 30 (N.J. 1977).
592. *People v. Stamp*, 2 Cal. App. 3d 203, 210 (1969).

murder. Today, modern statutes divide murders into two degrees: (a) first degree and (b) second degree.

First Degree Murder

Most jurisdictions have two types of first-degree murder: (i) first degree felony murder and (ii) intent to kill with premeditation and deliberation.[593]

First-Degree Felony Murder

G is guilty of first-degree felony murder because the boy's death occurred during the commission of a felony that is inherently dangerous to human life.[594] Felonies that are commonly enumerated as inherently dangerous to human life are burglary, arson, rape, robbery, and kidnapping.[595]

Intent to Kill

G likely intended to kill the boy. See rules and analysis above. (Greg's Crimes: Intent to Kill).

Premeditation

Premeditation requires that the defendant reflected on the idea of killing; mere seconds is enough.[596] Here, G will argue he did not reflect on the killing because G instinctively reacted to the boy's bad attitude. G grabbed his pocketknife in a moment of frustration. G did not come to the warehouse with a weapon to kill the boy. However, the prosecution will argue G threatened to kill the boy before the boy spit in G's face, which means G considered killing the boy before being provoked. Moreover, even if G was provoked, G took time to consciously grab the knife rather than leaving the boy alone. G likely premeditated the killing.

Deliberation

Deliberation requires that the defendant made the decision to kill in a cool and dispassionate manner.[597] Here, G will argue he did not act with a cool head because he panicked after seeing the news report featuring the boy and was frustrated after the boy spit in his face. G's reaction was clouded and an

---

593. *Terry v. Potter*, 111 F.3d 454, 458 (6th Cir. 1997).
594. *People v. Smith*, 733 N.W.2d 351, 365 (Mich. 2007).
595. *Id.*
596. *United States v. Frady*, 456 U.S. 152, 173 (1982).
597. *State v. Dellinger*, 79 S.W.3d 458, 492 (Tenn. 2002).

impulsive reaction to the boy's failure to cooperate. Thus, G is not guilty of first-degree murder because there was no deliberation.

2nd Degree

All other killings at common law and killings during non-enumerated felonies are considered second-degree murder.[598] If the court finds there was no intent to kill with premeditation or deliberation or that felony murder did not apply, then G would be guilty of second-degree murder under intent to cause serious bodily harm or depraved heart murder. But G will argue his second-degree murder charge should be mitigated to voluntary manslaughter.

Voluntary Manslaughter

Voluntary manslaughter is a killing in the heat of passion.[599] For the defendant to reduce murder to voluntary manslaughter, (a) there must be reasonable provocation, (b) the defendant must have been provoked, (c) a reasonable person would not have cooled off between the time of provocation and delivery of the fatal blow, and (d) the defendant must not have cooled offer during that interval.[600] Reasonable provocation is most frequently recognized as being subjected to a serious battery or threat of deadly force, or discovering one's spouse in bed with another person; mere words are usually not enough to constitute reasonable provocation.[601]

Cooling Off

(c) A reasonable person would not cool off because there was a short period of time between the altercation and the killing, the spitting and stabbing occurred within minutes. (d) G did not cool off because G took the pocket-knife and stabbed the boy immediately after the boy frustrated him.

Provocation

(b) Here, G was provoked because the boy spit in his face after refusing to give the contact information, which frustrated G. (a) Here, G will argue an ordinary person dealing with financial crisis, martial problems, a missing person's search, and a failed ransom plan would have a short temper. Thus, disrespectful acts, such as spitting, would reasonably frustrate the person and cause them to react violently. However, the prosecution will argue the boy never

---

598. *United States v. Delaney*, 717 F.3d 553, 556 (7th Cir. 2013).

599. *Girouard v. State*, 321 Md. 532, 539 (1991).

600. *U.S. v. Jack,* 483 Fed.Appx. 427, 428 (10th Cir. 2012).

601. *Girouard v. State*, supra note 599.

threatened to harm G. The boy stayed in the warehouse for a week and merely refused to cooperate with G's kidnapping plans. A simple spit in the face is not deadly and does not warrant a stabbing reaction. Thus, G cannot mitigate his second-degree charge to voluntary manslaughter.

(3) Jared's (J) Crimes

Felony Murder

As a member of the conspiracy to kidnap the boy, J is guilty of murder under the felony murder rule if the death was in furtherance of the conspiracy and a foreseeable consequence of the conspiracy.[602]

Here, J will argue G's actions were unpredictable and not within the scope of the felony because J specifically told G that he did not want anyone to get hurt and G promised that he only wanted money. However, the boy's death was likely foreseeable because J knew G's temper was out of control, which means G was unpredictable; and kidnapping is a dangerous felony because the victim might resist.

J will argue the death was not in furtherance of the conspiracy, kidnapping for ransom, because killing the boy did not help them discover the boy's contact information to request money from his parents. However, the prosecution will argue that G's extra force was necessary to extract information from the boy to further the conspiracy.

In conclusion, J is liable for felony murder because he knew about G's temper and still decided to work with G. J should not have trusted G.

---

602. *People v. Billa*, 31 Cal. 4th 1064, 1068 (2003).

Answer 3

Alicia's (A) Crimes

Homicide

Homicide is the killing of a human being.[603] Here, the actus reus is met because B died. The issue is whether the appropriate mens rea for murder was met.

Mens Rea

Murder is an unlawful killing with malice aforethought.[604] There are four types of common law murder: (a) intent to kill, (b) intent to inflict great bodily harm, (c) depraved heart murder, and (d) felony murder.[605] Intent to kill is a form of express malice and the remaining murders are forms of implied malice.[606]

(a) (b) Intent to Kill and Intent to Cause Serious Bodily Injury

Here, there is no intent to kill or cause serious bodily injury because A wanted to trick B and not kill him. A thought it would be funny to simulate B's accident, but no facts suggest she wanted B to get hurt.

(c) Depraved heart

A is guilty of depraved heart murder if she was subjectively aware that her conduct created a substantial and unjustified risk of death, but still consciously disregarded the risk.[607] Here, A consciously disregarded the risk of death by (i) driving 105 mph, (ii) unlatching B's seatbelt, and (iii) simulating B's car accident after he suffered from post-traumatic stress. However, the issue is whether the risk was substantial and if her actions were justified.

The prosecution will argue (i) A created a substantial risk of death by driving 105 mph because it is difficult to control a car at high speeds, and a high-speed collision is more likely to cause death. A's risk was not justified because it is illegal to drive more than 100 mph. Society's laws indicate driving fast on the highway is dangerous. (ii) A disregarded the risk that B could die if she

---

603. MPC § 2.10.1, supra note 580.
604. *U.S. v. Pearson*, supra note 581.
605. *Id.*
606. *Gutierrez Marquez v. Gunn*, supra note 583.
607. *United States v. Marrero*, 743 F.3d 389, 400 (3d Cir. 2014).

crashed the car while he was not wearing a seatbelt because she rigged his seat-belt to come undone and not reattach.

(iii) A knew B suffered from post-traumatic stress from his previous car accident because she purposefully pranked B to help him get over his trauma. A's actions were not justified because she mainly simulated the car accident for entertainment purposes. It is common knowledge that extreme fear or shock could cause a heart attack. A should have realized that B was more susceptible to a dangerously intense reaction because he suffered previous injuries from not wearing a seatbelt. A might try to argue that everyone reacts differently to stressful situations, such as high-speed driving and pranks, but her argument is weak. If the court entertains A's argument, then A will argue that the lesser charge of involuntary manslaughter is more appropriate.

Involuntary Manslaughter

Manslaughter differs from murder because it is a killing without malice aforethought. The difference between depraved heart murder and involuntary manslaughter is the seriousness of the risk of death. Second-degree murder involves a greater risk.[608] In the majority of states, involuntary manslaughter is a killing with criminal negligence.[609] A minority of the states uses ordinary recklessness or civil negligence to determine culpability.[610]

Criminal Negligence

Criminal negligence is a gross deviation from the standard of care of a reasonable person.[611] Here, the prosecution will argue a reasonable person would not break the law by driving 105 mph. A will argue that people often drive above the speed limit, but A's argument will not succeed because the speed limit was likely 65 mph to 70 mph. A reasonable person might drive 80 mph or 90 mph, but not 105 mph; 40 mph to 35 mph above the speed limit is a gross deviation.

The prosecution also has a strong argument that a reasonable person would not purposefully detach their friend's seatbelt while driving 105 mph because seatbelts are safety mechanisms that prevent deaths during accidents. A should have known that pranking B could cause a negative bodily reaction, such as a

---

608. *United States v. Hatatley*, 130 F.3d 1399, 1404 (10th Cir. 1997).

609. *United States v. One Star*, 979 F.2d 1319, 1321 (8th Cir. 1992).

610. *Santillanes v. State*, 849 P.2d 358, 363 (N.M. 1993).

611. *Williams v. State*, 235 S.W.3d 742, 750–51 (Tex. Crim. App. 2007).

heart attack because of B's accident history. In conclusion, A is guilty of involuntary manslaughter under the majority standard.

Ordinary Recklessness and Ordinary Negligence

Under the ordinary recklessness standard, the defendant must be aware of the substantial risk of death and disregard it.[612] See analysis above. (Alicia's Crimes: Depraved Heart). Ordinary negligence uses the civil negligence standard of care.[613] A meets the ordinary tort negligence standard because A was guilty under the gross negligence theory.

Felony Murder

For felony murder to apply the defendant must commit or attempt to commit the underlying felony.[614] Here, A committed the underlying felony by driving 105 mph. The scope of liability under the felony murder rule is broad, but there are limitations.[615]

Here, no limitations apply. (a) The underlying felony, driving over 100 mph, is independent of the killing. (b) The agency rule does not apply because B was not a co-felon. B did not know A planned to drive over 100 mph because A promised not to drive fast. (c) The killing was during the commission of the felony because B flew out of the window, suffered a heart attack, and was hit by oncoming traffic before A reached a point of temporary safety. (d) B's death was a foreseeable result of the felony because driving fast increases the chance of a collision and death. Thus, A is liable for homicide under the felony murder rule.

First-Degree Versus Second-Degree Murder

Today, modern statutes divide murders into two degrees: (a) first degree and (b) second degree. Most jurisdictions have two types of first-degree murder: (i) first-degree felony murder and (ii) intent to kill with premeditation and deliberation.[616] All other killings at common law are considered second-degree murder.[617]

---

612. MPC § 2.02(2)(c), supra note 568.
613. *Williams v. State*, supra note 611 at 751.
614. *Montoya v. U.S. Parole Comm'n*, 908 F.2d 635, 642 (10th Cir. 1990).
615. *Id.*
616. *Terry v. Potter*, supra note 593.
617. *United States v. Delaney*, supra note 598.

Here, A had no intent to kill and the killing did not occur during a commonly enumerated felony.[618] However, the killing might have occurred during the commission of an inherently dangerous felony because driving 105 mph could cause death if there is a high-speed collision. If driving over 100 mph is not considered inherently dangerous, then A would be guilty of second-degree murder under the felony murder and depraved heart doctrines.

Causation and Concurrence

The causation and concurrence elements are implicit in all crimes. Actual cause requires the defendant's act to be the cause of the prohibited result.[619] Proximate cause requires that the act be the direct cause of the social harm.[620] Concurrence requires the actus reus to be completed with the appropriate mens rea; they must occur simultaneously.[621] Here, concurrence is met because A disregarded the risk of death while driving fast and rigging B's seatbelt.

Actual Cause

Here, A will argue that driving 105 mph and the seatbelt prank were not the but-for causes because B died after being hit by another car. Her actions caused B's heart attack, but people survive heart attacks everyday. A's argument will fail because A's actions substantially contributed to B's death.[622] If A never asked B to take a joy ride, unlatched his seatbelt, and drove 105 mph, then B would have never have flown through the windshield, suffered a heart attack, or been hit by oncoming traffic. Thus, actual cause is met.

Proximate Cause

There must be no intervening causes between the defendant's voluntary act and the harm. A defendant is still the proximate cause of the victim's death if the intervening cause is dependent, which means the intervening cause is a result of the defendant's voluntary act.[623] If the intervening cause would independently have occurred without the defendant's actions, then the defendant is not the proximate cause unless that independent intervening cause was foreseeable.[624]

618. *People v. Smith*, supra note 594.
619. MPC § 2.03, supra note 557.
620. *Id.*
621. *Morissette v. United States*, supra note 559.
622. *Univ. of Texas Sw. Med. Ctr. v. Nassar*, 133 S. Ct. 2517, 2525 (2013).
623. *State v. Dunn*, 850 P.2d 1201, 1215 (Utah 1993).
624. *Id.*

Here, B's heart attack and the car killing B on impact were intervening causes because they occurred between A's actions and B's death. However, these intervening causes were likely dependent causes because B would have never flown through the window or suffered a heart attack if A never detached his seatbelt and drove 105 mph. A's actions left B unprotected and injured on the highway. Thus, proximate cause is met.

Overall Conclusion

A is guilty of first-degree felony murder if driving over 100 mph is an inherently dangerous felony. If not, then A is liable for second-degree murder under the felony murder rule and depraved heart murder. If A did not consciously disregard a substantial risk, then A is guilty of involuntary manslaughter.

Answer 4

Percy's (P) Crimes

(1) Embezzlement of Funeral Money

Embezzlement is the fraudulent conversion of the property of another by a person in lawful possession of that property.[625]

Lawful Possession

The defendant must have honestly received the goods, chattels, or money.[626] Here, P was Marie's (M) in-home care provided, which means P's daily duties likely included handling M's finances. P did not steal the money. P had lawful possession over the money when M gave P cash for her funeral expenses.

Fraudulent Conversion

The defendant must deal with the property in a manner inconsistent with the trust arrangement he made with the other person.[627] Here, P's actions were inconsistent with his trust arrangement because M asked P to deposit the funeral money into the bank, but P used the money to pay off his gambling debt.

Mens Rea

The defendant must have the specific intent to fraudulently convert the property;[628] borrowing and failing to return money is not embezzlement.[629] Here, no facts state P intended to reimburse M's money. P transferred possession of the money to a third party, which means P probably cannot retrieve M's money. Thus, P is guilty of embezzlement because all the elements are met.

(2) Larceny of Marie's (M) Jewelry

The difference between larceny and embezzlement is larceny is a wrongful possession.[630] Larceny is a taking and carrying away of tangible personal property of another by trespass with the intent to permanently deprive.[631] Larceny by trick is a taking induced by misrepresentation.[632] Larceny by false

---

625. *United States v. Young*, 955 F.2d 99, 102 (1st Cir. 1992).
626. *Lewis v. People*, 60 P.2d 1089, 1097 (Colo. 1936).
627. *Id.*
628. *United States v. Young*, supra note 625 at 105.
629. *Id* at 104.
630. *United States v. Waronek*, 582 F.2d 1158, 1161 (7th Cir. 1978).
631. *Id.*
632. *Bell v. United States*, 462 U.S. 356, 359 (1983).

pretenses also requires a misrepresentation to obtain the victim's consent, but involves taking title and not possession of the property.[633] Here, the most appropriate charge is larceny by trick because P lied that M's daughter poisoned the cake to induce M to give P her jewelry. P did not have lawful possession and did not receive title to the jewelry.

Intent to Permanently Deprive

The defendant must have the specific intent to create a substantial risk of loss; good faith intent to borrow is not sufficient.[634] Here, P will argue he lied about who poisoned the cake to avoid liability for M's death and not to deprive M of her jewelry. However, the prosecution will argue P's ultimate goal was to isolate M from her family to obtain M's fortune. M's jewelry is part of her fortune and would fit perfectly into P's plan. Thus, P likely intended to eventually deprive M of her jewelry, especially because he subsequently sold the jewelry for thousands of dollars.

Property of Another

The person must have a possessory interest superior to that of the defendant.[635] M had superior possessory rights to P because she was the original owner of the jewelry and P had no interest in the property.

Taking

The defendant must obtain control of the property; mere destruction or movement of the property is not sufficient to constitute a taking.[636] This element is met because M gave P the jewelry, P sold the jewelry for thousands of dollars, and P likely kept the money. Thus, P controlled the property.

Asportation

At common law, the movement only needs to be slight.[637] P sold the jewelry for thousands of dollars, which means P moved the jewelry from the mansion to the dealer.

---

633. *Id.*
634. Model Penal Code § 223.0 (AM. LAW INST., Official Draft 1962).
635. *United States v. Waronek*, supra note 630.
636. *United States v. Mafnas*, 701 F.2d 83, 84 (9th Cir. 1983).
637. *Jones v. Commonwealth*, 349 S.E.2d 414, 418 (Va. Ct. App. 1986).

Misrepresentation

Larceny by trick requires the defendant to knowingly make a false statement of past or existing fact with the intent to defraud another.[638] Here, P will argue he did not lie to obtain the jewelry, but to protect himself from liability for M's death. P will argue he didn't care about the jewelry. However, P's argument is weak because P knew M's daughter did not sprinkle peanut oil on the cake. P was the true culprit, but still accused the daughter. P's actions suggest he wanted to further isolate M from her family to encourage M to devise her fortune to him. Thus, P committed a misrepresentation with the proper intent because the jewelry is considered part of M's fortune. P is guilty of larceny by trick.

(3) Homicide

Homicide is the killing of a human being.[639] Here, the actus reus is met because M died from an allergic reaction to peanut oil. The issue is whether the appropriate mens rea for murder was met.

Mens Rea

Murder is an unlawful killing with malice aforethought.[640] There are four types of common law murder: (a) intent to kill, (b) intent to inflict great bodily harm, (c) depraved heart murder, and (d) felony murder.[641] Intent to kill is a form of express malice and the remaining murders are forms of implied malice.[642]

(a) Intent to Kill

Here, the prosecution will argue P intended to kill M by sprinkling peanut oil on the icing because P wanted M's fortune. However, this is a weak argument because P changed his mind before the incident. P decided not to kill M because he enjoyed her company and wanted to use her funeral money to pay off his debts. P did not have the intent to kill. P wanted to trick M into hating her daughter.

---

638. *Sutro Bros. & Co. v. Indem. Ins. Co. of N. Am.*, 264 F. Supp. 273, 287-88 (S.D.N.Y. 1967).

639. MPC § 2.10.1, supra note 580.

640. *U.S. v. Pearson*, supra note 581.

641. *Id.*

642. *Gutierrez Marquez v. Gunn*, supra note 583.

(b) Intent to Cause Serious Bodily Injury

Here, the prosecution will argue P may not have intended to kill M, but he definitely wanted to cause serious bodily injury. P knew M was allergic to peanuts, but still sprinkled the peanut oil on the cake. P likely wanted M to blame her daughter for her injuries. However, P did not intend for M to have such an extreme reaction and searched for M's EpiPen to save her. P's actions suggest he did not want M to suffer seriously bodily harm.

(c) Depraved Heart

P is guilty of depraved heart murder because he was subjectively aware that his conduct created a substantial and unjustified risk of death, but still consciously disregarded the risk.[643] Here, the prosecution will argue that there was a substantial risk of death because P induced M's peanut allergy with peanut oil without an EpiPen nearby. An extreme allergic reaction causes a person's airways to close, failure to breath, and ultimately death. P might argue he did not know M's allergy was serious, but this is a weak argument because P was M's in-home care provided and likely knew M's medical history. Moreover, P's risk was not justified because he induced M's allergy to cover up his lies about M's family and isolate M from her daughter.

If P was subjectively aware of the high risk of death, then P is guilty of depraved heart murder. If P only intended M to have a small allergic reaction, then he might be acquitted.

First-Degree Versus Second-Degree Murder

Today, modern statutes divide murders into two degrees: (a) first degree and (b) second degree. Intent to kill with premeditation and deliberation is considered first-degree murder.[644] All other killings at common law, excluding felony murder, are considered second-degree murder.[645] P would likely be guilty of second-degree murder under the depraved heart theory if the court determines P was subjectively aware of the risk. However, the prosecution will argue P should be guilty of first-degree murder.

---

643. *United States v. Marrero*, supra note 607.
644. *Terry v. Potter*, supra note 593.
645. *United States v. Delaney*, supra note 598.

Intent to Kill with Premeditation and Deliberation

Premeditation requires that the defendant reflected on the idea of killing; mere seconds is enough.[646] Deliberation requires that the defendant made the decision to kill in a cool and dispassionate manner.[647] Here, the prosecution will argue P reflected on his killing because P used his position as M's in-home care provider to create a relationship of dependency, which likely took months. If M agreed to devise her fortune to P, then P would have killed M earlier. No facts suggest P was panicking when he sprinkled the peanut oil on the cake.

However, P will argue he did not intend to kill M because he enjoyed her company. The extreme reaction was an accident because he was nervous and not thinking clearly, which is why he quickly retreated to the kitchen. P's argument is likely stronger and P is not guilty of first-degree murder.

Voluntary Manslaughter

P will argue his second-degree murder charge should be mitigated to voluntary manslaughter. Voluntary manslaughter is a killing in the heat of passion.[648] For the defendant to reduce murder to voluntary manslaughter: (a) there must be reasonable provocation, (b) the defendant must have been provoked, (c) a reasonable person would not have cooled off between the time of provocation and delivery of the fatal blow, and (d) the defendant must not have cooled offer during that interval.[649]

Here, P will argue he acted in the heat of passion because he quickly retreated to the kitchen after M confronted him. P's actions suggest he panicked because M might discover his manipulation. However, P's argument is weak for two reasons. First, a reasonable person would not induce a deadly allergic reaction to cover up a lie. M did not reasonably provoke P when she confronted him about his deception. Second, the facts suggest P was not enraged, but thinking clearly about how to frame M's daughter using the cake. Thus P's charge will not be mitigated.

Involuntary Manslaughter

Manslaughter differs from murder because it is a killing without malice aforethought. The difference between depraved heart murder and involuntary

---

646. *United States v. Frady*, supra note 596.
647. *State v. Dellinger*, supra note 597.
648. *Girouard v. State*, supra note 599.
649. *U.S. v. Jack*, supra note 600.

manslaughter is the seriousness of the risk of death. Second-degree murder involves a greater risk.[650] In the majority of states, involuntary manslaughter is a killing with criminal negligence.[651] A minority of the states uses ordinary recklessness or civil negligence to determine culpability.[652]

Criminal Negligence

Criminal negligence is a gross deviation from the standard of care of a reasonable person.[653] Here, the prosecution will argue a reasonable person would not induce a peanut allergy, especially if they know the person has an EpiPen. People with EpiPens usually have life-threatening allergies. Thus, P is likely guilty of involuntary manslaughter.

Ordinary Recklessness and Ordinary Negligence

Under the ordinary recklessness standard, the defendant must be aware of the substantial risk of death and disregard it.[654] See analysis above. (Percy's Crimes: Depraved Heart). Ordinary negligence uses the civil negligence standard of care.[655] P meets the ordinary tort negligence standard because P was guilty under the gross negligence theory.

Concurrence and Causation

The causation and concurrence elements are implicit in all crimes. Actual cause requires the defendant's act to be the cause of the prohibited result.[656] Proximate cause requires that the act be the direct cause of the social harm.[657] Concurrence requires the actus reus be completed with the appropriate mens rea; they must occur simultaneously.[658]

Here, actual cause is met because M died after P sprinkled peanut oil on the cake and fed M the cake. Proximate cause is also met because there were no intervening causes between P actions and M's consumption of the cake.

However, the concurrence element is likely not met because P changed his mind about killing M. Although P originally intended to kill M, at the time he

---

650. *United States v. Hatatley*, supra note 608.

651. *United States v. One Star*, supra note 609.

652. *Santillanes v. State*, supra note 610.

653. *Williams v. State*, supra note 611 at 751.

654. MPC § 2.02(2)(c), supra note 568.

655. *Williams v. State*, supra note 611 at 751.

656. MPC § 2.03, supra note 557.

657. *Id.*

658. *Morissette v. United States*, supra note 559 at 254–55.

committed the actus reus, P decided he enjoyed M's company and did not want to kill her.

Conclusion

P might be guilty of second-degree murder under the depraved heart theory, but the more appropriate charge is involuntary manslaughter because P did not intent to kill M when he sprinkled peanut oil on the cake.

Answer 5

Felicia's (F) Crimes

(1) Burglary

Common law burglary requires (a) breaking and (b) entering a (c) dwelling of another (d) at night with the (e) intent to commit a felony therein, but modern burglary only requires an entering of a (c) structure with (e) intent to commit a crime therein.[659]

Here, (a) breaking requires actual movement, but minimal force is sufficient.[660] F used her employee ID to enter the building, which means she needed to at least open the door. (b) Entering requires the defendant or any type of apparatus to enter the structure; a brief moment of entry is enough.[661] F physically entered the building to retrieve Rhonda's (R) scarf. (c) A dwelling is a place where people live whereas a structure is a building.[662] At common law, F entered an office building and not a dwelling because no one lived in the office. The building was empty at 5:45 PM because people went home after work. However, under the modern statutes, the office building is considered a structure and this element is met. (d) Modern statutes eliminated the night requirement.[663] At common law, whether 5:45 PM is nighttime will depend on the season because the sun sets earlier in the winter. Most people consider sunset the beginning of nighttime. (e) The defendant must have the specific intent to commit a felony or crime at the time of entry.[664] Here, F intended to steal the scarf from R's desk when she entered the building because F saw R leave the scarf on the desk, purchased black clothes, and arrived that evening prepared to steal the scarf. Larceny is a felony.

Conclusion

At common law, F would not be guilty of burglary because 5:45 PM might not constitute nighttime and the office building is not a dwelling. However, F is guilty of burglar under modern statutes.

---

659. Model Penal Code § 221.1(1) (AM. LAW INST., Proposed Official Draft 1962).
660. *Rex v. Samuel Hall*, 168 Eng. Rep. 842 (1818).
661. *Hebron v. State*, 627 A.2d 1029, 1038 (Md. 1993).
662. Model Penal Code § 221.0(1) (AM. LAW INST., Proposed Official Draft 1962).
663. *Taylor v. United States*, 495 U.S. 575, 576 (1990).
664. *United States v. Cooper*, 473 F.2d 95, 96-97 (D.C. Cir. 1972).

(2) Attempted Murder

Attempts are failed or incomplete efforts to commit a substantive offense. A criminal attempt occurs when a person, with the specific intent to commit an offense, performs acts towards the commission of that offense.[665]

Actus Reus

The defendant must commit an overt act that goes beyond mere preparation.[666] The two common tests are: the (a) dangerous proximity test and (b) substantial step test. The first test requires an act that is dangerously close to success; courts focus on how much remains to be done before the crime is committed.[667] The second test requires a substantial step; the courts focus on how much of the crime was already completed.[668]

Here, (a) F almost completed the crime because R is in coma. F's use of extreme force caused R to fall on the floor. F will argue that more actions were necessary to kill R, such as punching or using a weapon, but this is weak because F had nothing else left to do but wait for R to die. (b) F took a substantial step toward killing R because F yelled, "I'll kill you" and pushed R to the ground. F's actions were beyond mere planning. Thus, under both tests, F satisfied the actus reus requirement.

Mens Rea

The defendant must specifically intend to perform the actus reus and commit the underlying offense.[669] Here, F will argue that she could not control her anger, which means F did not intend to kill R. F did not continually attack R after R fell to the ground and F immediately called the paramedics, which means R's coma was likely an accident. However, F's argument is weak because F acted out of her own free will. Even if F felt a moment of rage, F could have walked away. Moreover, F yelled "I'll kill you" before she pushed R, which suggests F intended to kill R. F's statements are strong evidence of her internal thoughts. The mens rea is likely met.

---

665. Model Penal Code § 5.01(1) (AM. LAW INST., Official Draft 1962).

666. *United States v. Howard*, 766 F.3d 414, 419-20 (5th Cir. 2014).

667. *Hyde v. United States*, 225 U.S. 347, 387-88 (1912) (Holmes, J., dissenting).

668. MPC § 5.01(1), supra note 665.

669. *United States v. Howard*, supra note 666.

Conclusion

If F had the subjective intent to kill, then F is guilty of attempted murder because the actus reus is met.

(3) Insanity

Although there are four different insanity tests, each test similarly requires the defendant to suffer from a mental disorder or defect.[670] Here, F was bipolar, suffered from obsessive-compulsive disorder (OCD), and had a disability that made it difficult for her to understand social situations. These disorders are mental defects because they all affect the brain.

Burglary Charge

M'Naghten Test

A defendant is not guilty by reason of insanity if, at the time of his actions, the mental defect caused the defendant to lack the ability to know the wrongfulness of his actions or understand the nature and quality of his actions.[671] Here, the prosecution will argue F's decisions to wear all black and sneak into the building after work hours indicated F knew stealing was wrong because F took precautions to conceal her bad acts from others.

However, F will argue she only burglarized the building because she believed R created a theft condition to gain ownership of R's scarf. F did not realized her acts were wrong because F's disability made it difficult for her to understand social situations. F did not know R was joking. If F believed her acts were wrong, then F would not have worn the scarf to work the next day to show off her accomplishment. F would have concealed the scarf from R. Moreover, F told R, "I fulfilled your condition. This scarf is mine." F did not acknowledge she did anything wrong. Thus, F did not understand the nature of her actions and should be acquitted.

Irresistible Impulse Test

A defendant is not guilty by reason of insanity if the mental illness makes her unable to control her actions.[672] Here, F will argue her OCD caused her to steal the scarf because she was obsessed with the scarf. However, this is a weak

---

670. *Redfield v. United States*, 328 F.2d 532, 533 (D.C. Cir. 1964).

671. *U.S. v. Currens*, 290 F.2d 751, 774 (3d Cir. 1961).

672. *Wade v. United States*, 426 F.2d 64, 67 (9th Cir. 1970).

argument because F purchased black clothes and created a plan to enter the building without any coercion.

Durham Test

A defendant is not guilty by reason of insanity if the crime was a product of a mental disease.[673] Here, the facts imply that F burglarized the building because she had OCD and did not understand the social situation. If the court agrees, then F will be acquitted.

MPC Approach

A defendant is not guilty by reason of insanity if the defendant lacked substantial capacity to appreciate the criminality of his conduct, or confirm his conduct to the requirements of the law.[674] This test combines M'Naghten and the irresistible impulse tests. F will be acquitted under this standard.

Attempted Murder Charge

M'Naghten Test

See rule above (Insanity: Burglary Charge). Here, F said she could not control her anger, which suggests F knew pushing R over a scarf was wrong. F also called the paramedics immediately because she felt horrible. F's subsequent actions show F knew her behavior was not acceptable. F will not be acquitted under this theory.

Irresistible Impulse Test

See rule above (Insanity: Burglary Charge). Here, F will argue she only pushed R because her bipolar disorder kicked in and caused uncontrollable anger. F will claim the bipolar disorder made it impossible to think clearly and took away her free will. The prosecution will argue F's illness may cause anger, but F could still decide to walk away or handle the conflict differently, such as yelling versus pushing. If F could control her actions, then F will not be acquitted.

Durham Test

See rule above (Insanity: Burglary Charge). Here, F's bipolar disorder probably caused F to yell "I'll kill you" and push R in a moment of rage. F will be

---

673. *Durham v. U.S.*, 214 F.2d 862, 874–75 (D.C. Cir. 1954).
674. Model Penal Code § 4.01(1) (Am. Law Inst., Proposed Official Draft 1962).

acquitted under this standard because F may have handled the situation in a calm manner if she was not bipolar.

MPC Approach

See rule above (Insanity: Burglary Charge). It is likely F would not be acquitted under the MPC approach.

Answer 6

(1) Ben (B), Carl (C), and Danny's (D) Conspiracy

Conspiracy to Run an Illegal Drug Trafficking Business

Conspiracy does not merge with the completed crime and carries its own penalty.[675] Conspiracy is an agreement by two or more persons to commit a criminal act or to accomplish a legal act by unlawful means.[676]

Agreement

An explicit or implicit agreement is sufficient to satisfy the actus reus requirement.[677] The parties do not need to know all the details or agree to all the acts, but the parties must be aware of the agreement's essential nature.[678] The bilateral approach requires two guilty minds,[679] and the unilateral approach requires one guilty mind.[680] A guilty mind requires genuine criminal intent to commit the underlying crime and join the conspiracy. An undercover police officer feigning the agreement does not have a guilty mind.[681]

Under both approaches, there is a valid agreement between B, C, and D to run an illegal drug trafficking business. Although B was hesitant in the beginning, he eventually agreed. The defendants cannot use Argo's (A) lack of criminal intent to invalidate the agreement because there were more than two guilty minds.

Overt Act

One of the conspirators must perform an overt act to show the conspiracy is in process and not purely in the minds of the conspirators.[682]Most jurisdictions require the overt act to further the conspiracy.[683] Here, C sold drugs, B met with D about conspiracy assignments, and A handled accounting. Thus, every conspirator committed an overt act that furthered the conspiracy.

---

675. *Iannelli v. U. S.*, 420 U.S. 770 (1975).

676. Model Penal Code § 5.03 (Am. Law Inst., Proposed Official Draft 1962).

677. *United States v. Johnston*, 789 F.3d 934, 940 (9th Cir. 2015).

678. *United States v. Jimenez Recio*, 537 U.S. 270, 274-75 (2003).

679. *United States v. Harris*, 733 F.2d 994, 1005 (2d Cir. 1984).

680. MPC § 5.03, supra note 676.

681. *United States v. Harris*, supra note 679.

682. MPC § 5.03, supra note 676.

683. *Id.*

Mens Rea

Conspirators must specifically intend to make the agreement and accomplish what was agreed upon.[684] Here, A was the only person without the genuine intent to join the drug-tracking business because he was an undercover police officer. D ran the whole business and C believed the conspiracy was a good idea. B will argue he did not intend to sell drugs, but this is a weak argument because B changed his mind after speaking to C.

In conclusion, B, C, and D are guilty of conspiracy.

(2) Carl's (C) Solicitation

Solicitation is inciting, inviting, requesting, counseling, advising, inducing, urging, or commanding another to commit a felony with the specific intent that the person will commit the inchoate offense.[685] The person does not need to agree to complete the crime.[686] At common law, solicitation is a crime independent of any other offense, but in modern jurisdictions, solicitation merges with conspiracy.[687] Here, no facts suggest B or D asked anyone to join the conspiracy. A asked B to join the family business, but A did not genuinely intend for B to commit any crimes because A was an undercover police officer. However, C convinced B to join the conspiracy after B said no. Thus, C is guilty of solicitation at common law, but solicitation will merge with conspiracy under modern jurisdictions.

(3) Ben (B) and Danny's (D) Conspirator Liability for Argo's (A) Death

A co-conspirator is vicariously liable for the acts done by another co-conspirator, whether or not they agreed upon the acts, if those acts were (a) in furtherance of the conspiracy and (b) a natural and probable consequence of the conspiracy.[688] A defendant is not liable for offenses committed by co-conspirators prior to his joining the conspiracy.[689]

---

684. *United States v. Feola*, 420 U.S. 671, 688 (1975).

685. *Prakash v. Holder*, 579 F.3d 1033, 1039 (9th Cir. 2009).

686. *Salinas v. United States*, 522 U.S. 52, 65 (1997).

687. *Bishop v. State*, 98 A.3d 317, 337 (Md. 2014).

688. *Pinkerton v. United States*, 328 U.S. 640, 647-48 (1946).

689. *United States v. Blackmon*, 839 F.2d 900, 908-09 (2d Cir. 1988).

(a) A's death was in furtherance of the conspiracy to run an illegal drug trafficking business because A was an undercover police officer who intended to end the business. C killed A because A tried to stop C from collecting the drugs hidden in the newspapers. (b) B and D will argue the killing was not foreseeable because C's assignment was to get drugs. No one told C to kill anyone and no facts suggest C had a history of violence. The killing was an accident that occurred when C tried to escape. However, the prosecution will argue that drug trafficking is commonly known as a dangerous activity because it is illegal and often includes interactions with unpredictable criminals. Both B and D knew the risks involved with intercepting the newspapers because D provided guns for protection, which suggests they knew the business was dangerous and could result in death.

B and D are liable for A's death as co-conspirators unless they withdrew from the conspiracy.

Ben's Withdrawal

Withdrawal is not a defense to the crime of conspiracy, but is a defense to the subsequent crimes of co-conspirators.[690] A defendant can limit his liability for subsequent acts of co-conspirators by affirmatively notifying co-conspirators about his withdrawal or engaging in acts inconsistent with the conspiracy.[691] The defendant's withdrawal must be genuine.[692] Here, B told A and C that he would call the police because he believed their actions were wrong. B's statement implied that he no longer wanted to be a member of the drug-trafficking business. B's intent was genuine because he did not follow C to the interception point and offered to help A stop the conspiracy. B's willingness to help indicates his withdrawal was truthful.

Prevent the Completion

In some jurisdictions, withdrawal requires the conspirator to prevent the completion of the conspiracy by convincing the other co-conspirators to abandon their undertaking or exposing the conspiracy to the authorities.[693] Here, B intended to call the police to stop the conspiracy, but likely decided not to contact the authorities because A revealed he was a police officer and would handle the situation. A reasonable person in B's position would believe

---

690. *U.S. v. Read*, 658 F.2d 1225, 1232–33 (7th Cir. 1981).
691. *Id.*
692. *Id. at 1231.*
693. *United States v. Escobar de Bright*, 742 F.2d 1196, 1199 (9th Cir. 1984).

a cop's statement and not take additional actions to stop C from going to the interception point. Thus, under all jurisdictions, B validly withdrew from the conspiracy and would not be liable for A's death.

Accomplice Liability

Accomplice liability attaches to the crime committed by the principal if the accomplice knowingly aided in that crime.[694] At common law, the principal in the first degree (P1) is a party who commits the acts that constitute the crime. The principal in the second degree (P2) is a party who is present with P1 during the commission of the crime and intentionally assists P1. Accessory before the fact is a party who was not present with P1 during the commission of the crime, but intentionally assists P1 before the crime. Accessory after the fact is a party who was not present with P1 during the commission of the crime, but immediately assists P1 after the crime.[695] In modern jurisdictions, most courts do not distinguish between P1s, P2s, and accessories before the fact.[696] Here, C is the P1 because C killed A. B and D are not P2s because they were not at the scene of the crime, but they might be accessories before the fact.

Danny's (D) Accomplice Liability for Argo's (A) Death

Actus Reus

The accomplice's assistance does not need to be substantial; any aid will suffice, such as physical or psychological assistance, or failing to act when there is a duty to act.[697] Here, D provided the guns, clothes, and vehicles to help C intercept the newspaper delivery. D likely provided the gun used to kill A.

Mens Rea

The accomplice must knowingly help the principal commit the underlying prohibited conduct; the accomplice does not need specific knowledge of the elements of the principal's crime or to engage in any illegal conduct.[698] Here, D will argue he did not intend for C to kill A. D provided guns to help C protect himself when obtaining the drugs from the newspaper bundles. The prosecution will argue D knowingly helped C commit homicide because D supplied guns, which suggests D knew someone might be killed during the assignment.

---

694. *Waddington v. Sarausad*, 555 U.S. 179, 192 (2009).

695. *State v. Hamilton*, 13 Nev. 386, 391 (1878).

696. *Id.*

697. *Waddington v. Sarausad*, supra note 694 at 185.

698. *Id.* at 198.

Thus, D did not specifically intend to kill A, but did intend to help C kill any-one who jeopardized the drug trafficking business. D likely had the necessary mens rea and will be guilty of homicide under accomplice liability.

Ben's (B) Accomplice Liability for Argo's (A) Death

Although the prosecution will argue B helped C obtain the guns from D, B likely did not have the necessary mens rea because B withdrew from the con-spiracy and refused to help C with the newspaper assignment. B repudiated his encouragement by threatening to tell the police, which means B is not guilty of A's homicide. See analysis above (Ben's Withdrawal).

Answer 7

(1) Mr. Liam's (Mr. L) Homicide of Neil (N)

Defense of Property

Defense of property requires the defendant to honestly and reasonably believe it was necessary to use non-deadly force to prevent the imminent dispossession of personal or real property.[699] Here, whether Mr. L believed the force was necessary is irrelevant because Mr. L cannot use a bow and arrow to protect his home. A defendant may never use deadly force to protect property.[700] Deadly force is only justified under self-defense or defense of habitation.

Self-Defense

Self-defense is a complete defense, which means the defendant is acquitted if the defendant has an honest and reasonable belief that (a) the victim threatened imminent force and (b) it was necessary to use force to repel the threat of force.[701] (c) The force used must be proportional to the force threatened.[702]

(a) <u>Imminent</u>: Self-defense for homicide requires an imminent threat of serious bodily injury or death.[703] Here, the prosecution will argue a reasonable person would not believe an imminent threat existed because N merely egged Mr. L's home. Mr. L was protected inside his house. Even if an egg hit Mr. L, he would not suffer serious bodily injury. However, Mr. L will argue he honestly believed N and M would soon break into his house and physically harm him because they egged his house every weekend for a month. Mr. L will argue that criminals are unpredictable and their crimes could quickly increase in intensity. If Mr. L's belief was reasonable, then this element is met.

(b) <u>Necessary</u>: The court looks at the defendant's relevant knowledge about the aggressor, physical attributes of all persons involved, and any prior experiences of the defendant to determine if deadly force was necessary.[704] Here, Mr. L subjectively believed a trap was necessary to stop N from egging his house and to protect himself. The issue is whether Mr. L's reasonably believed deadly force was necessary.

---

699. *U.S. v. Lesmeister*, 742 F.Supp.2d 1064, 1070 (D.S.D. 2010).

700. *Wallace v. U.S.*, 162 U.S. 466, 473–74 (1896).

701. *Davis v. Strack*, 270 F.3d 111, 125 (2d Cir. 2001).

702. *United States v. Peterson*, 483 F.2d 1222, 1229-30 (D.C. Cir. 1973); *United States v. Black*, 692 F.2d 314, 318 (4th Cir. 1982).

703. *State v. Stewart*, 763 P.2d 572, 577 (Kan. 1988).

704. *People v. Goetz*, 497 N.E.2d 41, 52 (N.Y. 1986).

Mr. L will argue a reasonable person would set a trap to prevent the criminals from breaking into the home because N egged his house consistently for one month and would eventually elevate his crimes. However, the prosecution will argue N never threatened Mr. L's physical safety. Thus, N's previous behavior indicated a bow and arrow was not necessary to stop the egging. Mr. L could have deterred N by yelling, calling the police, or setting up an alarm system.

(c) Proportional: Here, a bow and arrow is considered deadly force because an arrow can kill someone. Mr. L's use of deadly force is not proportional to egging someone's house because eggs are fragile and unlikely to cause serious bodily harm.

Effect of Imperfect Self-Defense

If the defendant raises self-defense, but the claim fails because the belief was honest, but not reasonable; or deadly force was used when only non-deadly was required; or the defendant was the initial aggressor, then self-defense mitigates a murder charge to voluntary manslaughter.[705] Here, Mr. L will likely be charged with voluntary manslaughter because his belief was not reasonable and deadly force was not necessary to repel N's egging of the house.

Defense of Habitation

Under the castle doctrine, a defendant can use deadly force to prevent an intruder from entering his residence because individuals have the utmost bodily security and privacy in the home.[706] Defense of habitation is broader than self-defense because it permits the defendant to use deadly force before a personal threat is imminent.[707]

There are three common law approaches. The first approach allows an actor to use deadly force if he honestly and reasonably believes that deadly force is necessary to prevent imminent, unlawful entry. The second approach adds an element that the defendant believes the aggressor intends to commit a felony once inside. The third approach requires the felony to be a violent felony, such as rape, robbery, murder, arson, or aggravated assault.[708]

---

705. *Burch v. Corcoran*, 273 F.3d 577, 586–87 (4th Cir. 2001).
706. *People v. Ceballos*, 526 P.2d 241, 249 (Cal. 1974).
707. *Id.*
708. *People v. Brown*, 8 Cal. Rptr. 2d 513, 518 n.6 (Cal. Ct. App. 1992).

Here, Mr. L will argue a reasonable person would believe N would eventually enter the home because N entered the gate to egg Mr. L's house, which means N was likely near the entrance. However, the prosecution will argue no facts suggest N tried to enter Mr. L's home. N never tried to break down the front door. Thus, Mr. L is not acquitted because there was no threat of entry into Mr. L's home.

Conclusion

If imperfect self-defense applies, then Mr. L is guilty of voluntary manslaughter. If not, then Mr. L could be liable for murder.

(2) Matthew's (M) Crimes

Attempted Murder

Attempts are failed or incomplete efforts to commit a substantive offense. A criminal attempt occurs when a person, with the specific intent to commit an offense, performs acts towards the commission of that offense.[709]

Actus Reus

The defendant must commit an overt act that goes beyond mere preparation.[710] The two common tests are: the (a) dangerous proximity test and (b) substantial step test. The first test requires an act that is dangerously close to success; courts focus on how much remains to be done before the crime is committed.[711] The second test requires a substantial step towards committing the crime; the courts focus on how much of the crime was already completed.[712]

Here, (a) the prosecution will argue M's actions were beyond preparation because M threw the arrow at Mr. L and caused Mr. L physical harm. However, M will argue the arrow hit Mr. L's arm, which means there was still much to be done before Mr. L would die. M's argument is weak because if M aimed properly, M could have hit Mr. L in a vital organ and caused immediate death. (b) The prosecution will argue that throwing an arrow is a substantial step because M engaged in a physical attack against Mr. L. The actus reus is met under both tests.

---

709. MPC § 5.01(1), supra note 665.
710. *United States v. Howard*, supra note 666.
711. *Hyde v. United States*, 225 U.S. 347, 387-88 (1912) (Holmes, J., dissenting).
712. Model Penal Code § 5.01 (Am. Law Inst., Official Draft 1962).

Mens Rea

The defendant must specifically intend to perform the actus reus and commit the underlying offense.[713] Here, the prosecution will argue M intended to kill Mr. L because M yelled, "You won't get me," took the deadly weapon, and then threw it at Mr. L. M's words suggest he wanted to kill Mr. L to protect himself. However, M will argue he never intended to kill Mr. L, but only acted to prevent Mr. L from attacking them again. The arrow hit Mr. L's arm and not his heart, which suggests M did not want Mr. L to die.

Thus, if M did not intend to kill Mr. L, then M is likely not guilty of attempted murder. If M did have the intent, then M would argue that he acted in self-defense and to defend N.

Self-Defense

See rules above. (Mr. Liam's Homicide of Neil: Self-Defense). Here, M subjectively believed the threat was imminent because M screamed, "You won't get me," immediately before he threw the arrow at Mr. L. A reasonable person would believe Mr. L would initiate another physical attack because Mr. L set off a trap that killed N and yelled, "Got you. Get off my property!" M had no previous interactions with Mr. L, which means M likely believed Mr. L was serious about killing M. A reasonable person, who watched their friend die, would believe deadly force, such as throwing the arrow at the aggressor, was necessary to escape the yard alive. Thus, M will be acquitted unless M was the initial aggressor or had a duty to retreat.

Initial Aggressors

A defendant cannot be acquitted due to self-defense if the defendant was the initial aggressor.[714] Here, the prosecution will argue M was the initial aggressor because M trespassed on Mr. L's property. However, M will argue he never threw an egg at Mr. L's property or threatened Mr. L's physical safety. M merely entered the gate, which is an action visitors must do to reach Mr. L's front door. If M's act of entering the gate with eggs is enough to be an initial aggressor, then M is guilty of attempted murder.

---

713. *United States v. Howard*, 766 F.3d 414, 419 (5th Cir. 2014).

714. *Jenkins v. State*, 942 So. 2d 910, 915-16 (Fla. Dist. Ct. App. 2006).

Duty to retreat

Some jurisdictions required the defendant to retreat before resorting to deadly force if there are reasonably safe avenues of retreat while other jurisdictions allow the defendant to use deadly force without retreating if the defendant had a lawful right to be present.[715] Here, under all jurisdictions, M did not have the legal right to be on Mr. L's property because M was trespassing with the intent to cause property damage. Thus, M had the duty to retreat if there was a safe avenue available.

M will argue he had no safe avenue of retreat because the whole yard could have been equipped with traps. M feared for his life because N died immediately upon entrance. However, M's argument is weak because N was killed after they entered the front gate, which means M was near the gate. M could have easily turned around and ran away instead of trying to fight with Mr. L, who was likely still at the front door. If the jurisdiction requires a duty to retreat, then M could be guilty of attempted murder.

Defense of Others

A defendant is acquitted of a crime if the defendant honestly and reasonably believed that force was necessary to repel a threat of imminent harm to a third party.[716] The force must be proportional to the threat of harm; deadly force can only be used to repel the threat of imminent deadly force.[717] Here, M yelled, "Don't worry Neil! I'll protect you!" M's statements suggest M believed N needed protection. M's belief was reasonable because N was hit by Mr. L's bow and arrow and fell to the floor. N could not get up to protect himself from Mr. L who was yelling "Got you. Get off my property!" M's use of deadly force was likely reasonable because Mr. L used deadly force first. See analysis above. (Matthew's Crimes: Self-Defense).

Conclusion

In conclusion, M could likely use defense of others as a way to avoid conviction for attempting to murder Mr. L unless M and N were considered the initial aggressors.

---

715. *United States v. Peterson*, supra note 702 at 1236.
716. *United States ex rel. Rooney v. Housewright*, 568 F.2d 516, 523 (7th Cir. 1977).
717. *United States v. Black*, supra note 702.

Robbery

Robbery requires a taking of another's personal property from their person or presence using force or intimidation with the intent to permanently deprive the person of their property.[718]

Force or Threat

The defendant's threat must be of immediate death or serious physical injury to the victim, family, relative, or person in presence at the time; a threat to property is not enough unless it is to destroy the victim's dwelling.[719] The threat must be used to obtain the property or immediately retain it.[720] Here, M will argue that egging Mr. L's house was not a threat to destroy Mr. L's dwelling. However, the prosecution's argument is stronger because M threw an arrow that hit Mr. L's arm before M attempted to steal Mr. L's wallet. Thus, M's actions were a threat of immediate, serious physical harm to Mr. L's person.

Person or Presence

The property does not need to be taken from the victim's person, but must be taken from a location reasonably close to the victim.[721] Here, M ran up to Mr. L and put his hand in Mr. L's pocket, but realized there was no wallet to steal. This element is not met because no property was stolen. In conclusion, M is not liable for robbery, but might be liable for attempted robbery.

Attempted Robbery

See rules above. (Matthew's Crimes: Attempted Murder). Here, the actus reus is met under both tests because M did everything necessary to complete the crime. M hit Mr. L with an arrow to immobilize Mr. L and put his hand in Mr. L's pocket to take the wallet. The mens rea is also met because M's actions indicate he specifically intended to rob Mr. L. However, M will argue he is not guilty because he mistakenly believed that Mr. L had a wallet to steal.

Mistake of Fact

Mistake of fact negates the necessary mens rea. For specific intent crimes, the defendant is not guilty if the defendant's mistake about the factual circumstances was honest. For a general intent crime, the defendant is not guilty if his

---

718. *Carter v. United States*, 530 U.S. 255, 261 (2000).
719. Model Penal Code § 3.06 (Am. Law Inst., Proposed Official Draft 1962).
720. *Id.*
721. *United States v. Edwards*, 231 F.3d 933, 936 (5th Cir. 2000).

mistake was honest and reasonable.[722] Attempted robbery is a specific intent crime. Here, M's mistake was honest because he physically reached into Mr. L's pocket and found no wallet. M's actions suggest he believed Mr. L had a wallet.

However, mistake is not an available defense if the defendant would be guilty if the situation had been as he supposed.[723] If Mr. L did have a wallet in his pocket, then M would have taken the wallet and been guilty of robbery. Thus, mistake of fact is not a defense and M is guilty of attempted robbery.

(3) Karen's (K) Crimes

Accomplice Liability

Accomplice liability attaches to the crime committed by the principal if the accomplice knowingly aided in that crime.[724] At common law, the principal in the first degree (P1) is a party who commits the acts that constitute the crime. The principal in the second degree (P2) is a party who is present with P1 during the commission of the crime and intentionally assists P1. Accessory before the fact is a party who was not present with P1 during the commission of the crime, but intentionally assists P1 before the crime. Accessory after the fact is a party who was not present with P1 during the commission of the crime, but immediately assists P1 after the crime.[725] In modern jurisdictions, most courts do not distinguish between P1s, P2s, and accessories before the fact.[726] Here, K is an accessory after the fact because she hid M in her home after M attempted to rob and kill Mr. L.

Actus Reus

The accomplice's assistance does not need to be substantial; any aid will suffice, such as physical or psychological assistance, or failing to act when there is a duty to act.[727] Here, K agreed to physically conceal M from the authorities until things settled down. This element is met because M would have been apprehended earlier if K never hid him.

---

722. MPC § 2.04, supra note 564.
723. *Id.*
724. *Waddington v. Sarausad,* supra note 694.
725. *State v. Hamilton,* supra note 695.
726. *Id.*
727. *Waddington v. Sarausad,* supra note 694.

Mens Rea

The accomplice must knowingly help the principal commit the underlying prohibited conduct; the accomplice does not need specific knowledge of the elements of the principal's crime or to engage in any illegal conduct.[728] Here, no facts suggest K wanted M to kill or rob Mr. L, which means she did not want to bring about the prohibited conduct. K seemed to be helping a friend in need. Thus, K is not liable as M's accomplice.

---

728. *Id.* at 198.

Answer 8

(1) Sue's (S) Crimes
Rae's (R) Homicide

Homicide

Homicide is the killing of a human being.[729] Here, the actus reus is met because R died. The issue is whether the appropriate mens rea for murder was met.

Mens Rea

Murder is an unlawful killing with malice aforethought.[730] There are four types of common law murder: (a) intent to kill, (b) intent to inflict great bodily harm, (c) depraved heart murder, and (c) felony murder.[731] Express malice exists when there is intent to kill while implied malice refers to all other types of common law murder.[732]

(a) Intent to Kill

The use of a deadly weapon authorizes a permissive inference of intent to kill.[733] A deadly weapon is any instrument used in a manner likely to produce death or serious bodily injury.[734] Here, S will argue she had no intent to kill because a steak knife is not a deadly weapon. A steak knife is an eating utensil and not an object used for killing. However, this is a weak argument because a steak knife could cause serious bodily injury by piercing someone's skin and S screamed, "I should have killed both of you and not Tracy," before she grabbed a steak knife and stabbed R. S likely had the intent to kill.

(b) Intent to Cause Serious Bodily Injury

Here, S had intent to cause serious bodily injury because she intended to kill R.

---

729. MPC § 2.10.1, supra note 580.
730. *U.S. v. Pearson*, supra note 581.
731. *Id.*
732. *Gutierrez Marquez v. Gunn*, supra note 583.
733. *Perez v. Rozum*, supra note 584.
734. MPC § 2.10.0(4), supra note 585.

First-degree Versus Second-degree Murder

Today, modern statutes divide murders into two degrees: (a) first degree and (b) second degree. Most jurisdictions have two types of first-degree murder: first-degree felony murder and intent to kill with premeditation and deliberation.[735] All other killings at common law are considered second-degree murder.[736]

Here, S intended to kill R because she stabbed R with a knife after yelling "I should have killed both of you and not Tracy." The prosecution will argue S had at least mere seconds to reflect on her actions because it takes time to grab a knife from a nearby table. However, S will argue she did not reflect on the killing because R and Penny (P) surprised her at the bar. S did not prepare in advance to kill R, which is why S grabbed the first available weapon. Moreover, S was screaming and drunk when she killed R, which suggests she was acting in the heat of passion. The nightmares of Tracy's (T) murder clouded S's judgment. S was not acting with a cool head and cannot be guilty of first-degree murder.

S would be guilty of second-degree murder because she intended to cause serious bodily harm by stabbing R. But S will argue her murder charge should be mitigated to voluntary manslaughter.

Voluntary Manslaughter

S will argue her second-degree murder charge should be mitigated to voluntary manslaughter. Voluntary manslaughter is a killing in the heat of passion.[737] For the defendant to reduce murder to voluntary manslaughter, (a) there must be reasonable provocation, (b) the defendant must have been provoked, (c) a reasonable person would not have cooled off between the time of provocation and delivery of the fatal blow, and (d) the defendant must not have cooled offer during that interval.[738] Reasonable provocation is most frequently recognized as being subjected to a serious battery or threat of deadly force, or discovering one's spouse in bed with another person; mere words are usually not enough to constitute reasonable provocation.[739]

Here, S had a sudden and intense passionate response when P and R showed up to the bar because S suddenly started screaming and attacked them.

---

735. *Terry v. Potter,* supra note 593.

736. *United States v. Delaney,* supra note 598.

737. *Girouard v. State,* supra note 599.

738. *U.S. v. Jack,* supra note 600.

739. *Girouard v. State,* supra note 599.

Cooling Off

(c) The prosecution will argue a reasonable person would have cooled off by the time R entered the bar because T's death occurred weeks ago. However, this is a weak argument because a reasonable person would suffer from severe trauma if she was forced to kill a friend. A few weeks would not be enough to cool off and seeing the person who caused her friend's death could spark an angry reaction. (d) S did not cool off because she immediately confronted R and blamed R for T's death by screaming, "I should have killed both of you and not Tracy."

Provocation

(b) Here, S was actually provoked because she screamed and attacked P and R when she saw them in the bar. (a) The prosecution will argue no reasonable provocation existed because R never spoke a word to S when she entered the bar. A reasonable person would not try to kill people at the bar because she was upset about their past interactions. A reasonable person would have reported the incident to the police. However, S will argue a reasonable person, who was forced to kill her friend, would want revenge if she saw the people responsible for her friend's death. A reasonable person would feel scared, angry, and threatened and likely unable to control their emotional reactions. The prosecution has a stronger argument because reasonable people do not kill people who upset them.

Conclusion

If a reasonable person would have been provoked and not cooled off, then S would be guilty of voluntary manslaughter unless a defense applies.

Intoxication

Intoxication is not an affirmative defense, but it negates the mens reas of a crime.[740] Voluntary intoxication is only a defense to specific intent crimes; homicides are usually general intent crimes except for intent to kill with premeditation and deliberation.[741] If someone else is at fault for a defendant's intoxication, or the intoxication is a result of an innocent mistake, then the involuntary intoxication negates the mens rea for both specific intent and general intent crimes.[742] Here, S will argue she is not guilty because she was drunk when she confronted and stabbed R. However, S voluntarily drank at the bar to make the guilt and nightmares go away. Thus, S's argument is weak

---

740. *Montana v. Egelhoff*, 518 U.S. 37, 37-38 (1996).
741. *Id.* at 46.
742. *City of Minneapolis v. Altimus*, 238 N.W.2d 851, 858-59 (Minn. 1976).

and intoxication won't negate an element because no one forced S to get drunk. S is guilty of voluntary manslaughter if her reaction was reasonable enough to mitigate it from 2nd degree.

Attempted Murder of Penny (P)

Attempts are failed or incomplete efforts to commit a substantive offense. A criminal attempt occurs when a person, with the specific intent to commit an offense, performs acts towards the commission of that offense.[743]

Actus Reus

The defendant must commit an overt act that goes beyond mere preparation.[744] The two common tests are: the(a) dangerous proximity test and (b) substantial step test. The first test requires an act that is dangerously close to success; courts focus on how much remains to be done before the crime is committed.[745] The second test requires a substantial step towards completing the crime; the courts focus on how much of the crime was already completed.[746]

Here, S stabbed R, who was right next to P, and then chased P out of the bar with the steak knife. (b) S's actions are enough to constitute a substantial step towards killing P because S had a weapon and already used it to kill P's friend. (a) If S caught P, then the only step left would be to stab P, which is dangerously close to completion of the murder. Thus, the actus reus is met under both tests.

Mens Rea

The defendant must specifically intend to perform the actus reus and commit the underlying offense.[747] Here, S screaming, "I should have killed both of you and not Tracy," combined with her subsequent actions of chasing P with a steak knife is enough to show S intended to kill P. Thus, S is guilty of attempted murder.

(2) Defenses to Tracy's (T) Homicide

Duress

Duress is a complete defense if (a) another person threatened the defendant with imminent deadly or serious bodily injury; and (b) the defendant

---

743. MPC § 5.01(1), supra note 665.
744. *United States v. Howard*, supra note 666.
745. *Hyde v. United States*, supra note 667.
746. MPC § 5.01(1), supra note 665.
747. *United States v. Howard*, supra note 713.

reasonably believed the threat was real and would be carried out; and (c) the defendant had no reasonable opportunity to escape.[748]

Here, (a) P held S at gunpoint and threatened to kill S if S refused to kill T. (b) A reasonable person would believe P's threat was real because the gun was loaded and the women were in a desperate situation. The women faced possible death because they only had enough supplies to last a few days, which can cause individuals to act insane. (c) S had no route of escape from P because she was trapped in a cave. All the elements of duress are met, but duress is not a defense to intentional homicide.[749] In some jurisdictions, if the defendant kills someone and satisfies the elements of duress, then she is entitled to an imperfect duress defense, which mitigates mitigate murder to voluntary manslaughter.[750] Thus, S is guilty of voluntary manslaughter because she committed the killing under duress.

Mistake of Fact

Mistake of fact negates the necessary mens rea. For specific intent crimes, the defendant is not guilty if the defendant's mistake about the factual circumstances was honest. For a general intent crime, the defendant is not guilty if his mistake was honest and reasonable.[751] Homicide is usually a general intent crime except for intent to kill with premeditation and deliberation. However, mistake is not an available defense if the defendant would be guilty if the situation had been as he supposed.[752]

Here, S's belief was honest because S struggled to kill T and felt guilty after T's death. S believed T was still alive. A reasonable person might not check to see if T was alive before killing T because T was already in poor condition. However, the prosecution will argue mistake of fact is an invalid defense because if T was alive, then S administering the deadly dose of morphine would have killed T. S's stronger argument is that the actus reus, the killing of a human being, was not met because T was already a corpse and not alive.[753] Thus, S cannot be responsible for killing a dead person.

---

748. Model Penal Code § 2.09(1) (AM. LAW INST., Proposed Official Draft 1962).

749. *United States v. Mitchell*, 725 F.2d 832, 835 n.4 (2d Cir. 1983).

750. *Beardslee v. Woodford*, 358 F.3d 560, 576 (9th Cir. 2003).

751. MPC § 2.04, supra note 564.

752. *Id.*

753. *Beardslee v. Woodford*, supra note 750 at 577.

(3) Penny's (P) Crimes

Conspiracy to Kill Tracy

Conspiracy does not merge with the completed crime and carries its own penalty.[754] Conspiracy is an agreement by two or more persons to commit a criminal act or to accomplish a legal act by unlawful means.[755]

Agreement

An explicit or implicit agreement is sufficient to satisfy the actus reus requirement.[756] The parties do not need to know all the details or agree to all the acts, but the parties must be aware of the agreement's essential nature.[757] The bilateral approach requires two guilty minds,[758] and the unilateral approach requires one guilty mind.[759] A guilty mind requires genuine criminal intent to commit the underlying crime and join the conspiracy.

Here, P, R, and S never explicitly agreed to kill T. However, P and R likely had an implicit agreement to work together because P held S at gunpoint while R supplied S with the needle of morphine. P and R's actions suggest they conspired to kill T.

Overt Act

One of the conspirators must perform an overt act to show the conspiracy is in process and not purely in the minds of the conspirators.[760] Most jurisdictions require the overt act to further the conspiracy.[761] Here, P held S at gunpoint and R gave S morphine to kill T. Both conspirators committed an overt act.

Mens Rea

Conspirators must specifically intend to make the agreement and accomplish what was agreed upon.[762] Here, P intended to kill T because she believed T was sick and would die anyway. P likely had an implicit agreement with R to

---

754. *Iannelli v. U. S.*, supra not 675.
755. MPC § 5.03(4), supra note 676.
756. *United States v. Johnston*, supra note 677.
757. *United States v. Jimenez Recio*, supra note 678.
758. *United States v. Harris*, supra note 679.
759. MPC § 5.03, supra note 676.
760. *Id.*
761. *Id.*
762. *United States v. Feola*, supra note 684.

kill T, but more facts are necessary to determine P's actual intent. Thus, if P had the intent to enter an agreement with R, then P is guilty of conspiracy.

Accomplice Liability

Accomplice liability attaches to the crime committed by the principal if the accomplice knowingly aided in that crime.[763] At common law, the principal in the first degree (P1) is a party who commits the acts that constitute the crime. The principal in the second degree (P2) is a party who is present with P1 during the commission of the crime, and intentionally assists P1. Accessory before the fact is a party who was not present with P1 during the commission of the crime, but intentionally assists P1 before the crime. Accessory after the fact is a party who was not present with P1 during the commission of the crime, but immediately assists P1 after the crime.[764] In modern jurisdictions, most courts do not distinguish between P1s, P2s, and accessories before the fact.[765] Here, P is a P2 because she was present at the scene of the crime when S killed T.

Actus Reus

The accomplice's assistance does not need to be substantial; any aid will suffice, such as physical or psychological assistance, or failing to act when there is a duty to act.[766] Here, P did not provide physical assistance to S because R gave S the morphine. But P did provide psychological assistance by telling S that she must kill T to save herself.

Mens Rea

The accomplice must knowingly help the principal commit the underlying prohibited conduct; the accomplice does not need specific knowledge of the elements of the principal's crime or to engage in any illegal conduct.[767] Here, P told S to kill T or die in T's place. P's words show P wanted someone to kill T. P used S as the principal to commit the deed. Thus, P is guilty of T's murder under accomplice liability.

---

763. *Waddington v. Sarausad,* supra note 694.
764. *State v. Hamilton,* supra note 695.
765. *Id.*
766. *Waddington v. Sarausad,* supra note 694 at 185.
767. *Waddington v. Sarausad,* supra note 694 at 198.

Real Property Answers

Answer 1

(1) Cheng's (C) Interest in Wildwood (WW)

Discovery

For undiscovered land, the first possessor with the intent to possess the land and actual control of the property acquires ownership.[768] Here, WW was unclaimed land that C discovered while sailing. C intended to possess the land because she placed a flag on WW to claim the land. C had actual control because she asked her attorney to draft and record the deed to WW. Thus, as the original owner of WW, C could freely transfer the land to anyone.

(2) Amelia (A), Deborah (D), Phillip (P), and Nick's (N) Interests in Wildwood

At the Time of the Grant

C exercised her right to transfer the property by drafting a will. The issue is what type of interests C granted to A, D, P, and N. A present interest vests and becomes possessory at the moment of its creation.[769] Here, at the time of the grant, C had a life estate in WW. A life estate is a present interest given to a grantee for his or her life.[770]

A future interest requires a party to wait until a future time to obtain possession of the property.[771] A shifting executory interest is a future interest that cuts short a preceding estate and goes to a third party[772] whereas a remainder is an interest created in a third party that comes after the natural termination

---

768. *Johnson v. M'Intosh*, 21 U.S. 543, 569-570, 574 (1823).
769. Restatement (First) of Prop. § 153(3) (Am. Law Inst. 1936).
770. Restatement (First) of Prop. § 18 (Am. Law Inst. 1936).
771. Restatement (First) of Prop. § 153(1) (Am. Law Inst. 1936).
772. Restatement (First) of Prop. § 25 cmt. e (Am. Law Inst. 1936).

of the preceding estate.[773] A contingent remainder is subject to a condition precedent or limited to a person who is not ascertained.[774] But if the remainder is limited to an ascertained person and not subject to a condition precedent, then the remainder is vested.[775] A vested remainder can be subject to open, partial divestment, or total divestment, which means the party in possession can lose their interest partially or completely if a condition subsequent is satisfied. If a vested remainder is subject to open, then it means the grant went to a group of persons identified by a description and not by a name, and that others can enter the class until it closes.[776]

C's brother (B) had a vested remainder in a life estate because he would get the property when C died, which is after the natural end of C's life estate. M's children, A and D, had a vested remainder subject to open in fee simple because they existed at the time of the grant and would receive the property after the natural end of B's life estate. The gift to M's children was defeasible because more people could enter the class since M was still alive. An unborn child of M had an executory interest because the child's interest would divest the interest of the existing members of the class, A and D. M's existing and unborn children also had a vested remainder subject to total divestment because if A or D used the land for residential or commercial purposes, then the land would go to N for life.

N had a shifting executory interest in life estate because N's interest would cut off M's children's interests in WW. N's heirs had a contingent remainder in fee simple absolute because, before N's heirs' can obtain the property, A and D must use the land for residential or commercial purposes. N's heirs' have a remainder and not an executory interest because it comes after the natural end of N's life estate.

Rule Against Perpetuities (RAP)

RAP applies to executory interests, contingent remainders, and vested remainders subject to open or partial divestment.[777] RAP states no interest is good unless it vests within 21 years after some life in being at the time of the creation of the interest.[778] RAP limits the power of an owner to create future

---

773. *Doe, Lessee of Poor v. Considine*, 73 U.S. 458, 460 (1867).
774. *Id.* at 476.
775. *Id.* at 460.
776. *Id.* at 475.
777. Restatement (First) of Prop. § 372 (Am. Law Inst. 1944).
778. *Hopkins v. Grimshaw*, 165 U.S. 342, 355 (1897).

interests.[779] At common law, courts look at what might happen rather than what will actually happen.[780] If there is a logically probable result where the interest will fail to vest, then the grant is void.[781] Here, A and D will argue that the clause limiting the use of the land to exploring and granting N a future interest is void because the clause violates RAP. However, their argument is weak because the clause specifically limits the restricted use to A and D. Thus, A and D are the validating lives because they were alive at the time C created the grant. The clause is valid because N's interest will vest or not vest within A and D's lifetime.

Rule Against Restraints on Alienation

A grantor cannot prevent grantees from disposing of the property.[782] Any absolute restraint on alienation of a fee simple is void unless it is in a trust.[783] Partial restraints on alienation are allowed if reasonable.[784] To determine whether a provision is reasonable, the courts look at the purpose, nature, and duration of the restraint.[785]

Here, A and D will argue that limiting their right to sell and use the land was an unreasonable restraint on alienation because C completely restricted their right to do anything besides explore the land within their lifetime. If the court disagrees and determines the clause is a partial restraint, then A and D will argue the duration was unreasonable because it applied to their entire time of ownership. However, N will argue the nature of the restraint was reasonable because the provision did not apply to the entire group of grantees, M's children, but only two people, A and D. The purpose of the restriction was also reasonable because C wanted to preserve the land by preventing industrialization that would demolish the natural habitats. Thus, the restraint is likely a valid partial restraint.

The Rule in Shelley's Case and Merger Rule

Shelley's Case prevents grantors from creating remainders in a grantee's heirs.[786] For *Shelley's Case* to apply, the freehold estate must be given to the first

---

779. *Duke of Norfolk's Case*, 22 Eng. Rep. 931 (1682).

780. *Blackhurst v. Johnson*, 72 F.2d 644, 646 (8th Cir. 1934).

781. *Id.*

782. *Mountain Brow Lodge No. 82, Indep. Order of Odd Fellows v. Toscano*, 64 Cal. Rptr. 816, 821 (Cal. Ct. App. 1967).

783. Restatement (Second) of Prop.: Donative Transfers § 4.1(1) (Am. Law Inst. 1983).

784. Restatement (Second) of Prop.: Donative Transfers § 4.1(2) (Am. Law Inst. 1983).

785. *Id.*

786. *Webster v. Cooper*, 55 U.S. 488, 496 (1852).

transferee and the remainder must be limited to the heirs of the first transferee in the same instrument.[787] Here, N has a contingent remainder in life estate and N's heirs have a contingent remainder in fee simple. Under *Shelley's Case*, N's heirs' contingent remainder in fee simple will transform into N's contingent remainder because N has the right to name his heirs. Thus, because N holds both the remainder in life estate and remainder in fee simple in the same property, N's interests will merge into a fee simple absolute. In conclusion, N has a remainder in fee simple absolute in the property and not just a life estate.

After Cheng and Cheng's Brother's Death

Under the rule of convenience, an open class closes when a member of the class demands possession or distribution of the estate.[788] Members of the class cannot demand possession until the natural termination of the previous life estate, term of years, or until the divesting condition occurs.[789] Here, when C and B died in the car accident, their life estates ended and WW automatically passed to A and D, who were M's living children at the time B's life estate ended. The class closed when A demanded distribution of the interests. Once the class closed, none of M's future children could share in the gift. Thus, P, who was not born at the time A demanded distribution, has no interest in WW. A and D are joint owners and have a fee simple subject to an executory interest because if A or D sold the land or used it for another purpose other than exploring, then the property would pass to N in fee simple absolute.

After Amelia built a home on WW in 1996

A violated the land restriction provision because she used the land for residential purposes when she built a three-story house for her family. When the condition subsequent was satisfied, A and D were divested of their property and WW passed to N. Thus, N is the true owner of WW in 1996 and could only lose his interest if T adversely possessed against his interest.

(3) Theresa's (T) Interests in Wildwood

Adverse Possession

T's best argument is that she acquired superior title through adverse possession, which requires (a) actual, (b) exclusive, (c) open and notorious, (d)

---

787. *Id.* at 498–99.

788. Restatement (Third) of Prop.: Wills and Other Donative Transfers § 15.1 (Am. Law Inst. 2011).

789. *Cent. Trust Co. of N. Ohio v. Smith*, 553 N.E.2d 265, 271–72 (Ohio 1990).

adverse, and (e) continuous possession (f) for the statutory period.[790] Under color of title, a person with a title to the land will gain ownership of all the land described in the title, even if they never actually possessed the whole property.[791] The person only needs to possess a portion of the land in the deed.[792] Here, T cannot gain ownership of North, South, and West WW because she did not have the written deed to WW. However, if all the elements of adverse possession are met, T is the true owner of East WW because she actually possessed East WW.

(a) <u>Actual</u>: T must physically occupy the land in the same manner as a reasonable owner.[793] N will argue a reasonable owner would leave the island in its natural state so people could enjoy the land. However, T will argue a reasonable owner would operate a live-work coffee house to make a profit. It is more likely an owner would develop the property than leave it stagnant.

(b) <u>Exclusive</u>: T must exclude others in the way a reasonable owner would and not share possession with the true owner or general public.[794] Here, N will argue T was not exclusively possessing WW because A built a three-story house on West WW and T never asked to her leave. However, T did exclude others from East WW because T asked D to leave East WW. T's request showed she did not want to share her land with a stranger.

(c) <u>Open and Notorious</u>: The possession must be visible and obvious enough for a reasonable owner to receive actual or constructive notice of the adverse title claim.[795] Here, any reasonable owner inspecting WW would discover T's coffee shop because T's coffee shop regularly served sailors for more than ten years and was visible from the ocean, which means it was not hidden on the island. However, N will argue a reasonable owner would not constantly inspect an extremely large, uninhabited, and undeveloped island for settlers when C's grant restricted the use to exploring; this means that parties with an interest in the land could not develop the land. N's argument is weak because a reasonable owner would have discovered T's coffee shop within 11 years if they properly maintained their property.

---

790. *Ward v. Cochran*, 150 U.S. 597, 609 (1893).
791. *Bradshaw v. Stott*, 4 App. D.C. 527, 533 (D.C. Cir. 1894).
792. *Id.*
793. *Van Valkenburgh v. Lutz*, 106 N.E.2d 28, 31 (N.Y. 1952).
794. *Ward v. Cochran*, supra note 790 at 606.
795. *Bradshaw v. Stott*, supra note 791 at 534.

(d) <u>Adverse</u>: T's possession must be without permission from the true owner.[796] The majority rule does not consider the adverse possessor's state of mind, but the minority rule requires the trespasser to honestly believe she owns the land.[797] A rare minority requires the trespasser to know that she is possessing the land without permission from the owner; a mistaken possession would not constitute hostility.[798] Here, A and D filed a lawsuit after discovering T's presence, and N believes he is the sole owner of WW, which suggests no one gave T permission to use the land. Under the majority and minority, T honestly believed she was the owner because she asked D to leave her property. However, under the rare minority, T would lose because she did not purposely trespass on the land; the facts suggest T did not know someone else owned the land.

(e) <u>Continuous</u>: T must occupy the land in a reasonably continuous manner that is consistent with ownership of that land.[799] Here, this element is met because T set up the coffee shop in 1986, and the facts suggest T never stopped serving sailors since the opening. T's use of the land was also reasonable. See analysis above. (Theresa's Interests in Wildwood: Actual).

(f) <u>Statutory Period and Tacking</u>: T will argue that the statutory period of 10 years was met because T openly and adversely ran the coffee shop for 11 years. However, the statutory period does not begin to run against a person with a future interest until the future interest vests and becomes possessory.[800] If the adverse possessor enters before the grantor divides his interest in the land, then the subsequent owners' possessions can be tacked to satisfy the statutory period. However, if the adverse possessor enters after the interests were divided, then the owners' interests cannot be tacked.[801]

Here, T cannot tack A, D, and N's interests because T entered East WW in 1986, which was after C divided the interests through her will in 1980. N's future interest did not vest until A satisfied the condition precedent by using West WW for residential purposes in 1996. A year later, A and D discovered T's coffee shop and filed a lawsuit. This means T only adversely possessed against N for one year after N's interest vested. Thus, T is not the true owner of WW because she did not adversely possess for 10 years.

---

796. *Chaplin v. Sanders*, 676 P.2d 431, 434 (Wash. 1984).
797. *Id.*
798. *Id.* at 434-435.
799. *Ward v. Cochran*, 150 U.S. 597, 607 (1893).
800. *Baylor v. Soska*, 658 A.2d 743, 745 (Pa. 1995).
801. *Id.*

Answer 2

(1) Ownership of Marshlands

(a) At the Time of the Grant

Garrett (G) had a life estate because Michelle (M) granted the property to him for the duration of his lifetime.[802] Elly (E) had a contingent remainder because E's interest followed the natural end of G's life estate and whether E's interest became possessory depended on if she satisfied the condition precedent,[803] which was graduating from college.

G's children, Alice (A) and Francis (F), and E had alternative contingent remainders because, depending on whether the condition was met, only one of the named parties in the grant would take the property.[804] Either E would take the land if she graduated from college within her lifetime or G's children would have the option to purchase the land if E did not graduate. Rachel (R) had a contingent remainder in fee simple absolute because her interest would not become possessory unless E failed to graduate from college and G's children refused to purchase the land.

Rule Against Perpetuities (RAP)

RAP applies to executory interests, contingent remainders, and vested remainders subject to open or partial divestment.[805] RAP states no interest is good unless it vests within 21 years after some life in being at the time of the creation of the interest.[806] RAP limits the power of an owner to create future interests.[807] At common law, courts look at what might happen rather than what will happen.[808] If there is a logically probable result where the interest will fail to vest, then the grant is void.[809] Here, A will argue that E's remainder violates RAP, but A's argument is weak because E is the validating life; we will know if E graduated from college within 21 years of her life. Thus, E will succeed in preserving her future interest in Marshlands.

---

802. R. of Prop. § 18, supra note 770.
803. *Doe, Lessee of Poor v. Considine*, supra note 773.
804. *Boal v. Metropolitan Museum of Art of City of New York*, 298 F. 894, 903 (2d Cir. 1924).
805. R. of Prop. § 372, supra note 777.
806. *Hopkins v. Grimshaw*, supra note 778.
807. *Duke of Norfolk's Case*, supra note 779.
808. *Blackhurst v. Johnson*, supra note 780.
809. *Id.*

(b) Garrett's Death

At common law, a contingent remainder is destroyed if it does not vest at or before the termination of all preceding life estates.[810] However, almost all jurisdictions have abolished this rule and instead give a reversion to the transferor and an executory interest to the third-party who originally had the contingent remainder.[811] Here, when G died, E had not graduated from college. Thus, because the condition precedent was not met and E's interest had not vested, Marshlands went back to M in a reversion. M had a fee simple subject to E's springing executory limitation, which was springing because it cut off the interest of the transferor, M, and did not follow a natural end.[812] A, F, and R still had contingent remainders because E was still alive and could graduate from college before her death.

(c) Michelle's Sale to Alice and Francis

A and F will argue that M had a fee simple in Marshlands, which made M the true owner and allowed M to freely transfer the land so long as it did not violate another person's right in the property. Thus, M could sell the land to A and F because E had not fulfilled the condition precedent. However, A and F's argument is incorrect because E had the remainder of her lifetime to graduate from college. M should have transferred the land with the caveat that the ownership is subject to the same limitations attached to M's interest. A and F could only purchase a fee simple subject to total divestment.

(d) Elly Graduates from College

A and F were the valid owners of the home for the two years between G's death and E's graduation from college. However, once E graduated from college, the condition precedent was met and E's interest vested. E had a fee simple absolute, A and F no longer had the option to repurchase the land, and R had no future interest in the land.

True Owner

The true owner is E. A and F will need to sue M to collect losses from the sale.

---

810. *District of Columbia v. Clark*, 175 F.2d 821, 824 (D.C. Cir. 1948).
811. *Id.*
812. R. of Prop. § 25 cmt. e, supra note 772.

(2) Waste on Marshlands

An implied covenant to not commit waste exists in every grant unless the grant specifically states the life tenant would not be impeached for waste.[813] Any act of a life tenant that permanently injuries the property is actionable by the remainderman.[814] Wear and tear is allowed, but the land must be presented to future interest holders in the same condition it was received.[815] Voluntary waste is when a life tenant actively uses or changes the property's condition in a way that significantly decreases the property's value.[816] Permissive waste is when inaction occurs or the owner fails to exercise reasonable care to prevent harm to the property.[817] Future interest owners can be compensated for both voluntary and permissive waste.

Here, the future interest owners, E, A, F, and R, have a claim for permissive waste because the floors and walls were infested with mold. G's failure to clean is a form of neglect because a reasonable owner would regularly maintain the home. G is also liable for voluntary waste because his house parties damaged the grass and fence. A reasonable owner would not host uncontrollable parties. Thus, G decreased the property's value because the ruined grass makes the yard unattractive, the mold needs to be removed to prevent people from falling sick, and the fence will need to be repaired.

Ameliorating Waste

A life tenant is allowed to make reasonable changes in the use or condition of the property if it increases the property's value.[818] Ameliorating waste is not compensable if the current property was no longer suitable for the purpose it was being used.[819] Here, G's renovated granite kitchen increased the value of the property. Although tearing down the old kitchen seems wasteful, a reasonable owner would have replaced the broken stoves with equipment that worked properly.

---

813. *United States v. Bostwick*, 94 U.S. 53, 65–66 (1876).

814. *Id.*

815. *Id.* at 54.

816. *Id.* at 69.

817. *Kimbrough v. Reed*, 943 P.2d 1232, 1233 (Idaho 1997).

818. *Melms v. Pabst Brewing Co.*, 79 N.W. 738, 739 (Wis. 1899).

819. *Id.*

Conclusion

When a life tenant commits waste, he is liable for the amount that was wasted and shall lose the thing wasted.[820] G will be liable for his voluntary and permissive waste minus the value he added for installing the new kitchen. G would normally lose the land, but because G died and the land is now in possession of another, his estate only needs to pay damages to the future interest owners.

(3) Rights and Duties of Co-Tenants

Joint Tenancy

If two or more persons own an interest in the same land, then they are co-owners and considered one entity in joint tenancy, tenancy in common, or tenancy by the entirety. To create a joint tenancy, four unities must be met: (a) the interests must vest at the same time, (b) the interests must be acquired in the same written instrument, (c) the interests must be equal shares of the same estate, and (d) each must have the right to possess the whole.[821] Joint tenants have a right of survivorship, which means when one joint tenant dies, the deceased tenant's interest goes to the surviving tenant.[822]

Here, A and F obtained the property (a) at the same time and (b) in the same instrument because they purchased the land from M together. (d) Although F let A live in the home, A never told F he could not use the property. Thus, each has the right to possess the whole. (c) However, their interests in the property are unequal because A paid $80,000 and F paid $40,000. The default presumption is the additional payment was a gift.[823] The presumption can be rebutted by evidence that the parties intended the extra payment to be a loan or intended to take as tenants in common by dividing the land pro rata.[824] F and A were likely not joint tenants because F said A owned more of the house. F's comment indicates they did not have equal shares because they intended to divide the house according to their contributions. F and A were likely not joint tenants. Thus, A's share in the property did not transfer to F upon A's death.

---

820. *Kimbrough v. Reed*, supra note 817 at 1233-1234.
821. *Riddle v. Harmon*, 162 Cal. Rptr. 530, 531 (Cal. Ct. App. 1980).
822. *Id.*
823. *In re Shelton*, 334 B.R. 174, 176–77 (Bankr. D. Md. 2005).
824. *Id.*

Tenants in Common

If one of the four unities does not exist, then the co-ownership is a tenancy in common where both parties have the right to possess the whole, cannot exclude each other, and can freely assign, alienate, devise, and divide the property.[825] When A died, her two-thirds share in Marshlands went to R because she devised her shares to R and the right of survivorship did not exist. As a result, R and F owned the land as tenants in common. F cannot eject R from the land because he is not the sole owner and R has a right to possess the whole property.

Right to Rent

The majority rule states the tenant in possession does not owe rent to other cotenants for reasonable exclusive use of the property.[826] However, the tenant in possession must share net profits from the lease with a third party based on each cotenant's pro rata share of the property.[827] Net means the cotenant may offset rent revenues by costs associated with generating and collecting rent. Here, F is entitled to one-third of the monthly rental proceeds from the tenant minus any costs A incurred from renting the property.

Right to Contribution for the Mortgage

The tenant in possession can demand the pro rata share of expenses from his cotenant in carrying charges, such as property taxes and interests on mortgages, even if the cotenant is not in possession of the property.[828] Here, F must pay one-third of the mortgage payments even though he is out of possession. If F does not pay the mortgage, then R can seek contribution.[829]

Right to Contribution for Repairs

Cotenants have no duty to make repairs unless ordered by a city ordinance.[830] However, a cotenant can seek contribution for necessary repairs that were not for cosmetic purposes.[831] If the cotenant in possession seeks contribution for repairs, then the cotenant out of possession can offset these expenses

---

825. *Second Realty Corp. v. Krogmann*, 235 F.2d 510, 512 (D.C. Cir. 1956).
826. *Spiller v. Mackereth*, 334 So. 2d 859, 861 (Ala. 1976).
827. *Id.*
828. *Reitmeier v. Kalinoski*, 631 F.Supp. 565 (D.N.J. 1986).
829. *Id.*
830. *Melnick v. Press*, 809 F.Supp.2d 43 (E.D.N.Y. 2011).
831. *Reitmeier v. Kalinoski*, supra note 828 at 581.

against the reasonable value of the cotenant in possession's exclusive use and occupation of the property.[832] Here, R is only entitled to contribution if the repairs made by A were necessary. A's repairs were likely necessary because if the mold was not removed, then the home would be uninhabitable. F will argue fixing the fence and grass were cosmetic repairs, but his argument is weak because "A's repairs made the home a livable space." Thus, R can collect one-third of the $50,000 from F minus the reasonable value of A and R's exclusive possession of Marshlands.

---

832. *In re Fazzio*, 180 B.R. 263 (Bankr. E.D. Cal. 1995).

Answer 3

(1) Max's (M) Ownership Claim

Joint Tenancy

If two or more persons own an interest in the same land, then they are co-owners and considered one entity in joint tenancy, tenancy in common, or tenancy by the entirety. To create a joint tenancy, four unities must be met: (a) the interests must vest at the same time, (b) the interests must be acquired in the same written instrument, (c) the interests must be equal shares of the same estate, and (d) each must have the right to possess the whole.[833] Joint tenants have a right of survivorship, which means when one joint tenant dies, the deceased tenant's interest goes to the surviving tenant.[834]

Here, Katherine (K) and Shane (S) were joint tenants because they (a) purchased the condo at the same time and (b) the deed included both their names. (c) K and S's interests were equal because they evenly shared the costs of the home and (d) they moved in together, which showed they each had a right to possess the whole.

Tenancy by the Entirety (TBE)

TBE requires the same four unities as JT, but also requires the parties to be married at the time they acquired the property; engagement is insufficient.[835] Here, K and S were engaged when they purchased the condo. They did not get married until after they moved into the home. Thus, there was no TBE, and K and S were joint tenants.

Severance

One spouse cannot unilaterally sever a TBE and neither spouse can seek judicial partition.[836] TBE can only be terminated by the death of a spouse, divorce, or mutual agreement, such as legal separation.[837] However, for a joint tenancy, unilateral separation and judicial partition are available.[838] If one party conveys his or her interest to another party, then the conveyance severs the joint

---

833. *Riddle v. Harmon*, supra note 821.
834. *Id.*
835. *United States v. Craft*, 535 U.S. 274, 280 (2002).
836. *Id.* at 281.
837. *Deutsche Bank Nat. Trust Co. v. Evans*, 421 B.R. 193, 197 (W.D. Pa. 2009).
838. *United States v. Craft*, supra note 835 at 281.

tenancy and right of survivorship.[839] Severance results in the transferee and other joint tenant(s) holding the property as tenants in common where both parties have the right to possess the whole, cannot exclude each other, and can freely assign, alienate, devise, and divide the property.[840]

Here, S will argue that K could not sell the land to Max (M) because the property belonged to S and K as husband and wife. S never consented to the sale and they were legally married because they never filed for a divorce. However, this argument is weak because S and K were not married when they obtained the property; they were joint tenants. Thus, K could unilaterally alienate her property. K's sale to M severed the joint tenancy; K no longer had an interest in the condo, and S and M became tenants in common.

Adverse Possession

S and K can argue they acquired superior title to M if they acquired the condo through adverse possession, which requires (a) actual, (b) exclusive, (c) open and notorious, (d) adverse, and (e) continuous possession (f) for the statutory period.[841] Under color of title, a person with a title to the land will gain ownership of all the land described in the title, even if they never actually possessed the whole property.[842] The person only needs to possess a portion of the land in the deed.[843] Here, S and K possessed the whole condo by living in the home. If all the elements of adverse possession are met, then they will get title to the entire property.

(a) <u>Actual</u>: S and K must physically occupy the land in the same manner as a reasonable owner.[844] Here, this element is met because S and K were reasonably using the property as a residential space by living in the condo.

(b) <u>Exclusive</u>: S and K must exclude others the way a reasonable owner would and not share possession with the true owner or general public.[845] No facts suggest S and K shared ownership with anyone. S and K excluded M from the condo because M was not successful in evicting them.

---

839. *Id.* at 280.

840. *Second Realty Corp. v. Krogmann*, 235 F.2d 510, 512 (D.C. Cir. 1956). See also *United States v. Craft*, supra note 835.

841. *Ward v. Cochran*, supra note 799 at 609.

842. *Bradshaw v. Stott*, supra note 791.

843. *Id.*

844. *Van Valkenburgh v. Lutz*, supra note 793.

845. *Ward v. Cochran*, supra note 799 at 606.

(c) <u>Open and Notorious</u>: The possession must be visible and obvious enough for a reasonable owner to receive actual or constructive notice of the adverse title claim.[846] Any owner who viewed the apartment would see S and K were living in the condo. When M returned after his prison sentence, he immediately realized S and K occupied the property. This element is met.

(d) <u>Adverse</u>: S and K's possession must be without permission from the true owner.[847] The majority rule does not consider the state of mind of the adverse possessor, but the minority rule requires the trespasser to honestly believe she owns the land.[848] Here, S cannot adversely possess the condo because he has a right to possess the whole property as a tenant in common.[849] The statutory period only begins to run when one tenant in common ousts another tenant in common by providing unequivocal and actual notice of his adverse claim to the other party; mere acts inconsistent with the other cotenant's rights is not enough.[850] S's possession was not adverse because he entered the apartment using his own key and lived in the condo as the cotenant in possession for five years. However, K will argue she adversely possessed against M's interest because she was not a tenant in common. K's argument will fail because K had permission from S, one of the true owners, to live on the property.

(e) <u>Continuous</u>: S and K must occupy the land in a reasonably continuous manner that is consistent with ownership of that land.[851] This element is met because S and K lived in the condo for five years without interruption.

(f) <u>Statutory Period and Tacking</u>: S and K lived in the home for the statutory period of 5 years. However, a disability that exists at the time the adverse possession began will toll the statute of limitations.[852] Disabilities include infancy, imprisonment, and mental incompetence.[853] However, once the statute of limitations begins to run, then it continues without interruption, notwithstanding any subsequent disabilities that befalls the owner.[854] Here, M will argue the statutory period was tolled during the four years he was imprisoned. M's argument will fail because M was not sentenced until a year after S and K

---

846. *Bradshaw v. Stott*, supra note 791 at 534.
847. *Chaplin v. Sanders*, supra note 796.
848. *Id.*
849. *Elder v. McClaskey*, 70 F. 529 (6th Cir. 1895).
850. *Id.* at 545.
851. *Ward v. Cochran*, supra note 790 at 607.
852. *McDonald v. Hovey*, 110 U.S. 619, 621 (1884).
853. *Id.* at 620.
854. *Id.* at 624.

moved into the condo. Thus, M's disability began after the statutory period started to run.

Conclusion

S and K did not acquire the land through adverse possession because S had the right to possess the condo and K had permission to live on the land.

Good Faith Improvements

Although S and K are unlikely to gain legal title, they can claim reimbursement for improvements that increased the property's value.[855] If the improvements were made in good faith, then M must pay the fair market value of the improvements.[856] Here, K was not a good-faith improver because two years before she reconciled with S, she conveyed her interest in the condo to M. K should have remembered that she sold the property to a third party.

S honestly believed he owned the property because he did not know that K sold the land to M. However, a cotenant cannot seek contribution for cosmetic repairs; co-tenants can only claim contribution for necessary repairs.[857] Here, a new fireplace and home stereo system are cosmetic renovations because they are not essential to the habitability of the home. Thus, S is unlikely to recover for his improvements.

Fixtures

When a person attaches his property to the land of another without an agreement permitting him to remove it, then the thing affixed belongs to the owner of the land.[858] A fixture becomes permanent if: (a) it is attached to the property, physically or constructively, (b) it was connected to the property for a particular use and used in that manner, and (c) the person who attached it had the actual or inferred intent to make it permanent.[859]

Here, M will argue the fixtures became permanent. S and K (a) attached the fireplace because it was built into the home. S and K also attached the home stereo system by latching it onto the walls. (b) The fireplace was connected to make the home warmer and the home stereo system improved the in-home entertainment experience. (c) S and K likely intended to attach the fireplace

---

855. *Anderson v. Reid,* 14 App.D.C. 54, 60 (D.C. Cir. 1899).
856. *Id.* at 76.
857. *Reitmeier v. Kalinoski,* supra note 828 at 581. See also *Melnick v. Press,* supra note 830.
858. *Ballard v. Alaska Theater Co.,* 161 P. 478, 482 (Wash. 1916).
859. *In re Joseph,* 450 B.R. 679 (Bankr. E.D. Mich. 2011).

and home stereo system permanently because they attached them to the walls and lived in the house as true owners for five years. No facts suggest S and K planned to move when they affixed the objects. Thus, the fireplace and stereo system became part of the condo. However, M does not have the sole right to the property because S is a cotenant. Thus, S owns 50% of the fireplace and home stereo system. S can make changes and remove the fixtures as long as he does not commit waste that will negatively impact M's interest.

(2) Shane's (S) Claims

S will argue that since they were married, he had a 50% interest in K's sale to M. However, S and K never created a TBE. See analysis above. (Max's Ownership Claim: Tenancy by the Entirety). Thus, S has no interest in K's sale to M and will receive $0 of the $100,000.

(3) Bank's Claims

K is no longer responsible for the mortgage payments. M assumed K's benefits and liabilities related to the condo when he purchased the property. Thus, the bank cannot collect mortgage payments from K and must sue the tenants in common, S and M.

Answer 4

(1) Landlord (L) vs. Arthur (A)

Type of Leasehold

A lease is a non-freehold estate that gives the tenant exclusive possession of the property for a period of time in exchange for rent; the owner retains a reversion.[860] A lease term longer than a year must be in writing.[861] Here, the writing is satisfied because L and Tenant (T) entered a written contract. The leasehold is a tenancy for years because the lease has a definite start date and end date; February 1, 2000 to January 31, 2003.[862]

Renewed Lease

No notice is required to end a tenancy for years because the expiration is automatic and self-executing.[863] However, for a periodic tenancy, where the terms indefinitely continue day-to-day, week-to-week, month-to-month, or year-to-year, notice of termination is required.[864] Notice must be equal to the length of the tenancy and include an explicit termination date.[865] The only exception is the yearlong lease that allows a six-month notice rather than a year.[866] If the term's length is not stipulated, then the term conforms to the frequency of rent payments.[867] Here, the tenancy for years ended automatically on January 31, 2003. A will argue that after January 31st, the lease became a month-to-month periodic tenancy because the rental payments were due on the 1st of every month. Thus, A could terminate the lease anytime with proper notice. However, A will be liable for the remainder of the lease term for the final month because he moved out without giving L notice a month in advance.

L will argue A renewed the original lease by staying on the property after the lease term ended. A tenancy at sufferance is a type of wrongful occupation where the tenant remains on the land in a voluntary, wrongful, and nontrivial

---

860. *City of Los Angeles v. San Pedro Boat Works*, 635 F.3d 440 (9th Cir. 2011).

861. *U.S. Postal Service v. American Postal Workers Union*, 367 Fed.Appx. 971 (11th Cir. 2010).

862. *National Bellas Hess, Inc. v. Kalis*, 191 F.2d 739, 740 (8th Cir. 1951).

863. *In re Reef Petroleum Corp.*, 51 B.R. 949, 951 (Bankr. W.D. Mich. 1985).

864. *In re Van Vleet*, 383 B.R. 782, 791 (Bankr. D. Colo. 2008).

865. *Id.*

866. *In re Foote*, 277 B.R. 393, 397 (Bankr. E.D. Ark. 2002).

867. *Ruiz v. New Garden Tp.*, 376 F.3d 203, 206 (3d Cir. 2004).

manner after the lease term ends.[868] In these situations, the landlord has three options: (a) the landlord can enter a tenancy at will with the holdover tenant, (b) consent to tenant's continued possession and renew the original lease, or (c) evict the tenant as a trespasser and recover damages.[869] Under the majority rule, the landlord consents to the tenancy by accepting rent.[870] If the landlord consents, then the new term is the same duration as the original lease.[871] However, courts are unlikely to make holdover tenants liable for more than a year because it is too harsh.

Here, L had the right to renew the original lease rather than enter a tenancy at will because A stayed on the property until May 15th. L will argue the three-year tenancy in the original lease should apply, but the court is more likely to enforce a lease term of one year. A will argue that L accepted monthly payments, which shows L consented to a month-to-month periodic tenancy. A's argument is weak because A stopped paying rent in December 2002, a month before the least term ended. The month-to-month payments applied to the original lease that existed before the holdover tenancy began. Thus, A is liable for another year of rent plus the last month of rent from the original lease unless L violated the terms of the lease first.

Duty to Pay Rent

The assignee is in privity of estate because both the landlord and assignee have an interest in the leased property; the assignee has the current right to possess the land and the landlord has a reversion after the lease term ends.[872] Here, A breached a covenant in the lease by failing to pay rent while in possession of the premises. However, A will argue he validly withheld rent because L failed to repair the plumbing and breached the implied warranties in the lease.

Duty to Repair

A residential tenant is responsible for minor repairs to the property, but the landlord must ensure the premises meets basic health and safety standards.[873] Here, the clause requiring the tenant to repair everything inside the apartment

---

868. *Herter v. Mullen*, 53 N.E. 700, 702 (N.Y. 1899).

869. *Semmes v. U.S.*, 14 Ct.Cl. 493, 503 (Ct. Cl. 1878).

870. *Dale v. H.B. Smith Co., Inc.*, 136 F.3d 843, 847 (1st Cir. 1998).

871. *Security Life & Acc. Ins. Co. v. U. S.*, 357 F.2d 145, 150 (5th Cir. 1966).

872. *Hillside Metro Associates, LLC v. JPMorgan Chase Bank, Nat. Ass'n*, 747 F.3d 44, 50 (2d Cir. 2014).

873. *Towers Tenant Ass'n, Inc. v. Towers Ltd. Partnership*, 563 F.Supp. 566, 573 (D.D.C. 1983).

will not preclude A from recovery because L cannot waive his duty to make necessary repairs.[874] Humans need a clean and safe place to defecate. Thus, L's failure to repair the plumbing constituted a constructive eviction and A had the right to withhold rent.

Implied Warranty of Habitability

This covenant only applies to residential leases and requires the landlord to keep the premises in a safe and habitable state for the tenant.[875] A breach of this warranty requires: (a) notice of the defective condition to the landlord, (b) a substantial defect, which is determined by the effect on the tenant's health and safety, length of time it exists, and whether it violates housing codes, and (c) failure by the landlord to make the repair within a reasonable time.[876]

Here, (a) A immediately notified L that the plumbing in one of the bathrooms was not working. (c) L failed to make the repair within a reasonable time because the plumbing remained broken for five months. (b) A will argue the defect was substantial because he paid rent for two working bathrooms and one was broken for almost half a year. Plumbing problems cause sewage backup and water damage, which generates mold that can seriously impact a tenant's health. However, L will argue A never mentioned mold or sewage problems and there was another bathroom that A could have used as an alternative. L's argument is weak because the length of time and potential health hazards were substantial. A had the right to withhold rent.

Implied Covenant of Quiet Enjoyment

Tenants have the right to quiet and peaceful possession of the property for the term without the landlord or anyone else interfering with their use and enjoyment.[877] A breach of this covenant requires: (a) intentional acts of the landlord or someone acting on behalf of the landlord (b) that cause a substantial interference with the tenant's enjoyment of the premises or renders the premises unfit for the purpose for which it was leased, and (c) that the tenant vacates the premises (d) within a reasonable time after landlord's actions.[878]

---

874. *Id.*
875. *Miller v. Christian*, 958 F.2d 1234, 1238 (3d Cir. 1992).
876. *Hilder v. St. Peter*, 478 A.2d 202, 210 (Vt. 1984).
877. *Blackett v. Olanoff*, 358 N.E.2d 817, 818 (Mass. 1977).
878. *Id.*

Here, (a) L intentionally interfered with A's peaceful possession because L sent a debt collector to A's home every weekend to request payment. (b) A will argue that a debt collector's weekly request for money is a substantial interference of someone's enjoyment of the land because it is harassment. L will argue A had a duty to pay rent and the debt collector was protecting L's rights. Moreover, A's use of the property was not compromised because the debt collector only came on weekends for a month, which is a total of four times. (c) A vacated the property on May 15th, which was a month after the debt collector's first appearance, which is (d) a reasonable time because most people take more than a month to relocate. In conclusion, L breached the implied covenant of quiet enjoyment because L trespassed through a debt collector.

Self-Help

L should have used proper channels to evict A. Before a landlord can evict a tenant, the landlord must give the tenant notice to remedy the default or vacate the premises.[879] For a residential lease, the majority rule is that a landlord cannot use self-help, which is any excessive force to regain possession of the leased premises, to evict a tenant who failed to pay rent.[880] The landlord must use the state's summary eviction proceedings or ejectment to evict tenants.[881] Here, L incorrectly used self-help by changing the locks. L inappropriately prevented A from entering his home. L will argue a minority of jurisdictions allows self-help to be carried out without a breach of peace.[882] L never used violence, but peacefully limited L's access to the building. However, L's argument will fail because peaceful self-help tends to apply to personal property, such as repossession of vehicles.

Total and Partial Eviction

In conclusion, L breached several implied covenants in the lease before A breached the duty to pay rent. A complete eviction occurs when the landlord excludes the tenant from the premises[883] whereas a partial eviction occurs when part of the property is withheld from the tenant.[884] A constructive eviction is

---

879. *Kassan v. Stout*, 507 P.2d 87, 89 (Cal. 1973).
880. Restatement (Second) of Prop.: Landlord and Tenant § 14.2 (Am. Law Inst. 1977).
881. *Velazquez v. Thompson*, 451 F.2d 202, 204 (2d Cir. 1971).
882. *Albertorio-Santiago v. Reliable Financial Services*, 612 F.Supp.2d 159 (D.P.R. 2009).
883. *In re Full House Foods, Inc.*, 279 B.R. 71 (Bankr. S.D.N.Y. 2002).
884. Restatement (Second) of Prop.: Landlord and Tenant § 6.1 cmt. h (Am. Law Inst. 1977).

when the landlord violates an implied covenant in the lease.[885] If these covenants are violated, then the tenant can terminate the lease and sue for damages if they vacate within a reasonable time. If the tenant does not vacate within a reasonable time, then the tenant waived the implied covenants.[886] Here, A vacated the premises on May 15th; A can sue for damages, claim constructive eviction and terminate the lease, stop paying rent, or reduce the rent until the repairs are completed.

(2) Landlord (L) v. Tenant (T)

Assignment or Sublease

An assignment is the transfer of an entire property interest for the unexpired remainder term.[887] A sublease is a partial transfer to a sublessee for less than the full remaining term of the lease; the tenant retains some interest in the term.[888] Here, T assigned her interest to A because she transferred the remainder of the lease to A. T lived on the property for two years out of the three-year lease term and transferred the final year of her interest to A. Thus, T retained no interest in the property.

Consent from Landlord

A leasehold is freely transferable absent an express condition in the contract that creates a reasonable restriction on transfers. Transfers without consent are not void, but voidable at the option of the landlord.[889] The landlord can accept the rent from the transferee and waive consent or evict the transferee.[890] Here, the lease stated T could not assign the lease without written consent from the landlord. T violated this term by transferring the property without written consent from L. However, L accepted rent from A for 11 months, which means L consented to the transfer and cannot sue T for any damages caused by A's failure to pay rent after the lease term ended. However, L can still sue T for the last month of rent because T is in privity of contract with L.

---

885. *Id.* at cmt. e.

886. *Lavin v. Emery Air Freight Corp.*, 980 F.Supp. 93 (D. Conn. 1997).

887. *Mire v. Sunray DX Oil Co.*, 285 F.Supp. 885, 890 (W.D. La. 1968).

888. *Id.*

889. *Ring v. Mpath Interactive, Inc.*, 302 F.Supp.2d 301 (S.D.N.Y. 2004). See also *Amjems, Inc. v. F.R. Orr Const. Co., Inc.*, 617 F.Supp. 273 (S.D. Fla. 1985).

890. *Id.*

Tenant's Liability for Rent

After an assignment, the original tenant is no longer in privity of estate with the landlord because the tenant has no right to possess the property.[891] However, the original tenant is in privity of contract because the lease is a valid contract.[892] The landlord can sue the original tenant, but the original tenant can assert the same defenses as the assignee who possessed the land. Here, L sued T for rent payments up to May 15, 2003. After January 31, 2003, T is not responsible for payments because the contract term expired. However, T is liable for the final month of rent that A failed to pay unless A successfully proves he had the right to withhold rent. See analysis above. (Landlord v. Arthur).

---

891. *Jack Burton Management Co. v. American Nat. Ins. Co.*, 77 F.Supp.2d 1102, 1105 (E.D. Mo. 1999).

892. *Mire v. Sunray DX Oil Co.*, supra note 887.

Answer 5

(1) Building a Large Billboard

Express Easements

An easement is a non-possessory right to enter and use another's land for specific purposes; the landowner cannot unreasonably interfere with the easement holder's use.[893] To create an express easement there must be a writing that includes the precise location of the easement, specifies the use of the easement, and identifies who is burdened by the easement.[894] Here, an express easement was created because Charlie (C), Mia (M), and Jerry (J) agreed in writing that they would not build any structure on the roof. Each party was burdened by the easement because they could not develop their property upwards. However, Sylvia (S) is only bound by this easement if the negative easement transferred to her purchase of C's property.

Types of Easements

Easements in gross benefit a specific person regardless of whether that person owns any specific property[895] whereas an appurtenant easement benefits the owner or possessor of that particular parcel of land.[896] Negative easements prevent the owner of the burdened estate from acting[897] whereas affirmative easements give the holder of the easement the right to use the burdened estate for a specific purpose.[898] Unless a statute says otherwise, the only recognized negative easements are rights to airflow, light, channeled water flow, and lateral support.[899]

Here, C, M, and J created a negative appurtenant easement because their agreement prevented owners of Shopacre from erecting structures on the roof of their properties. The easement was not attached to a single person and restricted the use and enjoyment of the property. However, under common law, blocking someone's view of the mountains is not recognized as an easement.

---

893. Restatement (Third) of Property (Servitudes) § 1.2 (2000).

894. Restatement (Third) of Property (Servitudes) § 2.1 (2000).

895. *Sunset Lake Water Service Dist. v. Remington*, 45 Or.App. 973 (Or. Ct. App. 1980).

896. *In re Flyboy Aviation Properties, LLC*, 501 B.R. 808 (Bankr. N.D. Ga. 2013).

897. *Sabine River Authority v. U.S. Dept. of Interior*, 951 F.2d 669, 679 (5th Cir. 1992).

898. *C/R TV, Inc. v. Shannondale, Inc.*, 27 F.3d 104 (4th Cir. 1994).

899. *Petersen v. Friedman*, 162 Cal.App.2d 245 (1958). See also *Moore v. Shoemaker*, 10 App.D.C. 6, 16 (D.C. Cir. 1897).

Thus, the easement is invalid unless there is a statute that says parties can protect their right to a view.

Transferability of Easements

An easement's transferability depends on the type of easement created. An
appurtenant easement runs with the land unless the buyer is a bona-fide purchaser with no notice.[900] Here, S was not a bona-fide purchaser without notice
because S received a copy of the original agreement between C, M, and J. The
original agreement included the terms of the easement. Although S did not
have actual notice of the easement because she did not read the original agreement, S had constructive notice. A reasonable buyer would have reviewed the
terms of the agreement before purchasing the land. Thus, if the negative easement is recognized under a statute, then S must remove the billboard, or pay
M and J damages caused by her violation.

(2) Using the Back Lot for Storage

License

An easement is not revocable, but a license is revocable by the licensor at
will if the license was not exchanged for valuable consideration.[901] If M
granted C a license, then M could revoke the right to use the back lot for personal storage. A license is an authorization from an owner to enter the premises for a limited purpose without liability for trespass.[902] A license can be oral
and no consideration is needed.[903] Here, M will argue she granted a license
because their agreement was not in writing. Thus, no express easement existed,
which means no easement could transfer to S when she purchased the land.
However, S will argue M granted C an easement through implication.

Implied Easement

An implied easement does not require a written agreement because it is
implied by prior use.[904] It arises when there is common ownership in a parcel
that is subdivided.[905] An implied easement is created if: (a) unity of ownership is

---

900. *In re Flyboy Aviation Properties, LLC,* supra note 896.
901. Restatement (Third) of Property (Servitudes) § 2.2 (2000).
902. *City of Waukegan, Ill. v. National Gypsum Co.,* 587 F.Supp.2d 997, 1010 (N.D. Ill.
2008).
903. *In re Yachthaven Restaurant, Inc.,* 103 B.R. 68, 73 (Bankr. E.D.N.Y. 1989).
904. Restatement (Third) of Property (Servitudes) § 2.11 (2000).
905. Restatement (Third) of Property (Servitudes) § 2.12 (2000).

severed, (b) the use was in place before the parcel was severed, (c) the use was visible or apparent at the time of severance, and (d) the easement is reasonably necessary for enjoyment of the dominate estate.[906]

Here, (a) unity of ownership was severed because M owned Shopacre, divided it into three stores, and sold one store to C and another to J. (d) S will argue the storage space was necessary to enjoy the land because owners need space to store their products. However, M has a stronger argument because owners can store products inside their building. Owners do not need a shared parking lot for storage. (c) Although C storing products in the back lot is visible and apparent, (b) M divided her shares before C began storing his belongings. Thus, no easement was created because the parking lot was not used for storage before the severance.

Termination of Easement in Gross

Even if the court determined C had an easement, the easement would not transfer to S because an easement in gross is not transferable and ends at death of the holder unless the parties agreed otherwise. But an easement in gross that is commercial, which means the easement furthers moneymaking activity, is assignable.[907]

Here, the easement is not assignable because M granted C an easement to store his personal belongings. C's storage use was unrelated to his burger restaurant and did not increase his revenue. Moreover, when C sold the land to S, C likely intended to abandon the easement because he stopped using the property to store his personal belongings.[908] Thus, the easement was terminated by C's subsequent nonuse.[909]

Prescriptive Easement

S will argue she acquired the right to use the back lot through prescription. An easement is created if the person (a) actually, (b) openly and notoriously, (c) adversely, (d) continuously, and (e) exclusively possesses the land (f) for the statutory period.[910]

---

906. *Id.*
907. *Orange County, Inc. v. Citgo Pipeline Co.,* 934 S.W.2d 472 (Tex.Ct.App.1996).
908. Restatement (Third) of Property (Servitudes) § 7.4 (2000).
909. *Id.*
910. Restatement (Third) of Property (Servitudes) §§ 2.16-2.17 (2000).

(a) Only affirmative easements can be implied by prescription because the actual use element prohibits negative easements from being prescriptive.[911] Here, S actually used the property because she built a storage shed in the back parking lot to store equipment. (b) S's use must be reasonably noticeable to a landlord.[912] M will argue the back lot is seldom used because most customers enter stores through the front door. However, this is a weak argument because a reasonable owner would have seen a shed in the back lot during regular inspections of the land. (c) S's never received permission from M to build the shed or use it for storage purposes.[913]

(d) S's use was continuous and consistent with a reasonable easement holder's use because she stored her belongings in the shed for at least half a year without interruption.[914] (e) S's use must be exclusive and not concurrent with others.[915] S used a portion of the back lot without J or M sharing her space. Only S and her husband used the storage shed. (f) S purchased the land from C in 1984, but M did not bring a claim against S until 1987, which was three years later. The statutory period is only two years. Thus, an easement was created through prescription and S had the right to use the back lot for personal storage.

(3) Right to Use the Parking Lots

Express Easement and Termination by Misuse

See rules and analysis above. (Building a Large Billboard: Express Easements). Here, C, M, and J created an express easement to use the parking lot. The easement was appurtenant and affirmative, which means the easement passed to S when she purchased the land from C. However, S likely terminated the easement by exceeding the scope of use.[916] Easements cannot be changed unilaterally; both holders must agree to the modification.[917] Any move will be considered a misuse and terminate the easement unless the increased use does not overburden the servient estate or promotes use within the scope of the easement.[918]

---

911. *Bills v. Nunno*, 4 Mass.App.Ct. 279, 346 N.E.2d 718 (1976).
912. R. 3d of Prop. § 2.17, supra note 910.
913. *Id.*
914. *Id.*
915. *Sun Yung Lee v. Clarendon*, 453 Fed.Appx. 270, 274 (4th Cir. 2011).
916. *Macy Elevator, Inc. v. U.S.*, 105 Fed.Cl. 195, 202 (Fed. Cl. 2012).
917. *Id.*
918. *Id.*

Here, S unilaterally decided to park her car in the front parking lot. The original agreement stated the owners' cars must be parked in the back parking lot. S disregarded the agreement and never asked M's permission to change the scope of the easement. However, S will argue that parking in the front lot promotes the use of the easement because the parking lot is for everyone who uses the buildings and not only customers. S's argument is weak because M likely required owners to park in the back lot to ensure customers had enough parking in the front parking lot. Thus, S's misuse terminated her right to use the parking lots.

Easement by Necessity

Even though S lost her right to use the parking lots, S will obtain an easement to access her property through necessity. An easement by necessity is created when: (a) a common owner severs the property, (b) a necessity for egress and ingress existed at the time of severance, and (c) the severance caused the parcel to become landlocked.[919] The servient estate owner has the opportunity to locate the easement by necessity, but if the servient estate owner makes unreasonably delays, then the benefited estate owner can locate the easement.

Here, (c) S's property is landlocked because S's salon is surrounded by M's land. M owns the right store, left store, and parking lots around the building. S's property is in the center of M's land. (b) A prior use of egress and ingress existed because, at the time M conveyed the property to C, M allowed C to cross M's land to access his burger store. M's severance caused S's land to become landlocked because M originally owned Shopacre, divided the land, and sold the center store to C and the left store to J while retaining the remaining property. Thus, C had an easement by necessity that will pass to S. M, as the servient owner, can locate the easement and determine the scope of use.

---

919. Restatement (Third) of Property (Servitudes) § 2.15 (2000).

Answer 6

(1) Homeowners' Association (H) v. Jasmin (J)

H created three affirmative covenants: (i) owners must pay annual maintenance dues; (ii) owners must use pastel colors to pain their homes; and (iii) owners must use their land for residential purposes. Real covenants and equitable servitudes bind the original owners, but can also bind subsequent owners. If the plaintiff requests money damages, then the rules for real covenants apply, but if the plaintiff requests injunctive relief, then the court applies the rules for an equitable servitude.[920] Here, both equitable servitudes and real covenants are an issue because H sued J for $200 in dues, asked J to repaint her house, and told her to close her music studio.

Real Covenants

An affirmative covenant requires the owner of a burdened estate to perform some act whereas a negative covenant restricts the use of the burdened property. A real covenant runs with the land if: (a) a writing exists, (b) the original owners intent to bind successors, (c) the restriction touches and concerns the land, (d) horizontal privity exists, (e) vertical privity exists, and (f) the subsequent owner had notice of the covenant.[921]

Here, (a) only two of the covenants were written in the bylaws, the pastel paint and maintenance dues requirements. (b) Intent is interpreted by looking at the deed's language and the nature of the restriction.[922] Words, such as "heirs and assignees" or "shall run with the land," suggest an intent to bind subsequent owners. Although no words of succession were used, a homeowners' association's bylaws are created to govern all members of the community, which includes subsequent owners of the properties.

(c) The covenant must physically affect the property or bear some relationship to the preservation, purpose, or value of the land.[923] Here, all three covenants touch and concern the land because they restrict J's use of the land. Most landowners can freely paint their house and use the property for any activity. J was deprived of these freedoms. Although money payments do not touch

---

920. *In re Hassen Imports Partnership*, 502 B.R. 851, 861 (C.D. Cal. 2013).
921. *In re Foster*, 435 B.R. 650 (B.A.P. 9th Cir. 2010).
922. *In re Daufuskie Island Properties, LLC*, 431 B.R. 612 (Bankr. D.S.C. 2009).
923. *In re T 2 Green, LLC*, 363 B.R. 753, 766 (Bankr. D.S.C. 2006).

and concern the land, the homeowners' association dues to maintain the common roads is an exception.[924]

(d) Horizontal privity is satisfied if, at the time the original parties entered into the covenant, the original parties shared some interest in the land that was independent of the covenant.[925] When Luther (L) created the homeowners' association, every member in the community that purchased the property had an interest beyond the covenant because L was the grantor and the purchaser was the grantee. (e) Vertical privity exists when the subsequent owner receives the entire durational interest of the prior party through gift, devise, inheritance, or purchase.[926] J purchased L's entire interest in the last lot. J is in vertical privity with L, who was an original party to the covenants created by the homeowners' association. (f) Actual or constructive notice of the covenant is required.[927] A property owner has constructive notice of any restriction appearing within the chain of title.[928] Here, J had constructive notice because homeowners' association bylaws are usually recorded, accessible by anyone in the community, and disclosed to potential buyers. Thus, J should have read the bylaws before purchasing the home.

In conclusion, the real covenants to use pastel colors and pay maintenance dues will run with the land and bind J unless the covenants were terminated. The residential use restriction will not bind J because it is not in writing unless L had a common scheme for the land.

Termination of Real Covenants

The maintenance dues requirement was not terminated, but J will argue the pastel paint requirement was terminated through abandonment. A real covenant is terminated if a high number of landowners in the area violate the covenant, which causes a substantial change in the neighborhood.[929] Here, J will argue the covenant was abandoned because half the community repainted their homes with bright colors. 50% is a high enough number of landowners to indicate a shift in the community's preferences. However, H will argue a substantial change in the neighborhood requires a majority of the homeowners

---

924. *In re Foster*, supra note 921 at 660.
925. *In re Midsouth Golf, LLC*, 549 B.R. 156, 179 (Bankr. E.D.N.C. 2016).
926. *Id.*
927. *In re T 2 Green, LLC*, supra note 923.
928. *Id.* at 766.
929. *Fink v. Miller*, 896 P.2d 649 (Utah Ct. App. 1995).

to abandon pastels colors and not only half. H's argument is stronger because substantial usually requires more than 50%.

J will argue the covenant was terminated through acquiescence because H allowed others in the community to violate the painting restriction. If an owner passively endures multiple violations by many lots in the community, then the owner cannot enforce the covenant against another.[930] However, J's argument will fail because she was the first person to violate the covenant. Thus, the covenant was not terminated and J must repaint her home.

Equitable Servitude

An equitable servitude requires all the same elements as a real covenant except for privity.[931] See rule and analysis above. (Homeowners' Association v. Jasmin: Real Covenants (a)-(c), and (f)). Here, H will argue the residential use restriction was an implied servitude that runs with the land.

Implied Servitudes from Common Scheme

An equitable servitude is created when a developer imposes the same restrictions on all his retained lots based on a common scheme on how the land should be used.[932] Here, H will argue the residential use restriction is an implied servitude because L built 20 homes on the 20 lots instead of selling undeveloped land to buyers. L also created a homeowners' association and divided the homes into cul-de-sacs, which are common in residential areas. The facts do not state whether L recorded a general plan for the area or included the covenant in the landowner's deeds, but H will argue the overwhelming number of homes indicates J could not use the land for commercial purposes. Thus, J likely must stop using her property as a music studio because the residential restriction will run with the land.

(2) Sam's (S) Right to Ride His Bike on Martha's (M) Land

Express Easements

An easement is a non-possessory right to enter and use another's land for specific purposes; the landowner cannot unreasonably interfere with the easement holder's use.[933] To create an express easement there must be a writing that

---

930. Restatement (First) of Property § 561 (1944).
931. *Excel Willowbrook, L.L.C. v. JP Morgan Chase Bank, Nat. Ass'n*, 758 F.3d 592 (5th Cir. 2014).
932. Restatement (Third) of Property (Servitudes) § 2.14 (2000).
933. R. 3d of Prop. § 1.2, supra note 893.

includes the precise location of the easement, specifies the use of the easement, and identifies who is burdened by the easement.[934] Here, a valid easement was not created because M orally agreed that S could use her driveway. No writing exists. However, J created an express easement by providing S with a written note that allowed S to use her driveway for BMX tricks. Thus, the issue is whether J's easement binds M.

Types of Easements

Richard (R) will argue the easement granted by J binds subsequent owners. Easements in gross benefit a specific person regardless of whether that person owns any specific property[935] whereas an appurtenant easement benefits the owner or possessor of that particular parcel of land.[936] An easement in gross is not transferable and ends at death of the holder unless the parties agreed otherwise.[937] Here, S's right to use M's driveway for his BMX tricks was an easement in gross because it was unrelated to where S lived. J granted S permission to use her driveway for his personal enjoyment. Thus, S's easement is not transferable and did not run with the land.

Easement by Estoppel

R will argue an easement was created by estoppel. M cannot use the lack of a writing to avoid liability if R (a) relied on M's conduct in a way that (b) prejudicially changed his position and (c) R had no knowledge or means to acquire knowledge of the truth of the facts in question.[938]

Here, (a) R relied on M's conduct because he only sold the house to M after she agreed that S could use her driveway. If M did not agree to R's terms, then R would not have sold the home to her. (b) M's conduct prejudicially changed R and S's position because S cannot use the driveway to practice his BMX tricks and R already sold the home. If R knew M's true intentions, then R could have sold J's home to a buyer that would have allowed S to use the driveway. (c) R did not know M would post "No Trespassing" signs on her lawn. R asked if S could use her driveway and M said, "Okay." M did not indicate any reservations and R could not read her mind.

---

934. R. 3d of Prop. § 2.1, supra note 894.
935. *Sunset Lake Water Service Dist. v. Remington,* supra note 895.
936. *In re Flyboy Aviation Properties,* supra note 896
937. *Kent's Run Partnership, Ltd. v. Glosser,* 323 B.R. 408 (W.D. Pa. 2005).
938. *Mahony v. Danis,* 95 N.J. 50, 60 (N.J. 1983).

R must also show (d) M's conduct was a false representation, (e) M could reasonably foresee that R would act as a result of her conduct, and (f) M had knowledge of the true facts.[939] Here, (d) M will argue she did not falsely represent her intentions because M's original agreement to R's terms was genuine. M only changed her mind after she thought about her garden. However, without more facts to prove M's internal intent, M's argument is weak because her verbal agreement and subsequent actions of posting signs suggest she lied to R. (e) M should have known R would rely on her statement because he explicitly said he would only sell her the home if S could use her driveway. (f) M is the only person with knowledge about the true facts related to her intent. Thus, all elements are met and an easement by estoppel was created. S has the right to use M's driveway or receive compensation for M's violation of the easement in gross.

---

939. *Id.*

Answer 7

(1) Wesley's (W) Rights

Mortgages and Foreclosures

A mortgage is a security interest in land intended by parties to be collateral for repayment of debt.[940] If the debt is not satisfied, then the creditor can foreclose by judicial sale. The proceeds of the foreclosure sale are distributed in the following order: attorney fees, foreclosure expenses and costs, interest on the foreclosure loan, the principal on the foreclosure, junior liens, and then any surplus is paid to the mortgagor.[941] If the foreclosure sale is not enough to settle the loan, then the debtor must bring a deficiency judgment against any person who is personally liable on the mortgage to obtain the remainder of the money.[942]

Here, the bank's (B) lien is senior to the loan agency's (L) lien because Heidi (H) borrowed money from B before she borrowed money from L. Priorities in foreclosures are determined by the first-in-time rule.[943] B had priority over all non-purchase money mortgages because B's loan helped pay the down payment on the real estate.[944] Thus, proceeds from the sale must be paid to B before L, but L should be paid before H receives any surplus.

W will argue he owes L nothing because when a lender forecloses on a property, the buyer takes the property subject to senior interests, but junior liens are extinguished.[945] However, L will argue that junior liens are not extinguished unless the junior lienor was joined as a party to the action.[946] Thus, because B failed to join L as a party, W took the property subject to L's lien. W had constructive notice of L's lien because it was properly recorded. Thus, W will likely need to pay the junior lien on the property and sue H to recovery his losses.

---

940. Restatement (Third) of Property (Mortgages) § 1.1 (1997).

941. *Wivell v. Wells Fargo Bank, N.A.*, 773 F.3d 887 (8th Cir. 2014). See also *In re Cowin*, 492 B.R. 858 (Bankr. S.D. Tex. 2013), and *In re Miller*, 459 B.R. 657 (B.A.P. 6th Cir. 2011).

942. Restatement (Third) of Property (Mortgages) § 8.4 (1997).

943. *C.D. Barnes Associates, Inc. v. Grand Haven Hideaway Ltd. Partnership*, 406 F.Supp.2d 801, 806 (W.D. Mich. 2005).

944. Restatement (Third) of Property (Mortgages) § 7.2 (1997).

945. *Theo. H. Davies & Co., Ltd. v. Long & Melone Escrow, Ltd.*, 876 F.Supp. 230, 234 (D. Hawaii 1995).

946. *Id.*

(2) Heidi's (H) Redemption

The mortgagor has an equitable right of redemption that allows the mortgagor to pay the amount due on the property anytime prior to the foreclosure sale to redeem the property.[947] Here, H's equitable right of redemption expired because she attempted to redeem her property three months after the foreclosure sale. Thus, she cannot repossess the property. The only way H can redeem her property is if state law has a statutory right of redemption that allows her to redeem for a fixed period of time after the foreclosure sale.[948]

(3) City's (C) Actions
(i) Daycare Center

Use Variance

A use variance allows an owner to use the land in a manner that is not permitted under local zoning ordinances.[949] A variance is granted if: (a) the variance would not be substantially incompatible with the intended zoning plan, (b) the landowner suffers a unique hardship related to the use of land because of the zoning provisions, (c) the landowner would suffer an undue or unnecessary hardship if the variance is denied, and (d) the variance will not be detrimental to public welfare.[950]

(a) H will argue the variance is compatible because C wants to protect children living in residential areas from pollutants, but the daycare center is in an industrial area. The daycare center does not interfere with the zoning ordinance's goal of separating homes and factories. However, C's argument is stronger because the underlying purpose of the ordinance is to protect children from pollutants regardless of the area. A daycare center next to a factory is incompatible because it could cause health problems, especially during the early stages of development.

(b) H's hardship is unique because most businesses can provide childcare services for their employees on site without violating a zoning ordinance. H cannot provide childcare benefits because the nature of her business is

---

947. *Blossom v. Milwaukee & C.R. Co.*, 70 U.S. 196, 202 (1865).

948. *Colon v. Option One Mortg. Corp.* 319 F.3d 912, 920–21 (7th Cir. 2003).

949. *Laurence Wolf Capital Management Trust v. City of Ferndale*, 61 Fed.Appx. 204, 213 (6th Cir. 2003).

950. *Id.* at 214. See also *Cellular Telephone Co. v. Zoning Bd. of Adjustment of the Borough of Ho-Ho-Kus*, 197 F.3d 64 (3d Cir. 1999).

deemed dangerous to children. (c) H experienced an undue hardship because the lack of childcare services caused her employees to seek other job opportunities. H's limited staffing hurt her production and profits. Eventually, H needed another loan, which indicates her income dramatically declined. However, C will argue H's hardship was necessary because children are not safe near a factory.

(d) H will argue C's denial of her variance is detrimental to the public welfare because her employees are members of the public who relied on H's childcare services for 10 years. H's daycare provided affordable services for her workers. The sudden loss of childcare benefits hurt employees enough that they left H's company for new employment. However, C will argue its denial of H's variance was beneficial to the public welfare because businesses must implement safe practices. If children are constantly exposed to the factory's pollutants, then their health could suffer.

Thus, the board correctly denied H's variance. H's only remedy is to reverse the board's decision by proving the ordinance is unconstitutional.

Unconstitutional Ordinance

The goal of zoning is to promote the health, safety, and general welfare of the public by restricting the use of certain districts. However, zoning ordinances must promote a (a) legitimate state interest that is (b) rationally related to the promotion of those interests.[951] If not, then the state has violated the Fourteenth Amendment, which prevents states from depriving any person of life, liberty, or property without due process.[952]

(a) Here, C's zoning ordinance keeps industrial properties separate from residential and commercial properties to limit children's exposure to pollutants. The ordinance promotes a legitimate interest because children are too young to understand the impact of pollutants on their health. Thus, the government must protect them. (b) Limiting industrial use to the outskirts of the city is rationally related to C's goal because the outskirts are likely less populated, which means the risk of exposure is reduced because fewer children are present. Thus, the ordinance is likely constitutional and H cannot continue her daycare unless the daycare is a legal, non-conforming use that existed prior to the ordinance.

---

951. *Village of Euclid, Ohio v. Ambler Realty Co.,* 272 U.S. 365, 392 (1926).
952. *Id.*

Non-Conforming Use

A non-conforming use of land that lawfully existed prior to the effective date of the zoning restriction is allowed to continue without a variance.[953] However, most statutes require the use to exist at the time the ordinance takes effect; mere ownership of the land or plan to use the property is not sufficient.[954] Here, if a statute exists, then H will be allowed to continue her daycare services because the property offered childcare services 10 years before the zoning ordinance was passed.

(ii) Free Legal Aid Center

Physical Taking

The government cannot take private property for public use without just compensation.[955] A physical taking occurs when the government intrudes upon the property or takes away the owner's right to possess the property.[956] The property can only be taken for a significant public purpose, such as economic development, creating jobs, health, and safety.[957] Just compensation is the fair market value of the property.[958]

Here, C seized half of H's undeveloped lot to create a legal aid center for members in the community. A free legal aid center serves a significant public purpose because H's factory likely has several employees who may need legal advice. Although the population of people in the outskirts of the city is likely low, people in the city can drive to the free legal aid center. The American legal system is confusing and a free clinic helps people, who cannot afford an attorney, to vindicate their rights. Thus, C validly seized the property for public use. C must pay H the fair market value for the property.

---

953. *Gavlak v. Town of Somers,* 267 F.Supp.2d 214, 221 (D. Conn. 2003).

954. *Outdoor Graphics, Inc. v. City of Burlington, Iowa,* 103 F.3d 690 (8th Cir. 1996).

955. *Kelo v. City of New London, Conn.,* 545 U.S. 469, 477 (2005).

956. *Tahoe-Sierra Preservation Council, Inc. v. Tahoe Regional Planning Agency,* 535 U.S. 302, 322 (2002). See also *Loretto v. Teleprompter Manhattan CATV Corp.,* 458 U.S. 419, 428 (1982).

957. *Daniels v. Area Plan Com'n of Allen County,* 306 F.3d 445, 467 (7th Cir. 2002).

958. *U.S. v. Miller,* 317 U.S. 369, 374 (1943).

(iii) Heidi's (H) Undeveloped Lot for Her Home

Non-Conforming Use

See rule above. (City's Actions: Daycare Center: Non-Conforming Use). A planned non-conforming use is only allowed if the owner (a) acted in good faith and (b) made a substantial expenditure toward the building; mere intentions are not enough to claim a non-conforming use.[959] (b) Here, H will argue her residential use of the undeveloped lot is a non-conforming use because she began building the home before the zoning ordinance was passed. (a) H acted in good faith because she built the home to decrease her commute time and increase her ability to care for her family. However, H likely did not spend a substantial expenditure toward the building because construction only began a week before C's seizure. Thus, because minimal construction was completed, H cannot build a home near a factory and must request compensation for the government's taking of her property.

Physical Taking

See rules above. (Free Legal Aid Center). Here, C will argue a physical taking did not exist because the government temporarily seized H's land, but returned half of the lot. Thus, H is now in possession of the property. However, this argument is weak because C must provide just compensation to H for the time C possessed the property, which is likely the market rental rate.

Regulatory Taking

Although C returned half of H's property, H will argue C's regulation constituted a regulatory taking because H was unable to build a home on the undeveloped lot. Courts use the following factors to determine if a regulatory taking occurred: (a) character of the government action, (b) economic impact of the regulation on the landowner and extent to which the regulation has interfered with distinct investment-back expectations, and (c) the property taken.[960]

(a) Courts analyze the benefit to the public, such as how many people are benefited; and if the government's taking is permanent or temporary.[961] Here, although H cannot build a home, she can still use the undeveloped land to expand her factory business. However, H will argue the public does not

---

959. *Bickerstaff Clay Products Co., Inc. v. Harris County, Ga. By and Through Bd. of Com'rs,* 89 F.3d 1481, 1487–1488 (11th Cir. 1996).

960. *Penn Cent. Transp. Co. v. City of New York,* 438 U.S. 104 (1978).

961. *Id.* at 130–31.

benefit from C's residential-use restriction on her land because only H's family would reside in the area. (b) To assess the economic impact, courts analyze if the land has other reasonable uses, the loss of value in the land, if the owner added improvements with expectations of future use, and if the owner will lose the improvements already completed.[962] H will argue she expected to use the lot for a family home to reduce her commute. H currently commutes more than two hours a day, is a single mother, and has two newborn twins. A long commute for a working mother can dramatically decrease her quality of life. H also already started building the home and will lose the improvements she completed. However, C will argue H left the lot undeveloped for 10 years, which suggests the need for a family home is not immediate. H can make other arrangements for childcare or hire someone to help her run the factory.

(c) Economic regulation that renders the property valueless is a taking.[963] Here, C will argue the property was not rendered valueless because C told H that she could use the land for industrial purposes. Thus, C did not prevent construction, but simply limited the types of acceptable activities on the land. In conclusion, although C suffers several hardships, the regulatory taking is likely valid. If C allowed H to deviate from its zoning requirements, then C would need to grant similar permissions to other people requesting to build homes in an industrial area. As a result, more children might be exposed to pollutants and the public's general health and safety could decrease. Thus, H cannot build a home, but the residential-use restriction on H's land is a regulatory taking and C must provide H just compensation.

---

962. *Id.* at 131.
963. *Id.*

Answer 8

(1) Kent (K) and Mary's (M) Ownership

A valid delivery of a deed requires (a) the grantor's clear, present intent to deliver the deed and (b) actual delivery; an agreement to deliver is not sufficient.[964] Recording is not required for valid delivery.[965] Title passes to the grantee upon valid delivery, but the grantor can revoke the delivery if a condition has not occurred or there is no written contract to enforce the delivery.[966]

(a) A grantor's intent is evidenced by a physical act of delivery or implied acts, such as words or conduct. Here, M will argue Polly (P) did not have the present intent to deliver the deed to K because P said, "if anything happens to me." The word "if" suggests P only wanted K to assume possession if P was unable to monitor the property. Thus, delivery was contingent upon P's incapacitation. The words "take care of the home" are also ambiguous. M will argue that P intended to pass M the home through P's will and only wanted K to complete the sale to Jim (J) and not inherit the home. However, K will argue P would have explicitly asked K to complete the sale instead of asking him to care for the home. Thus, P's words plus her actual transfer of the physical deed to K symbolizes K was the intended recipient of the home and not M. P did not reserve any control over the deed.

(b) Valid delivery requires physically transferring land, constructive delivery, such as access or means to gain control of the property, or symbolic delivery, such as the thing that stands in place of the property.[967] Here, constructive delivery occurred because P gave K the physical deed to the property. In conclusion, P validly transferred the property to K. M had no power to sell the land to Rebecca (R) because K, as the owner, had the authority to sell the property to J.

(2) Jim's (J) Ownership

A valid land sale contract requires consideration, the essential terms to be stipulated, and a valid writing to satisfy the statute of frauds.[968] Under the

---

964. *S & S Services, Inc. v. Rogers*, 35 F.Supp.2d 459, 463 (D.V.I. 1999).

965. *Bunten v. American Sec. & Trust Co.*, 25 App.D.C. 226, 230 (D.C. Cir. 1905).

966. *Id.*

967. *Estate of Davenport v. C.I.R.*, 184 F.3d 1176, 1185 (10th Cir. 1999).

968. *Redevelopment Agency of City of Stockton v. BNSF Ry. Co.*, 643 F.3d 668, 679 (9th Cir. 2011). See also Restatement (Second) of Contracts §§ 17, 22(1) (1981) and Restatement (Second) of Contracts § 110 (1981).

doctrine of equitable conversion, after a valid contract is created, the buyer becomes the equitable owner of the real property and the seller has the right to the proceeds.[969] The seller holds title in a trust and is entitled to possession until the closing.[970] Here, J and P entered a valid written contract that included the essential terms, the price, and parties involved in the transfer; $500,000 for a Victorian house. Thus, after the contract was executed, J became the owner of the Victorian house and P merely held the title for J until she would transfer the physical deed at closing.

However, M will argue she is the true owner because the land passed to M through P's will. P died before she physically delivered the deed to J. M's argument is weak because, if someone dies, then the deceased's heirs or assignees must honor the land sale contract and convey the land at closing.[971] Thus, the property must be transferred to J because the purchaser is the actual owner of the property.

Implied Promises with the Land Contract

A land contract includes the implied promise that the title is marketable, which means there are no defects in the record chain of title, no adverse possession claims, and the land is not subject to future interests, encumbrances, or zoning violations.[972] Here, the title is not marketable because P failed to record the deed, Carol (C) has a claim of adverse possession, and Rebecca (R) claims she purchased the land. J will argue that K, as P's heir, must honor the implied promise in the land sale contract by defending against C and R's claims to the Victorian house and curing the defects.

However, under the merger doctrine, a land sale contract and its warranties are extinguished at closing because the deed becomes the controlling document.[973] Here, the implied warranty of marketable title was extinguished when J completed the closing and K's quitclaim deed became the controlling document. A quitclaim deed includes no warranties or covenants and merely conveys the interest the grantor has in the property.[974] Thus, K does not need to defend in court to perfect J's title.

---

969. *Redevelopment Agency of City of Stockton v. BNSF Ry. Co.*, 643 F.3d 668, 678–679 (9th Cir. 2011).

970. *Id.*

971. *Id.*

972. *McCain v. Cox*, 531 F.Supp. 771, 780 (N.D. Miss. 1982).

973. *In re The Lovesac Corp.*, 422 B.R. 478, 489 (Bankr. D. Del. 2010).

974. *Aud v. Illinois Cent. R. Co.*, 955 F.Supp. 757, 759 (W.D. Ky. 1997).

Bonafide Purchaser (BFP)

A BFP purchases the property for consideration without notice of another's claim to title of the land.[975] Here, J will argue he is a BFP because he was unaware that C previously purchased the home or that P's deed was defective.[976] J could not check the chain in title because P did not record her title. However, C will argue J had constructive notice because C lived on the property for five years. If J inspected the property before closing, then J would have seen C's personal property in the house. Thus, C will retain possession of the home. Although J has superior rights to M and K, who received the property through devise and gift, J is unlikely to have superior title to C, another BFP, because he had constructive notice of C's ownership claim. Thus, C will retain possession of the home.

(3) Rebecca (R) and Carol's (C) Ownership

Bonafide Purchaser

See rule above. (Jim's Ownership: Bonafide Purchaser). Here, C and R are BFPs because neither had notice of the other's ownership claim to the property. The same seller sold P and C the property during the same month. C did not have notice of P's purchase because P never recorded her deed nor lived on the property. R had no notice of C's interest because, although C followed proper recording requirements, P never recorded the deed. Thus, C's deed was a wild deed, which is a recorded deed that is not in the chain of title.[977] C will argue R had constrictive notice because R saw C's personal property in the home. However, this argument is weak. R visited the property with M and asked who occupied the home. M lied about her ownership and R was reasonably unable to discover the truth. Thus, R is a BFP. When the same property is transferred to more than one BFP, the buyer who takes the property depends on the recording statutes of the state.

Recording Statutes

Under State X's race-notice recording statute, a subsequent BFP is entitled to priority if the subsequent BFP purchased the property without notice of the previous purchaser's interest and the subsequent BFP records first.[978] Here, R

---

975. *Berge v. Fredericks,* 591 P.2d 246 (1979).
976. *Vasko v. United States,* 112 Fed.Cl. 204, 220 (Fed. Cl. 2013).
977. *Wingers v. Sweet,* 190 Fed.Appx. 629, 632 (10th Cir. 2006).
978. *In re Walker,* 861 F.2d 597, 600 (9th Cir. 1988).

is the subsequent BFP and can only obtain priority over C's interest if she recorded her deed first. Although R recorded her deed, C is the true owner because C recorded her deed five years before M transferred the property to R. Thus, C can recover damages for R's trespass and nuisance.

Trespass

A person is liable for any intentional, physical, unauthorized entry onto another's land caused by the person.[979] Here, R intentionally trespassed because R refused to leave the property and set up camp in C's front yard. The entry was unauthorized because C asked R to leave. C did not want R on the property. Thus, because C was the true owner of the land, R is liable for trespass.

Private Nuisance

A private nuisance is a non-trespassory invasion of another's interest in the private use and enjoyment of their land.[980] The invasion must be an unreasonable and substantial interference.[981] A private nuisance involves a single or definite number of plaintiffs whereas a public nuisance involves rights common to the general public.[982] To recover damages in an individual action for a public nuisance, the plaintiff must suffer a harm that is different from that suffered by other members of the public.[983] Here, the appropriate action is a private nuisance because R is physically camping on C's land. No facts suggest R is disturbing the whole neighborhood.

C will argue R's action is unreasonable because landowners do not enjoy squatters in their front yards. A squatter is trespassing by using physical space on the land and ruining the aesthetics of the property. However, R will argue the interference was not substantial because she was only there for one night and C was likely sleeping during R's trespass. In conclusion, R's actions interfered with C's use and enjoyment of the land and the interference was likely substantial because some people are unable to sleep when a stranger invades their property.

---

979. Restatement (Second) of Torts § 158 (Am. Law Inst. 1965).

980. Restatement (Second) of Torts § 821D (Am. Law Inst. 1979).

981. *Cook v. Rockwell Intern. Corp.*, 273 F.Supp.2d 1175, 1201–1202. (D. Colo. 2003).

982. Restatement (Second) of Torts § 821C (Am. Law Inst. 1979). See also *N.A.A.C.P. v. AcuSport, Inc.*, 271 F.Supp.2d 435, 448 (E.D.N.Y. 2003).

983. *Id.*

(4) Covenants in Rebecca's (R) General Warranty Deed

The general warranty deed has six different covenants: covenant (a) of seisen, (b) of right to convey, (c) against encumbrances, (d) to insure grantee's quiet enjoyment of the property, (e) to warrant and defend the title to the property, and (f) further assurances.[984]

(a) The covenant of seisen grantees there is valid title.[985] Here, M violated this covenant because she did not have the physical deed to the property when she sold the Victorian house to R. M had to draft a replica of the deed for the sale because the original deed was with K, who transferred it to J. (b) The covenant of the right to convey guarantees that the grantor has the power and capacity to transfer title and does not suffer from incapacities, such as disability and age.[986] Here, M will argue she did not violate this covenant because she believed P devised the Victorian house to her. M thought she was the valid owner. However, M's argument is weak because she never received the original deed from P. M should have known that ownership of the Victorian house was under controversy, especially because C was physically living in the house. (c) The covenant against encumbrances guarantees that there is no physical encroachments, liens, or servitudes.[987] Here, there were no issues related to this covenant.

(d) The covenant of quiet enjoyment guarantees that the grantee will not be disturbed by a third party's lawful claim of title to the land.[988] Here, M violated this covenant because M knew a third party might be living in the home. M saw C's personal property in the Victorian house when R came to view the property. Thus, although R is not the true owner, R was disturbed by C's presence on the land because C prevented R from moving into the home. (e) The warranty covenant guarantees the grantor will defend against reasonable claims of title by a third party.[989] Here, M knew C, J, and K had claims to the land. Thus, requiring M to defend R's title is reasonable. (f) The covenant of further assurances guarantees the grantor will perform as reasonably necessary to perfect title.[990] Several people have claims to the Victorian house. Thus, M must defend R's title in court to perfect R's title.

---

984. *In re Health Science Products, Inc.*, 183 B.R. 903, 931 (Bankr. N.D. Ala. 1995).
985. *Id.* at 932.
986. *Id.*
987. *Id.*
988. *Id.* at 931.
989. *Id.*
990. *Lamb v. Burbank*, 14 F.Cas. 989 (C.C.D. Or. 1870).

Torts Answers

Answer 1

(1) Jessica (J) v. Homeless Man (HM)

Battery

An actor is liable for battery if he (a) voluntarily acts (b) intending to (c) cause harmful or offensive (d) contact with another person.[991] Intent is satisfied if the actor desires to cause the consequences of his act, or believes that the consequences are substantially certain to result from the act.[992] Bodily contact is offensive if it offends a reasonable sense of personal dignity.[993] The contact can be direct or indirect.[994]

Here, (a) HM voluntarily hit the sandwich out of J's hand; his actions were not coerced. (b) HM acted intentionally because he was upset by J's gesture. HM knocked the sandwich out of J's hand because he wanted money and not food. If J cannot prove HM's subjective intent, then HM was at least substantially certain that hitting an object out of someone's hand could cause the object to fall. (c) HM will argue J did not suffer any injuries because he hit the sandwich and not her body. However, J will argue that a reasonable person offering a gift would be offended if the recipient knocked the gift out of her hand. (d) Although HM never touched J's body, he touched her sandwich, which satisfies the indirect contact requirement because the sandwich is an extension of J's body. In conclusion, HM is liable for battery because all the elements are met.

---

991. Restatement (Second) of Torts § 13 (Am. Law Inst. 1965).
992. Restatement (Second) of Torts § 8A (Am. Law Inst. 1965).
993. Restatement (Second) of Torts § 19 (Am. Law Inst. 1965).
994. R. 2d of Torts § 13, supra note 991.

(2) Kirk (K) v. Homeless Man (HM)

Assault

An actor is liable for assault if he (a) voluntarily acts (b) intending to (c) cause harmful or offensive contact with another person and (d) the other person is put in imminent apprehension of that contact.[995] See rules for (a)-(c) above. (Jessica v. Homeless Man). Imminent apprehension is met if the person believes the defendant's act may result in imminent contact without self-defense, flight, or intervention of some outside force.[996]

Here, (a) see analysis above. (Jessica v. Homeless Man). (c) Although a sandwich is unlikely to cause physical injury because sandwiches are usually soft, throwing a sandwich at someone is offensive. (d) K ducked because he was scared the sandwich would hit his face. K's fear showed actual apprehension of the contact and K's action was a necessary intervention to prevent the offensive contact. If K did not duck, then the sandwich would have hit K. (b) K will argue HM was substantially certain that knocking the sandwich out of J's hand could have hit someone in the vicinity. People cannot control flying objects. HM will argue he did not intend to harm K. HM's anger was directed to J. But HM's argument is weak because K can use the doctrine of transferred intent to satisfy the intent element of assault.

Transferred Intent

If an actor intends to commit a battery, but an assault results, then the actor is still liable even though the act was not done with the intent to cause an assault. If an actor intends to commit a battery or assault against one person, but the tort causes harmful or offensive contact to another, then the actor is fully liable to the other victim as though he originally intended to affect him.[997] The doctrine of transferred intent applies to the following five torts: assault, battery, false imprisonment, trespass to land, and trespass to chattels. Here, HM intended to batter J. HM's intent can be transferred to the assault claim against K. In conclusion, HM is liable for assault because all the elements were met.

(3) Homeless Man (HM) v. Barry (B)

Battery: Rock Throwing

See rules above. (Jessica v. Homeless Man: Battery). (a) B voluntarily threw the rock; his actions were not coerced. (b) B yelled, "Stop Thief," before he threw

---

995. Restatement (Second) of Torts § 21 (Am. Law Inst. 1965).

996. Restatement (Second) of Torts § 24 (Am. Law Inst. 1965).

997. Restatement (Second) of Torts § 16 (Am. Law Inst. 1965).

the rock at HM. B's words suggest B intended to use the rock to stop HM from running away with the umbrella. (c) Impact from a rock can cause physical injury because a rock is hard. The rock caused HM's internal bleeding. (d) Direct contact occurred because the rock hit HM in the head. In conclusion, B is liable for battery unless there is a valid defense.

Defense of Others

An actor is privileged to defend a third person from harmful or offensive contact if the actor correctly or reasonably believes that (a) the third person was privileged to act in self-defense, and (b) the actor's intervention was necessary to protect the third person.[998]

Here, (a) K was privileged to defend himself because HM stole K's umbrella. A reasonable person would be offended if someone took his belongings without permission. However, HM will argue that he posed no threat of harm to K's person because HM was running away from K and not toward the couple. Thus, K was likely not privileged to act in self-defense. (b) B reasonably believed his intervention was necessary to prevent HM from running away with K's umbrella or returning to harm the couple. No facts suggest K chased after HM or was close to repossessing the umbrella. Instead, the facts suggest HM was violent, unstable, and unpredictable. If the court agrees with B, then the issue is whether B's use of force was excessive.

Extent of Force

When acting in self-defense, an actor cannot use force in excess of what the actor correctly or reasonably believes is necessary to protect himself or another.[999] Here, HM will argue that throwing a rock at his head was excessive force because the head is a vital body part and rocks can cause serious bodily injury. Some cultures use stoning as a form of capital punishment, which is evidence that rocks are dangerous weapons. A person's life is precious, but an umbrella is easily replaceable. B could have thrown the rock at HM's body. However, B will argue a reasonable person would react similarly because the incident occurred rather quickly and no facts suggest B was close enough to tackle HM or use less force. If B threw the rock at HM's body, then there is no guarantee HM would stop running away. Both arguments are reasonable and the fact finder will determine the prevailing party, and if K was privileged to use self-defense.

---

998. Restatement (Second) of Torts § 76 (Am. Law Inst. 1965).
999. Restatement (Second) of Torts § 70 (Am. Law Inst. 1965).

Battery: Punch

See rules above. (Jessica v. Homeless Man: Battery). (a) B voluntarily punched HM without any coercion. (b) B intended to punch HM because HM was running towards B with the umbrella raised and B needed to protect himself. (c) A punch can cause physical harm. B's punch was strong enough to render HM unconscious. (d) B's fist made direct contact with HM's face. In conclusion, B is liable for battery unless a defense applies.

Self-Defense

An actor is privileged to use (a) reasonable force, not deadly force, to defend himself if (b) he reasonably believes another is about to inflict unprivileged harmful or offensive contact upon him.[1000]

Here, (b) a reasonable person would believe HM would cause imminent harmful contact because HM hit the sandwich out of J's hand, stole K's umbrella, and was running towards B with the umbrella raised. HM's past actions suggest he is a violent person. (a) However, HM will argue B used more force than necessary because the punch knocked HM unconscious, which suggests B hit HM extremely hard. HM's argument will fail because, in a physical fight, punching is a normal way for people to defend themselves; B did not use a weapon. HM will also argue that B could have retreated into the store and closed the door rather than fighting, but this argument is weak because an actor is not required to retreat.[1001] Thus, B was privileged to use self-defense and is not liable if B was not the initial aggressor.

Initial Aggressor

An aggressor cannot assert self-defense if he purposefully provoked trouble.[1002] Here, HM will argue B was the initial aggressor because B threw the rock at HM's head. If B never threw a rock at HM, then HM would not have run towards B in a rage. However, this argument is weak if B was privileged to act under the defense of others doctrine. See analysis above. (Kirk v. Homeless Man: Defense of Others).

False Imprisonment

An actor is liable for false imprisonment if (a) he acts intending to confine the other person (b) within fixed boundaries, and his act directly or

---

1000. Restatement (Second) of Torts § 63 (Am. Law Inst. 1965).
1001. *Id.*
1002. *Rude v. Adeboyeku,* 552 F.Supp.2d 32, 36 (D.D.C. 2008).

indirectly results in such a confinement, and (c) the other is conscious of the confinement or harmed by it.[1003]

Intent

See rule above. (Jessica v. Homeless Man: Battery). Here, B's statement, "You must follow me into the store or I'm going to call the police," suggests B wanted to confine HM to prevent HM from running away.

Confinement

Confinement includes physical force, physical barriers, threats of physical force, duress, or assertion of legal authority.[1004] Physical confinement usually requires fixed boundaries with no reasonable means of escape.[1005]

Here, B will argue HM had several reasonable means of escape. HM was placed behind the counter without any doors or physical barriers. HM could have easily walked away while B was talking to K. No one forced HM to stay in the store. However, B's argument is weak because B threatened to call the police if HM tried to run away. No reasonable person wants to deal with the police. B also previously used physical force to stop HM from running away. HM likely feared that B would throw another rock if HM tried to escape. Thus, HM was confined because he was not free to leave B's store.

Awareness of or Harmed by Confinement

Here, B will argue HM did not suffer harm because HM was merely sitting behind the counter. Although HM physically fell on the floor from internal bleeding, this harm was not caused by the confinement. However, B's argument is weak because HM was aware he was confined. B told HM he would call the police if HM tried to leave. In conclusion, B is liable for false imprisonment unless a defense applies.

Consent

One who effectively consents to the conduct of another cannot recover in an action of a tort for that conduct.[1006] To be effective, consent must be (a) made by a person with the capacity to consent or by another empowered to consent for him, and (b) made to that particular conduct or substantially

---

1003. Restatement (Second) of Torts § 35 (Am. Law Inst. 1965).

1004. Restatement (Second) of Torts §§ 38–41 (Am. Law Inst. 1965).

1005. Restatement (Second) of Torts § 36 (Am. Law Inst. 1965).

1006. Restatement (Second) of Torts § 892 (Am. Law Inst. 1979).

similar conduct.[1007] If the actor exceeds the authorized consent, then the consenting party is not precluded from recovering damages for the excess harm.[1008] Consent is measured from an objective point of view and can be implied or expressed.[1009]

Here, HM never provided express consent because he silently followed B into the store. However, B will argue HM's actions implied consent because B did not verbally or physically protest. A reasonable person in B's position would assume HM agreed to wait in the store to resolve the situation. B's argument is weak because HM only agreed to wait in the store after B threatened to call the police. Prior to B's threat, HM attempted to avoid confinement by running away with the stolen umbrella. Thus, B's defense fails because a reasonable person would know HM was coerced into waiting behind the counter.

Shopkeeper's Privilege

One who reasonably believes that another has tortiously taken a chattel upon his premises, or has failed to make due cash payment for a chattel purchased or services rendered there, is privileged to detain the person on the premises for a reasonable amount of time to investigate the facts.[1010] Here, B will argue the detention of HM was privileged because B saw HM steal the property K had purchased from B's store. A reasonable person would believe HM failed to pay cash for the umbrella. However, HM will argue B was an uninvolved third party because B already received money for the umbrella. Thus, B was not privileged to act on behalf of K.

If B was allowed to detain HM, then the issue is whether 20 minutes is a reasonable amount of time to investigate the facts. B will argue 20 minutes is reasonable because the police take time to respond. However, no facts suggest B actually called the police until HM fell on the floor. HM will argue that 20 minutes to investigate a theft that B witnessed with his own eyes is unreasonable. B already knew K purchased the umbrella and that HM stole it. Moreover, B was talking to K for 20 minutes and not investigating the facts. Thus, 20 minutes was likely unreasonable.

In conclusion, B is liable for false imprisonment because no defenses apply.

1007. *Id.*
1008. *Id.*
1009. *Id.*
1010. Restatement (Second) of Torts § 120A (Am. Law Inst. 1965).

Answer 2

(1) Dakota's (D) Liability: Trespass to Chattels and Conversion

Trespass to Chattels

A person is liable for trespass to chattels if they (a) intentionally (b) dispossess, use, or intermeddle with chattel in (c) possession of another.[1011]

Intent

Intent is satisfied if the actor desires to cause the consequences of his act, or believes that the consequences are substantially certain to result from the act.[1012] Here, although D intentionally shut off the air conditioning, D will argue she did not intent to ruin F's sculpture because she tried to maintain it for a week. However, F will argue D was substantially certain the sculpture would be ruined because she originally kept the room at 55 degrees to prevent the chocolate from melting. Thus, she knew shutting off the air conditioning, especially during the summer, would melt the chocolate sculpture. This element is likely met.

Dispossess, Use, or Intermeddle

An actor must impair the condition, quality, or value of chattel or deprive the possessor of the use of chattel for a substantial time.[1013] A dispossession is committed if the actor takes the chattel through fraud or duress or without the other's consent, bars the other's access to chattel, or destroys chattel in the other's possession.[1014] Here, D did not dispossess F's chattel because F voluntarily put his chocolate sculpture on display in D's gallery. However, F will argue D impaired the condition of his chattel because she ruined the chocolate sculpture when she turned off the air conditioning. Thus, the melted sculpture was in poor condition and could not be displayed at F's conference. This element is likely met.

Possession of Another

A person in possession of a chattel is one who has physical control of the chattel with the intent to exercise such control.[1015] Here, F will argue D interfered with F's control over the sculpture because F was the rightful owner.

1011. Restatement (Second) of Torts § 217 (Am. Law Inst. 1965).
1012. Restatement (Second) of Torts § 8A (Am. Law Inst. 1965).
1013. Restatement (Second) of Torts § 218 (Am. Law Inst. 1965).
1014. Restatement (Second) of Torts § 221 (Am. Law Inst. 1965).
1015. Restatement (Second) of Torts § 216 (Am. Law Inst. 1965).

However, D will argue that she had a superior possessory interest because F abandoned his property when he failed to pick up the sculpture. D reminded F about the 10:00 AM deadline and waited a week before turning off the air conditioning. F's failure to claim his property indicated he no longer wanted the sculpture. Thus, D had the authority to exercise any control over the sculpture because it was on her land. If D had legal possession of the sculpture, then D is not liable. If D did not have legal possession, then D is liable if no defenses apply.

Conversion

Conversion is an (a) intentional exercise of dominion or control over a chattel, or destruction of a chattel, that materially alters the chattel's condition or identity.[1016] (b) The interference must be serious enough to justify the full value of the chattel.[1017] To determine the seriousness of the interference, the following factors are important: (i) the extent and duration of the actor's exercise of dominion or control; (ii) the actor's intent to assert a right inconsistent with the other's right of control; (iii) the actor's good faith; (iv) the extent and duration of the resulting interference with the other's right of control; (v) the harm done to the chattel; and (vi) the inconvenience and expense caused to the other.[1018]

Here, (a) see rule and analysis above. (Dakota's Liability: Trespass to Chattels: Intent). (b)(i) D had possession of the sculpture for a week, which is an extended period of time. However, D only had possession because F failed to pick up his sculpture. (ii) Although D knew the sculpture would likely melt if she turned off the air conditioning, D never intended to interfere with F's right to his sculpture because she reminded F to claim his sculpture by 10:00 AM. D's voicemail suggests she did not want to retain possession of F's property. (iii) D acted in good faith because she waited a week after the lease expired before turning off the air conditioning. D could have thrown away the sculpture much earlier. (iv) The extent and duration of D's interference was high because the sculpture could not be displayed at the conference. F would need to completely rebuild the sculpture, which would take another six months. (v) The harm was high because the sculpture was ruined. (vi) The inconvenience and expense were high because F was a featured artist at the conference. Without any artwork to display, F lost possible job offers from

1016. Restatement (Second) of Torts §§ 222A and 226 (Am. Law Inst. 1965).
1017. *Id.*
1018. *Id.*

recruiters. Thus, D is liable for conversion if she didn't have legal possession unless a defense applies.

Defense of Land or Chattels

One is privileged to commit an act, which would otherwise be a trespass to a chattel or conversion, if the act is, or is reasonably believed to be, necessary to protect the actor's land or chattels, and the harm inflicted is reasonable compared to the harm threatened.[1019] Here, D will argue she acted reasonably to protect her land and money. F's chocolate sculpture monopolized a leasing space that could be rented to another client and cost D money because the chocolate needed to be in a cold environment. D reminded F to pick up his property, but F never showed up. Thus, a reasonable person in D's position would assume F abandoned the sculpture and would remove the chattel trespassing on her land to save money. Thus, D is unlikely to be liable for trespass to chattels or conversion.

Consent

One who would otherwise be liable to another for trespass to a chattel or conversion is not liable to the extent that the other has effectively consented to the interference with his rights.[1020] Consent occurs if words or conduct are reasonably understood by another to be intended as consent.[1021] Here, D will argue F consented to her interference because F never picked up his sculpture at 10:00 AM. D told F his sculpture would be thrown away if he did not meet the 10:00 AM deadline. A reasonable person in D's position would believe F consented to her discarding his property because he never reclaimed his property when the lease expired.

Damages

If D is liable for trespass to chattels, then D is responsible for the damage done to the chocolate sculpture, which would include repairing the sculpture to its original state or the loss in value.[1022] If D is liable for conversion, then D must pay for the full value of the chocolate sculpture, which also includes the cost of all the chocolate materials F recovered from the dumpster.[1023]

1019. Restatement (Second) of Torts § 260 (Am. Law Inst. 1965).
1020. Restatement (Second) of Torts § 252 (Am. Law Inst. 1965).
1021. R. 2d of Torts § 892, supra note 1006.
1022. Restatement (Second) of Torts § 222 (Am. Law Inst. 1965).
1023. Id.

(3) Dakota's (D) Liability: Intentional Infliction of Emotional Distress (IIED)

One who by (a) extreme and outrageous conduct (b) intentionally or recklessly causes (c) severe emotional distress to another is subject to liability for such emotional distress and any bodily harm that results from the distress.[1024]

Intent or Recklessness

See rule above. (Dakota's Liability: Trespass to Chattels: Intent). An actor's conduct is reckless if he does an act knowing or having reason to know that his conduct creates an unreasonable risk of physical harm to another.[1025] The risk must be substantially greater than that which is necessary to make his conduct negligent.[1026] Here, D did not intend to cause F emotional distress because she thought F no longer wanted his sculpture and merely turned off the air conditioning to save money. D was not substantially certain F would experience emotional distress because no facts suggest she knew recruiters were interested in his work or that he would be featured at a conference. To D, the sculpture was simply a material object.

However, F will argue D acted recklessly because an owner of an art gallery should know that artwork is important to the creator. D should have realized F's main reason for displaying his work at her gallery was to promote himself and that destruction of the chocolate sculpture would cause emotional distress because he likely spent time creating the sculpture. Thus, the intent requirement is likely met.

Outrageous Conduct

Conduct is outrageous if it is so extreme that it goes beyond all possible bounds of decency, and is regarded as atrocious and utterly intolerable in a civilized community.[1027] Here, F will argue that D's actions were outrageous because D, as a professional in the art world, should have at least tried to contact him one more time before destroying his sculpture. However, D's argument is stronger because no one in a civilized community would yell, "outrageous," if they learned she turned off the air conditioning after someone abandoned

---

1024. Restatement (Second) of Torts § 46 (Am. Law Inst. 1965).
1025. Restatement (Second) of Torts § 500 (Am. Law Inst. 1965).
1026. *Id.*
1027. Restatement (Second) of Torts § 46 cmt. d (Am. Law Inst. 1965).

their artwork on her property for over a week. Most people would have thrown the sculpture away much earlier. Thus, D unlikely acted outrageously.

Severe Emotional Distress

Here, F's depression caused him to lose weight, stop eating, and abandon his art. F's extreme change in behavior and physical manifestations of distress occurred after D destroyed F's sculpture, which suggests the loss of the sculpture caused severe distress. However, because D's actions were not outrageous, D is not liable for IIED.

Defense of Land

An actor is privileged to use reasonable force to prevent or terminate another's intrusion upon the actor's land or chattels, if (a) the intrusion is not privileged, (b) the actor reasonably believes that the intrusion can be prevented or terminated only by the force used, and (c) the actor has first requested the other to desist and the other has disregarded the request, or the actor reasonably believes that a request will be useless or that substantial harm will be done before the request can be made.[1028]

Here, (a) F's use of D's land was not privileged because his lease of D's gallery space expired. F's sculpture was trespassing on D's land for a week. (b) D acted reasonably because she called F with a reminder to pick up his sculpture, but F ignored her request. Thus, D reasonably believed F abandoned his property. D's actions were necessary to make the leasing space available to new clients. (c) D warned F that his property would be thrown away if he missed the 10:00 AM deadline, but F disregarded her voicemail. Thus, D was likely privileged to defend her land.

(4) Flik's (F) Liability: Trespass to Land

An actor is liable for trespass to land, irrespective of whether he causes harm to any legally protected interest of the other, if he intentionally (a) enters land in the possession of the other, or causes a thing or a third person to do so, or (b) remains on the land after consent terminates, or (c) fails to remove from the land a thing which he is under a duty to remove.[1029] Here, F no longer had permission to use D's space after his lease ended. Thus, F's failure to remove the sculpture is trespass to land.

1028. Restatement (Second) of Torts § 77 (Am. Law Inst. 1965).
1029. Restatement (Second) of Torts § 158 (Am. Law Inst. 1965).

Consent

See rule above. (Dakota's Liability: Trespass to Chattels: Consent). F will argue D expressly consented to the chattel on her property because she allowed him to display the chocolate sculpture. However, D's consent ended when the lease expired. Thus, F's failure to remove the sculpture was a trespass and he may need to pay for the leasing space and air conditioning costs.

Answer 3

(1) Justin (J) v. Reporter (R)
Defamation

A plaintiff will succeed on a defamation claim if there was (a) a false and defamatory statement (b) concerning the plaintiff that was (c) published to a third party.[1030] (d) Libel is falsely publishing defamatory matter in a written form. One who commits libel is subject to liability even if no special harm results from the publication.[1031]

(a) The defamatory statement must lower the plaintiff's reputation in the community or deter others from associating with him.[1032] Here, R suggested J is not committed to marriage. R's article discussed the negative impact of popular culture on youth and featured a picture of J and his new wife in wedding clothes as its graphic. Reasonable people may view J in a negative light after reading R's article because they disapprove of J's multiple marriages and divorces.

(b) The recipient of the communication must correctly, or mistakenly, but reasonably understand that the statement referred to the plaintiff.[1033] Here, R will argue people would not associate J with the article because J's name was never mentioned in the photo caption. However, R's argument is weak because J is a famous actor who was married five times within a span of three years. The tabloids are relentless when covering celebrity gossip. J's desire to keep the wedding a secret is evidence that the media followed his history of failed marriages. Thus, a reasonable person would likely recognize J in the photo and understand why J was chosen as an example.

(c) Publication of defamatory matter must be intentionally, or negligently, communicated to someone other than the person defamed.[1034] Here, the picture and article were intentionally published in *The Future* magazine, which is read by third persons.

1030. Restatement (Second) of Torts § 558 (Am. Law Inst. 1977).
1031. Restatement (Second) of Torts § 569 (Am. Law Inst. 1977).
1032. Restatement (Second) of Torts § 559 (Am. Law Inst. 1977).
1033. Restatement (Second) of Torts § 564 (Am. Law Inst. 1977).
1034. Restatement (Second) of Torts § 577 (Am. Law Inst. 1977).

(d) Here, R's defamatory matter is in written form because *The Future* is a print magazine. Thus, J does not need to prove special damages and general damages are presumed. In conclusion, R is liable for defamation unless the Constitutional limitations, an exception, or a defense apply.

Constitutional Limits

To balance an individual's interest in his reputation with the interests of free speech among society, one who publishes a false and defamatory communication about a public figure is subject to liability only if he (e) knows that the statement is false, and (f) acts in reckless disregard of the statement's truth or falsity.[1035] The courts added the requirements of falsity and actual malice to avoid deterring members of society from commenting on activities of public concern, public officials, or public figures.[1036]

Public Concern

R will argue J's marriages were a matter of public concern because, as a famous actor, J has a heavy influence on the nation's youth. Sharing various points of views about J's actions will give the youth different perspectives. J will argue his personal life is private. J should not be responsible for the decisions of others in society, especially because parents are responsible for their children. Both arguments are reasonable. Thus, arguing that J is a public figure is stronger.

Public Figure

A public figure is someone who occupies a position of persuasive power, assumes a role of prominence in society's affairs, or thrusts themselves into the forefront of a particular public controversy to influence the issues involved.[1037] Here, J is a public figure because he is a famous actor. J likely has a significant impact on popular culture and is a role model for other members in society. J holding a secret wedding to avoid the media and R hiding in the bushes to catch a photo of J's wedding proves J's life influences the general public. Thus, J must prove falsity and fault to recover for defamation.

(e) <u>Falsity</u>: Here, R will argue that his statement was true because J was married five times within three years. J influences society because many teenagers copy famous actors and actresses. J's numerous marriages and divorces could

---

1035. Restatement (Second) of Torts § 580A (Am. Law Inst. 1977).

1036. *New York Times Co. v. Sullivan*, 376 U.S. 254. (1964).

1037. *Wolston v. Reader's Digest Ass'n, Inc.*, 443 U.S. 157, 164 (1979).

teach the youth that commitment is not important. However, J might argue that outside factors or events caused his failed marriages. J's actions do not necessarily prove he does not believe in commitment and R has no evidence that J's life decisions negatively affect society's youth. Thus, without more facts, R's statement is false.

(f) <u>Fault</u>: Here, R will argue that he did not act recklessly because he knew about J's five failed marriages. R did not fabricate J's marriages or the marriage to Carrie (C). R was merely reporting the truth and cannot control how others react. However, this argument is weak because R should have known that using J's photo in an article about popular culture's negative influence on the commitment to marriage would portray J in a negative light. R should have conducted more research to see if J's decisions impacted the youth before printing the article. Thus, R acted recklessly and J can recover for defamation if no defenses apply.

Truth

One who publishes a defamatory statement is not liable for defamation if the statement is true.[1038] See analysis above. (Justin v. Reporter: Defamation: Public Figure: (e) Falsity). Here, more facts are necessary to determine whether J's actions influenced the youth.

Opinion

Statements of opinion are not defamatory unless a reasonable person would believe there were facts to support the statement.[1039] Here, J will argue that readers accept statements in magazines as true facts. *The Future* is a magazine printed by the government. A reasonable reader would assume the government conducted research and checked its sources before publishing the articles. However, R will argue that the title suggests the magazine is a gossip-focused article. Reasonably people would treat *The Future* similar to a tabloid and not a newspaper article, especially if there are no statistics reported in the article. If R's statement is an opinion, then J will not recover for defamation.

Invasion of Privacy

The right of privacy is invaded by (a) unreasonable intrusion upon the seclusion of another; or (b) misappropriation of the another's name or likeness; or

---

1038. Restatement (Second) of Torts § 581A (Am. Law Inst. 1977).
1039. *New York Times Co. v. Sullivan*, supra note 1036 at 265–266.

(c) unreasonable publicity given to the other's private life; or (d) publicity that unreasonably places the other in a false light before the public.[1040]

(a) Intrusion on Seclusion

One who (i) intentionally intrudes upon the seclusion of another's private affairs is subject to liability, if (ii) the intrusion would be highly offensive to a reasonable person.[1041] Here, (i) J did not want the public to know about his wedding because he purposefully planned a secret wedding in his home. Thus, R physically intruded upon J's private affairs by hiding in the bushes and taking photos of J's wedding without J's permission. (ii) R's actions were highly offensive because a reasonable person would not want strangers hiding in his bushes or printing his photo with a negative message. Moreover, R was trespassing on J's property, which is illegal. R might argue that a reasonable celebrity should not be offended because famous people commonly experience this intrusive behavior from photographers. This argument is weak because celebrities likely still get offended by paparazzi, but decide not to sue. Thus, R is liable.

(b) Misappropriation of Another's Likeness

One who (i) uses a person's name, photo, signature, voice, or likeness (ii) without permission (iii) for commercial advantage is liable for invasion of privacy.[1042] Here, (i) although R did not use J's name, R used J's photograph. J is a famous actor, which means people will recognize a photo of him in the magazine. (ii) R did not have permission to use J's photo because R hid in the bushes to get a picture of J in his wedding attire. (iii) If the government sells the magazine for profit, then J's photo was used for commercial advantage. J's photo would likely catch the consumer's attention and encourage purchases of the magazine because J is a public figure. If the government distributed the magazines for free, then J's photo was not used for commercial advantage and J's claim would fail.

(c) False Light

One who places another before the public in a false light is subject to liability if (i) the false light is highly offensive to a reasonable person, and (ii) the actor had knowledge of or acted with reckless disregard as to the falsity of the publicized matter.[1043] See analysis above. (Justin v. Reporter: Defamation). (i)

1040. Restatement (Second) of Torts § 652 (Am. Law Inst. 1977).

1041. Restatement (Second) of Torts § 652B (Am. Law Inst. 1977).

1042. Restatement (Second) of Torts § 652C (Am. Law Inst. 1977).

1043. Restatement (Second) of Torts § 652E (Am. Law Inst. 1977).

J was placed in a highly offensive light because no reasonable person wants to be blamed for a societal problem. (ii) R should have checked his facts before he accused J of negatively influencing the youth's commitment to marriage. Thus, R is liable for placing J in a false light.

(d) Public Disclosure of Private Facts

One who gives publicity to a matter concerning the private life of another is subject to liability if the matter publicized is of a kind that (i) would be highly offensive to a reasonable person, and (ii) is not of legitimate concern to the public.[1044] (i) No reasonable person would want society to focus on his or her failed marriages in articles, photos, or any other medium. (ii) Whether J's actions are of a legitimate concern to the public is debatable. See analysis above. (Justin v. Reporter: Defamation: Constitutional Limits). Moreover, R will argue that implicitly referencing J's marriages through a photo is not publication of private facts because everyone already knew about J's previous marriages. The media follows J because he is a celebrity. However, at the time R published the article, no one knew about he secret wedding except for J and C's immediate family. Thus, although his previous marriages were public information, the photo with C was private.

In conclusion, R is liable for invasion of privacy unless a defense applies.

Privileges

An absolute privilege allows a person to publish defamatory matter.[1045] An absolute privilege only applies to judicial officers, attorneys at law, parties to judicial proceedings, witnesses in judicial proceedings, jurors, legislators, executive and administrative officers, and publications required by law.[1046] Here, R will argue that he was required to publish the article by law because *The Future* focuses on problems in society. Thus, as a government employee, R was privileged to write about popular culture's influence on the youth's commitment to marriage. However, R's argument is weak because R could have presented his opinion in several different ways that did not highlight J as a cause of the problem. No law required *The Future* to include an update on J's marriage life.

1044. Restatement (Second) of Torts § 652D (Am. Law Inst. 1977).

1045. Restatement (Second) of Torts § 585-592A (Am. Law Inst. 1977).

1046. *Id.*

Qualified Privilege

Qualified privilege is available as a defense if there is a socially useful context for the speech at issue.[1047] Statements are privileged if the speaker has a good faith belief that the statement is true, and the statements are within the scope of a useful purpose for the speech or made for the benefit of the speaker or audience.[1048]

Here, although no facts confirm R believed J influenced the youth, R will argue the qualified privilege applies because the article was necessary to provide information that may explain the cultural change among the new generation. The government created *The Future*, which suggests the government decided articles, like R's, were useful to the public. However, J will argue R's article does not benefit the public because it presents a singular point of view. The government should have presented both sides to ensure the article was viewpoint neutral. If the court determines that one point of view is better than no point of view, then R might be able to assert his speech was privileged.

(2) Carrie (C) v. Anna (A): Defamation

See rules above. (Justin v. Reporter: Defamation). Slander is falsely publishing defamatory matter in a spoken form. If a defendant commits slander, then the plaintiff must prove special harm resulted from the statement unless the publication imputes to the other (i) a criminal offense, (ii) a loathsome disease, (iii) a matter incompatible with his profession, or (iv) a serious sexual misconduct.[1049]

(a) Here, A's statement lowers C's reputation because, in some societies, marrying for money, and not love, is viewed as a negative. (b) A used C's name in her statement. (c) A will argue she did not want others to hear her statement because she whispered the information to her friend. The teenager was eavesdropping. However, A's conversation was at the grocery market, which is a public place. If A did not want her statement to become public, then A should have waited until she was in a private space. (d) A's statement was slander because it was spoken to her friend. C must prove special damages because none of the special slander per se categories apply.

1047. Restatement (Second) of Torts §§ 594–598 (Am. Law Inst. 1977).
1048. *Id.*
1049. Restatement (Second) of Torts §§ 570–574 (Am. Law Inst. 1977).

Special Damages

C will argue she suffered special damages because questions about her marriage lowered the quality of her life. C lost wages because she took days off from work to escape the publicity. A's statement also sparked blogs and magazine articles about A and C fighting over J, which were untrue and likely lowered C's reputation. A will argue gossip-related stress is not a special damage because it is not an economic harm, but emotional distress. C married a celebrity and should have expected some level of intrusion in her life. However, A's argument will likely lose because C lost wages due to the controversy, which means C's damages can be quantified.

Opinion

See rule above. (Justin v. Reporter: Defamation). A will argue that her statement was obviously an opinion. No facts suggest A personally knew C or why C married J. A said "I think" C is in it for the money. A did not say "I know." Thus, C cannot recover for defamation because it was obvious that A had no factual basis for the assertion.

Truth

See rule above. (Justin v. Reporter: Defamation). Here, A will argue that her statement was true because C married J for the money. However, C will argue the statement was presented to the public without context. Although C married J for the money, she also loved J and enjoyed his company. Thus, C was not the stereotypical gold-digger. If the court determines the statement was true, then A is not liable for defamation.

Answer 4

(1) Demi (D) v. Belle (B)

Negligence

To succeed on a claim for negligence, the plaintiff must prove the following elements: (a) the defendant owed a duty of care to the plaintiff; (b) the defendant breached that duty; (c) breach of that duty caused the plaintiff's injury; and (d) the plaintiff suffered harm.[1050]

Duty

Under the majority rule, people owe a duty to everyone within the zone of danger.[1051] A plaintiff is in the zone of danger if the plaintiff is someone who would reasonably be injured by the defendant's conduct.[1052] Under the minority rule, people owe a duty of reasonable care to the world at large.[1053]

Here, under the minority rule, D is a foreseeable plaintiff because D is a member of the world. Under the majority rule, D will argue she was within the zone of danger because she was a guest in B's house; D could be hurt by dangerous conditions while roaming around the property. B will argue the zone of danger only included the inside of the house and not the backyard because B placed a sign on the back door that said "Off Limits." However, D's argument is likely stronger because B should have realized that, without an extra lock on the backyard door, her whole house was accessible to guests.

Standard of Care

If the defendant is a possessor of land, then the applicable standard of care depends on if the plaintiff is a trespasser, licensee, or invitee.

Status of Plaintiff

A trespasser enters or remains on the land without the consent from the possessor of the land[1054] whereas a licensee has the possessor's consent to enter or remain on the property.[1055] An invitee is invited onto the land by the possessor

---

1050. Restatement (Second) of Torts § 281 (Am. Law Inst. 1965).
1051. *Palsgraf v. Long Island R. Co.*, 248 N.Y. 339, 343 (1928).
1052. *Id.*
1053. *Id.* at 350–51.
1054. Restatement (Second) of Torts § 329 (Am. Law Inst. 1965).
1055. Restatement (Second) of Torts § 330 (Am. Law Inst. 1965).

of the land for (a) a business purpose or (b) for the purpose on which the land is held open to the public.[1056]

Here, D was not an invitee because B's bed and breakfast was only accessible to B's close family and friends. Members of the public were not allowed on the property. D will argue she was a licensee because D had B's consent to stay overnight as a guest. However, B will argue D was a trespasser because D exceeded her privilege. B placed a sign on the back door that said, "Off Limits," to notify D that she did not have permission to enter the backyard.

Duty to Licensees

If D was a licensee, then B owed a duty of reasonable care to make undiscovered dangers on the property safe.[1057] Here, D will argue B knew the chair was unsafe because it was not maintained for more than five years. Most people would have inspected the chair and fixed or discarded the chair. B will argue she used reasonable care to make the danger safe. B put a sign on the back door to prevent guests from using the equipment in the backyard. B cannot control guests who ignore her warnings. However, D will argue B unreasonably posted a small sign that guests would overlook. A reasonable landowner would make a large sign and verbally warn guests to avoid the backyard.

Duty to Trespassers

If D was a trespasser, then B owed no duty of reasonable care.[1058] However, if a landowner knew or should have known someone would trespass on the land, then the landowner must warn the trespasser of any artificial conditions on the land that are (a) created or maintained by the landowner, and (b) likely to cause death or seriously bodily harm to trespassers, and (c) unlikely to be discovered by trespassers.[1059]

Here, D will argue B knew guests would access the backyard. If B believed people would stay inside the house or that the backyard was safe, then B would not have posted a warning sign. Thus, B likely had a duty to warn trespassers about dangerous artificial conditions, such as the lawn chair because (a) B was responsible for maintaining the furniture in the backyard. However, B will argue (b) a lawn chair cannot cause serious bodily injury or death and (c) any person could easily discover the screws were loose by checking the chair before sitting

---

1056. Restatement (Second) of Torts § 332 (Am. Law Inst. 1965).
1057. Restatement (Second) of Torts § 341 (Am. Law Inst. 1965).
1058. Restatement (Second) of Torts § 333 (Am. Law Inst. 1965).
1059. Restatement (Second) of Torts § 335 (Am. Law Inst. 1965).

down. Moreover, even if B did have a duty to warn D about the chair, B will argue she used reasonable care by posting a sign.

Learned Hand Formula

The Learned Hand Formula determines whether B acted reasonably by posting a small sign on the back door. If the probability (P) and magnitude (M) of the harm resulting from the accident exceed the burden to prevent the harm, then the defendant likely breached her duty by not taking the proper precautions.[1060] Here, the burden is low because B could have told D not to enter the backyard within seconds. The P is high because the chair remained outside without any maintenance for five years, which means the chair likely deteriorated. The M is unknown because people who fall off a chair could suffer mere bruises or a serious concussion. Thus, it is likely B had a duty to warn D about the broken chair.

Breach

Conduct is negligent if it falls below the standard of care.[1061] Here, if D is a licensee or known trespasser, then B likely breached her duty of care by not verbally warning D about the chair. However, if D was an unknown trespasser, then B did not breach her duty because she owed no duty of care.

(2) Wilder (W) v. Belle (B)

Negligence

See rule above. (Demi v. Belle: Negligence).

Duty

See rules above. (Demi v. Belle: Duty). Here, under the minority rule, W is a foreseeable plaintiff because W is a member of the world. Under the majority rule, B will argue W was not within the zone of danger because he was not a guest in her home. However, W will argue that all children in the neighborhood are within the zone of danger because children are naturally attracted to trampolines. Whether B owed a duty to W depends on if a trampoline is an artificial condition highly dangerous to trespassing children.

1060. *United States v. Carroll Towing Co.*, 159 F.2d 169, 173 (2d Cir. 1947).
1061. Restatement (Second) of Torts § 282 (Am. Law Inst. 1965).

Child Trespassers

If an artificial condition on the land causes a trespassing child physical harm, then a possessor of land is only liable if (a) the possessor knows or has reason to know that children are likely to trespass; (b) the possessor knows or has reason to know the condition involves an unreasonable risk of death or serious bodily harm to children; (c) the children are unable to discover the condition or realize the condition is dangerous; (d) the utility to the possessor or burden to eliminate the danger are slight compared to the risk involved; and (e) the possessor fails to exercise reasonable care to protect the children.[1062]

(a) W will argue B should have known children were trespassing in her backyard because B saw W's jacket and notebook. A reasonable person, who previously operated a bed and breakfast that attracted children, would have realized that children might be trespassing to play on the trampoline. B should have investigated how the objects appeared on her property. However, B will argue she never saw W playing in her backyard because she was always grocery shopping. W went unnoticed for two weeks. Moreover, most children play in the front yard and do not break into their neighbor's backyard. B cannot be expected to monitor every child in the neighborhood. Thus, whether B seeing a jacket and notebook in her backyard is sufficient notification of trespassing children is debatable.

(b) B will argue a trampoline does not cause death or serious bodily harm to children because it is a toy and not a dangerous object, such as a knife. However, W's argument is stronger because trampolines are usually restricted to certain age groups. Retailers discourage young children from playing on trampolines without parental supervision because children may fall, break bones, or suffer serious injury. Moreover, B's trampoline was damaged because it was not maintained for over five years. Thus, the trampoline is likely a dangerous condition.

(c) B will argue children should appreciate the risk of playing on an old trampoline because it was not maintained and was outside for five years. Thus, it was likely obviously rusted. However, B's argument is weak because most nine year olds are unable to understand the risks of a trampoline ripping or falling apart. If a child finds something interesting, then the child will explore the structure.

1062. Restatement (Second) of Torts § 339 (Am. Law Inst. 1965).

(d) W will argue the trampoline has no utility because B did not use the trampoline for over five years and did not allow children on the property. B will argue the burden was high because it takes time and effort to dissemble the trampoline. But B's argument is weak because the risk of children discovering the trampoline is higher. B's bed and breakfast was popular because of the trampoline, which means children might learn about the trampoline, play on it, and get hurt. Thus, B likely needed to use reasonable care to make the trampoline safe.

(e) B will argue she used reasonable care because she put a sign on the back door that said "Off Limits" and enclosed her backyard using a fence. W climbed over the fence to play on the trampoline because B's property was not easily accessible. W will argue B should have put a sign on the trampoline to warn children who played in the backyard. However, this argument is weak because it is unreasonable to require landowners to post warning signs to protect trespassers who illegally accessed their private property, especially if a fence surrounds the backyard.

In conclusion, if B had reason to know that children were trespassing and acted unreasonable by not posting a sign on the trampoline, then B owed a duty to W and breached her duty by not eliminating or making the trampoline safe.

Negligence Per Se

The requirements of a law become the standard of care if: (a) the plaintiff is within the class of persons the statute was created to protect, and (b) the plaintiff's harm was the kind that the statute was enacted to prevent.[1063] If both elements are met and a defendant fails to comply with the statute, then the defendant breached their duty.[1064] However, compliance with the law does not prevent a finding of negligence if a reasonable man would take additional precautions.[1065]

Here, (a) W was within the class of persons the statute was created to protect because the statute required rubber tiles under any structures built for children. W is a child using a trampoline, which is a structure built for children and adults. B will argue a trampoline is not a structure because it is moveable and not bolted into the ground like playground equipment. (b) The statute aimed to eliminate the type of harm that resulted because if the ground was

---

1063. Restatement (Second) of Torts § 286 (Am. Law Inst. 1965).
1064. *Id.*
1065. Restatement (Second) of Torts § 288C (Am. Law Inst. 1965).

covered with rubber tile, then W would not have scratched his legs on the rocky terrain under the trampoline. In conclusion, unless an exception applies, B's failure to use rubber tiles would be considered breach if the trampoline is considered a structure.

Excused Violations

An excused violation of a law is not negligence. A violation is excused if (a) the violation is reasonable because of the actor's incapacity; (b) the actor neither knows nor should know of the occasion for compliance; (c) the actor is unable, after reasonable diligence or care, to comply; (d) the actor is confronted by an emergency not due to his own misconduct; or (e) compliance would involve a greater risk of harm to the actor or to others.[1066]

Here, B will argue she did not have reason to know the trampoline needed rubber tile because her bed and breakfast business was closed for several years, and B did not allow any children on her property; she refused all occupants under 18 years old. B could also not foresee W would trespass because W only played in the backyard while B was grocery shopping. Thus, placing rubber tile under an unused trampoline would be a waste of resources.

In conclusion, if B should have known W would trespass on her land, then there was an occasion for compliance and B breached her duty by violating the statute.

1066. Restatement (Second) of Torts § 288A (Am. Law Inst. 1965).

Answer 5

(1) Diego (D) v. Dr. Z (Z): Punctured Lung

Negligence

To succeed on a claim for negligence, the plaintiff must prove the following elements: (a) the defendant owed a duty of care to the plaintiff; (b) the defendant breached that duty; (c) breach of that duty was the actual and proximate cause of the plaintiff's injury; and (d) the plaintiff suffered harm.[1067]

Duty

Under the majority rule, people owe a duty to everyone within the zone of danger.[1068] A plaintiff is in the zone of danger if the plaintiff was someone who would reasonably be injured by the defendant's conduct.[1069] Under the minority rule, people owe a duty of reasonable care to the world at large.[1070] Here, under the minority rule, D is a foreseeable plaintiff because D is a member of the world. Under the majority rule, D was within the zone of danger because D was Z's patient. Z should know that any mistakes during surgery could harm his patient.

Standard of Care

The reasonable person standard is the default standard of care. However, D will use expert testimony to establish Z, as a practicing doctor, owed a higher standard of care. The standard of care for professionals is the skill and knowledge normally possessed by members of that profession in similar communities.[1071] Z will argue a lower standard of care applies because Z is paralyzed from the waist down. If an actor has a physical disability, then the actor is only negligent if his conduct does not conform to that of a reasonable person with the same disability.[1072] Here, both arguments are meretricious. Thus, Z will likely be required to act as a reasonable doctor in a wheelchair in that community.

1067. R. 2d of Torts § 281, supra note 1050.

1068. *Palsgraf v. Long Island R. Co.*, supra note 1051.

1069. *Id.*

1070. *Id.* at 350–51.

1071. Restatement (Second) of Torts § 299A (Am. Law Inst. 1965). See also *Brune v. Belinkoff*, 354 Mass. 102, 109 (1968).

1072. Restatement (Third) of Torts: Liab. for Physical & Emotional Harm § 11 (Am. Law Inst. 2010).

D will argue that a doctor with a special accommodation, who commonly operates on patients, would have checked the wheelchair's brake before starting the procedure. Z will argue he relied on the nurse because he could not check the breaks while sitting in the wheelchair. Although Z was justified to rely on the nurse's abilities, Z should have asked the nurse if the wheelchair was locked before beginning surgery.

Breach

Conduct is negligent if it falls below the standard of care.[1073] Here, Z likely breached his duty by failing to check the brakes. However, if a reasonable doctor would rely on the nurse, then Z did not breach his duty.

Actual Cause

The defendant's conduct is the factual cause if the harm would not have occurred absent the conduct,[1074] or if the conduct was a substantial factor in bringing about the harm.[1075] Here, Z will argue the nurse was the actual cause because she failed to lock the wheelchair. However, D will argue the wheelchair would not have bumped the table but for Z's failure to ensure the nurse locked the brake. Z was the substantial factor in bringing about the harm because he was the supervising doctor during the surgery. Thus, Z's actions were the actual cause.

Proximate Cause

An actor's liability is limited to the harm that resulted from the risks that made the actor's conduct tortious.[1076] The court must ask if there was a natural and continuous sequence between the cause and effect.[1077] A superseding cause, such as an intervention by a third person or another force, will prevent the actor from being liable even if the antecedent negligence is a substantial factor in bringing about the harm.[1078]

Here, D will argue that failing to confirm the brakes were locked would naturally cause the wheelchair to move during the operation. A punctured lung is

---

1073. R. 2d of Torts § 282, supra note 1061.

1074. Restatement (Third) of Torts: Liab. for Physical & Emotional Harm § 26 (Am. Law Inst. 2010).

1075. Restatement (Second) of Torts § 431 (Am. Law Inst. 1965).

1076. Restatement (Third) of Torts: Liab. for Physical & Emotional Harm § 29 (Am. Law Inst. 2010).

1077. *Palsgraf v. Long Island R. Co.*, supra note 1051 at 354.

1078. Restatement (Second) of Torts § 440 (Am. Law Inst. 1965).

a foreseeable result of the wheelchair bumping into the operation table because a moving wheelchair could cause the patient's injuries to increase or the doctor to make a mistake during surgery. However, Z will argue the nurse's failure to lock the brakes was a superseding cause because her actions caused the wheelchair to move. If the court agrees with Z, then the nurse's intervening act would absolve Z from liability.

Injury

D was physically harmed because D's rib punctured his lung. Z will be liable for D's full injury even though D's disease makes him heal slower than the average person because Z must take the plaintiff with all preexisting conditions. When an actor's tortious conduct causes harm to a person that, because of a preexisting physical or mental condition, is of a greater magnitude or different type than might reasonably be expected, the actor is nevertheless subject to liability for all such harm to the person.[1079]

In conclusion, if Z breached his duty to D, then Z is liable for negligence.

(2) Diego (D) v. Dr. Z (Z): Sponge

Negligence

See rule above. (Diego v. Dr. Z: Punctured Lung: Negligence).

Duty

See rules and analysis above. (Diego v. Dr. Z: Punctured Lung: Duty). D was within the zone of danger because he was Z's patient, which means Z's actions in the operation room would have an effect on D's physical state.

Res Ispa Loquitor

A plaintiff can use the doctrine of res ispa loquitor to prove breach through circumstantial evidence when no direct evidence that the defendant breached exists.[1080] Res ispa loquitor applies if the plaintiff can show (a) the defendant had exclusive custody or control of the instrumentality of the injury, and (b) that harm would not have occurred but for someone being negligent.[1081]

Here, (a) D will argue Z had exclusive control over the instrumentalities because Z was the supervising doctor of the surgery. Z physically used the tools

---

1079. Restatement (Third) of Torts: Liab. for Physical & Emotional Harm §31 (Am. Law Inst. 2010).
1080. Restatement (Second) of Torts §328D (Am. Law Inst. 1965).
1081. *Id.*

during the operation and directed the actions of the assisting nurses. No facts suggest other parties controlled Z. However, Z will argue he did not have exclusive control because the two nurses, who were present in the operating room, could have dropped the sponge during surgery. Z cannot be expected to micromanage professional nurses, especially when Z is focusing on the operation. (b) D will argue there is no way a sponge could have been left in his body without Z or one of the nurses negligently dropping the sponge during the surgery or failing to account for all the tools. In conclusion, if Z is determined to have exclusive control, then res ispa loquitor applies.

(3) Diego (D) v. Syaz (S)

Negligence

See rule above. (Diego v. Dr. Z: Punctured Lung: Negligence).

Duty to Act

If the law does not impose a duty, then no duty to aid another person exists.[1082] However, if an actor's actions cause an unreasonable risk of physical harm to another, then the actor is under the duty to exercise reasonable care to prevent that harm from occurring.[1083] Here, S had a duty to save D because S surprised D by yelling, "Boo," which caused D to trip on a branch and fall into the pool. S acted unreasonably because a reasonable person knows someone could fall off the roof if they were startled. Thus, S needed to use reasonable care to rescue D.

Standard of Care for Children

S will argue that reasonable children scare each other while playing games. Thus, S was not required to rescue D because the standard of conduct to which S must conform is that of a reasonable child of like age, intelligence, and experience under similar circumstances.[1084] S will argue that ten-year-old boys would not realize that scaring someone on the roof could cause them to fall into the pool and drown. If the court disagrees with S, then S had a duty to save D and to use reasonable care of a similarly situated child while rescuing D.

1082. Restatement (Second) of Torts § 314 (Am. Law Inst. 1965).
1083. Restatement (Second) of Torts § 321 (Am. Law Inst. 1965).
1084. Restatement (Second) of Torts § 283A (Am. Law Inst. 1965).

Rescues and Emergencies

If an actor, gratuitously or for consideration, renders services necessary to protect another, then the actor is liable for any physical harm resulting from his failure to exercise reasonable care while performing his undertaking.[1085] If the actor is confronted with an unexpected emergency that requires a rapid response, then this circumstance is taken into account when determining the appropriate standard of care.[1086]

Here, S will argue a reasonable child handling an emergency rescue would grab a pole to pull D out of the water and not jump into the pool because most ten-year olds are not trained lifeguards. A reasonable child would also drag their friend out of the water to avoid the subsequent risk of their friend drowning again. However, D will argue a reasonable child would not pull someone out of the water, but leave him at the poolside until the paramedics or an adult arrived. Moreover, S should not have attempted CPR because D was unconscious, but still breathing. A ten-year-old child should know that CPR is not necessary unless someone stops breathing.

Breach

See rule above. (Diego v. Dr. Z: Punctured Lung: Breach). S probably acted reasonable under the emergency circumstances because children often panic when they see a friend in trouble. S likely attempted CPR because ten-year-old children are impressionable. Most children learn how to handle situations from television shows that display CPR as a remedy after someone almost drowns. D will argue S broke D's ribs because S was untrained, but there are cases where trained adult lifeguards break ribs when conducting CPR. Thus, if a child would take D out of the water and give CPR, then S did not breach his duty.

Actual Cause

See rule above. (Diego v. Dr. Z: Sponge: Actual Cause). Here, but for S yelling "Boo," pulling D out of the water, and conducting CPR, D would not have fallen into the pool, hit his head, or broken a rib. Thus, S is the actual cause.

Proximate Cause

See rule above. (Diego v. Dr. Z: Sponge: Proximate Cause). Here, D will argue that falling into the pool is a natural consequence of scaring someone on the

---

1085. Restatement (Second) of Torts § 323 (Am. Law Inst. 1965).
1086. Restatement (Third) of Torts: Liab. for Physical & Emotional Harm § 9 (Am. Law Inst. 2010).

nearby roof because the person could trip and fall. The person almost drowning and needing CPR is also a foreseeable harm because some people don't
know how to swim and the shock from the scare or impact could immobilize
the person. However, S will argue that D tripping over the branch was a superseding cause. If the branch never existed, then D would not have fallen into
the pool and suffered injuries. S's argument is weak because tripping over
branches is a natural consequence of playing outside, especially with a pile of
leaves that is likely mixed with branches. Thus, S caused D's harm.

Injury

See rule above. (Diego v. Dr. Z: Sponge: Injury). This element is met because
D suffered from a head injury and a broken rib.

In conclusion, if S breached his duty to D, then S is liable for negligence.

(4) Diego (D) v. Mark (M)

Negligence

See rule above. (Diego v. Dr. Z: Punctured Lung: Negligence).

Duty to Control

There is no duty to control the conduct of a third party unless (a) a special
relationship between the actor and the third party imposes a duty to control
the third party, or (b) a special relationship exists between the actor and the
other that gives the other a right to protection.[1087] A special relationship
exists if the actor takes charge of a third party and knows or should know the
third party could cause bodily harm to others if not controlled.[1088]

Here, M will argue D and S were old enough to realize climbing on the roof
would be dangerous. Thus, he had no duty to control their actions. However,
this is a weak argument because a babysitter is hired to watch over children who
cannot care for themselves. D will argue a special relationship was created
between M and D because M accepted the responsibility of babysitting the boys.
M also had a duty to control S because M should have known that two young
boys left home alone would likely play games that could cause harm.

1087. Restatement (Second) of Torts § 315 (Am. Law Inst. 1965).
1088. Restatement (Second) of Torts § 319 (Am. Law Inst. 1965).

Standard of Care

M will argue he should not be held to a standard of reasonable care because he had short-term memory loss. However, his argument will fail because an actor's mental or emotional disability is not considered in determining whether conduct is negligent, unless the actor is a child.[1089] M is not a child because he is 20 years old. Thus, M was required to behave like a reasonable adult babysitting two young boys. A reasonable adult would stay on the property to monitor the boy's activities.

Breach

See rule above. (Diego v. Dr. Z: Punctured Lung: Breach). M breached his duty because he left the house to watch movies with his friends.

Actual Cause

See rule above. (Diego v. Dr. Z: Sponge: Actual Cause). Here, multiple causes lead to D's harm. However, M was a substantial factor in bringing about D's injury because if M had not left S and D alone, then they would not have played on the roof. Thus, M's negligent act started the chain of events.

Proximate Cause

See rule above. (Diego v. Dr. Z: Sponge: Proximate Cause). A criminal or tortious act of a third party is a superseding cause that will absolve the defendant from liability unless the defendant, at the time of his negligent conduct, realized or should have realized that the third party might avail himself to the opportunity to commit the crime or tort.[1090]

Here, M will argue S's assault of D was a superseding cause because S yelled, "Boo," which caused D to fall off the roof. Moreover, S battered D when pulling him out of the pool and conducting CPR. However, M's argument is weak because M should have known that leaving two children at home alone could cause harm. Children are naturally mischievous at the age of ten. Thus, S's tortious actions were likely foreseeable and will not shield M from liability.

Injury

See rule and analysis above. (Diego v. Syaz: Injury).

In conclusion, if S's acts were not a superseding cause, then M is liable for negligence.

1089. R. 3d of Torts: Liab. for Physical & Emotional Harm § 11, supra note 1072.
1090. Restatement (Second) of Torts § 448 (Am. Law Inst. 1965).

Answer 6

(1) Vicarious Liability

An employer is liable for the torts committed by employees acting within the scope of their employment.[1091] If the actor is an independent contractor, then the employer is not liable for the physical harm caused by the contractor or the contractor's servants.[1092] Here, Dr. Vivian (V) and the assistant are employees of D-Dental (D) because they work for the company. V's actions are within the scope of employment because she was likely extracting Alex's (A) wisdom teeth on D's property and using D's equipment. Similarly, the assistant's actions were within the scope of employment because she helped V with the surgery by informing Noni (N) about A's status. Thus, D is liable for any torts committed by V or the assistant.

(2) Alex (A) v. D-Dental (D)

Negligent Infliction of Emotional Distress (NIED)

An actor whose negligent conduct causes serious emotional harm to another is liable if (a) the actor places the other in danger of immediate bodily harm and the emotional harm results from the danger, or (b) the harm occurs in the course of specified categories of activities, undertakings, or relationships in which the negligent conduct is especially likely to cause serious emotional harm.[1093]

Here, (a) A's stomach contents regurgitating into his airways caused immediate bodily harm because it put stress on A's body. A suffered actual emotional distress because he was unable to sleep and needed therapy. A will argue it was foreseeable that he would be scared of dying in his sleep because he almost died during oral surgery while under anesthesia. Most people fear death, especially when their survival is in the hands of another. (b) A will argue that failing to give a patient proper instructions or failing to ensure the patient did not eat before the surgery could cause serious emotional harm. V, as a doctor, should have known that eating before a surgery would cause complications

---

1091. Restatement (Third) Of Agency § 2.04 (Am. Law Inst. 2006).

1092. Restatement (Second) of Torts § 409 (Am. Law Inst. 1965).

1093. Restatement (Third) of Torts: Liab. for Physical & Emotional Harm § 47 (Am. Law Inst. 2012).

during the procedure and result in a near-death experience. Thus, A can recover damages for his emotional distress if D acted negligently.

Negligence

To succeed on a claim for negligence, the plaintiff must prove the following elements: (a) the defendant owed a duty of care to the plaintiff; (b) the defendant breached that duty; (c) breach of that duty caused the plaintiff's injury; and (d) the plaintiff suffered harm.[1094]

Duty

Under the majority rule, people owe a duty to everyone within the zone of danger.[1095] A plaintiff is in the zone of danger if the plaintiff was someone who would reasonably be injured by the defendant's conduct.[1096] Under the minority rule, people owe a duty of reasonable care to the world at large.[1097] Here, under the minority rule, A was a foreseeable plaintiff because A is a member of the world. Under the majority rule, A was within the zone of danger because A was V's patient. V should know that mistakes during the operation could cause her patient harm.

Standard of Care

The reasonable person standard is the default standard of care. However, A will use expert testimony to establish V owed a higher standard of care as a practicing doctor. The standard of care for professionals is the skill and knowledge normally possessed by members of that profession in similar communities.[1098] Industry standards require physicians to reasonably disclose the dangers related to the proposed treatment because the patient must be fully informed before deciding to undergo the treatment.[1099]

Here, A will argue a reasonable physician would have ignored the patient's overconfidence about the surgery and finished explaining the risks and instructions. A reasonable physician would have also postponed the treatment after A indicated he ate "at bit" the morning of the operation. V should have asked

1094. R. 2d of Torts § 281, supra note 1050.

1095. *Palsgraf v. Long Island R. Co.*, supra note 1051.

1096. *Id.*

1097. *Palsgraf v. Long Island R. Co.*, supra note 1051 at 350–51.

1098. Restatement (Second) of Torts § 299A (Am. Law Inst. 1965). See also *Brune v. Belinkoff*, 354 Mass. 102, 109 (1968).

1099. *Canterbury v. Spence*, 464 F.2d 772, 782 (D.C. Cir. 1972).

A what he meant by "a bit" to ensure A read the packet of information and followed the instructions.

Breach

Conduct is negligent if it falls below the standard of care.[1100] Here, V was likely justified when she trusted A to review the instructions before the surgery. However, V should have finished her explanation of the risks and not ignored A's response that he ate before the procedure. Thus, V likely breached her duty.

Actual Cause

The defendant's conduct is the factual cause if the harm would not have occurred absent the conduct,[1101] or if the conduct was a substantial factor in bringing about the harm.[1102] Here, V's actions were not the but-for cause because A needed to eat breakfast for there to be stomach contents in his body during the surgery. However, V's actions were a substantial factor in bringing about the harm because V could have ensured A was properly prepared before beginning the surgery.

Proximate Cause

An actor's liability is limited to the harm that resulted from the risks that made the actor's conduct tortious.[1103] The court must ask if there was a natural and continuous sequence between the cause and effect.[1104] A superseding cause, such as an intervention by a third person or another force, will prevent the actor from being liable even if his antecedent negligence is a substantial factor in bringing about the harm.[1105] Here, a patient eating before surgery is a foreseeable result of neglecting to properly explain the operation's risks and instructions. Most people do not read large instruction packets. V should have realized A arrived unprepared when he admitted to eating that morning. By deciding to proceed with the surgery, V's actions were the proximate cause because she should have known stomach contents in the body could cause a near-death experience that would result in emotional distress.

1100. R. 2d of Torts § 282, supra note 1061.

1101. R. 3d of Torts: Liab. for Physical & Emotional Harm § 26, supra note 1074.

1102. R. 2d of Torts § 431, supra note 1075.

1103. R. 3d of Torts: Liab. for Physical & Emotional Harm § 29, supra note 1076.

1104. *Palsgraf v. Long Island R. Co.*, supra note 1051 at 354.

1105. R. 2d of Torts § 440, supra note 1078.

Injury

Here, A suffered physical harm from stomach contents regurgitating into his airways and suffered emotional distress from not being able to sleep and needing therapy.

In conclusion, V is likely liable for negligence unless a defense applies.

Contributory Negligence

If a plaintiff's unreasonable actions legally contribute to the plaintiff's harm, then the plaintiff is barred from recovering.[1106] Here, a reasonable patient would have listened to the doctor's explanation of the risks, read the packet of information, and fasted before the surgery. A stopped V from finishing her explanation, glanced at the packet without reading it, and had a breakfast buffet before the operation. Thus, unless the last clear chance exception applies, A cannot recover damages from D.

Last Clear Chance

A plaintiff who acts unreasonably may still recover damages if, immediately preceding the harm, (a) the plaintiff is unable to reasonably avoid the harm, and (b) the defendant is negligent in failing to utilize, with reasonable care, his existing opportunity to avoid the harm.[1107] The defendant must (i) know the plaintiff's situation and (ii) realize or should have realized the peril involved.[1108]

(b) Here, A will argue Dr. V had the last clear chance to avoid the harm because A stated he ate "a bit" that morning. V knew (i) the plaintiff was about to undergo surgery and (ii) that eating before could cause complications. Thus, V should have investigated A's response before administering the anesthesia. However, V has a stronger argument because A could have avoided the harm by not eating the breakfast buffet or responding honestly about the breakfast buffet. Thus, A is unlikely to recover for negligence in a contributory negligence jurisdiction.

Comparative Negligence

In a pure comparative negligence jurisdiction, the court apportions liability among the parties based on each party's fault.[1109] In a modified comparative negligence jurisdiction, apportionment is also based on fault, but only up

---

1106. Restatement (Second) of Torts § 463 (Am. Law Inst. 1965).
1107. Restatement (Second) of Torts § 479 (Am. Law Inst. 1965).
1108. *Id.*
1109. *Li v. Yellow Cab Co.*, 13 Cal. 3d 804, 827 (1975).

to the point where the plaintiff's negligence is equal to or greater than that of the defendant; when that point is reached, the plaintiff is barred from recovery.[1110] Here, A was negligent. See rule and analysis above. (Alex v. Dr. Vivian: Contributory Negligence). A's recovery will be lowered by the percent he was negligent under the pure comparative negligence standard. Under the modified comparative negligence standard, if A was 51% or more at fault, then he will recover nothing.

Assumption of the Risk

A plaintiff who voluntarily assumes the risk of harm arising from the defendant's negligent conduct cannot recover for such harm.[1111] A plaintiff can expressly accept the risks through a verbal or written agreement unless the agreement is contrary to public policy.[1112]

Here, A expressly assumed the risk because he signed the consent form without any pressure from V. A also voluntarily arrived the day of the procedure to undergo the surgery. However, A will argue his consent was invalid because he did not fully understand the risk of harm. A did not know he should fast before the surgery because he only heard part of V's explanation and glanced at the packet. V will argue A had every opportunity to learn about the risks involved, but refused to act reasonably. Moreover, A already knew about the procedure from his previous surgery. Thus, A likely had the actual knowledge and understood the risks associated with anesthesia when he signed the voluntary consent form.

Primary Implied Assumption of the Risk

If the voluntary consent form is invalid, then A assumed the risk by implication. A plaintiff who fully understands a risk of harm and voluntarily chooses to enter or remain within the area of risk is not entitled to recover for harm within that risk.[1113] Here, A arrived that morning for the surgery even though he knew the anesthesia treatment would make him unconscious. A's actions indicated he assumed the risk of any complications during the operation. A will argue he did not provide informed consent, but A's argument is weak because he had opportunities to learn more about the risks.

1110. *Id.*
1111. Restatement (Second) of Torts § 496A (Am. Law Inst. 1965).
1112. Restatement (Second) of Torts § 496B (Am. Law Inst. 1965).
1113. Restatement (Second) of Torts § 496C (Am. Law Inst. 1965).

Secondary Assumption of the Risk

In some jurisdictions, implied assumption of the risk does not survive as a separate and complete defense.[1114] If a plaintiff voluntarily encounters a known risk, then the plaintiff's contributory negligence is merged into the comparative fault scheme, and the trier of fact will apportion loss according to the fault of the parties.[1115] Secondary assumption of the risk is merely a variant category of contributory negligence.[1116] Here, A was comparatively negligent. See rule and analysis above. (Alex v. Dr. Vivian: Comparative Fault).

In conclusion, although V was likely negligent, A's recovery will be completely barred or reduced because A was negligent and assumed the risk.

(3) Noni (N) v. D-Dental (D)

Negligent Infliction of Emotional Distress

An actor who negligently causes sudden serious bodily injury to a third person is liable for serious emotional harm caused to any person who (a) perceives the event contemporaneously and (b) is a close family member of the third person suffering the bodily injury.[1117] Here, (b) N is a close family member of A because she is his wife. (a) N will argue she perceived the event contemporaneously because she was in the waiting room during A's procedure. The assistant told N about the complications while A was still under anesthesia. However, D will argue N never witnessed A's physical injuries on operating table or the stomach contents regurgitating into his lungs. Thus, N cannot recover for emotional distress because she was not at the scene of the incident and did not perceived anything. She only heard about the incident from the assistant.

1114. *Knight v. Jewett*, 3 Cal. 4th 296, 333 (1992).

1115. *Id.* at 315.

1116. *Id.*

1117. Restatement (Third) of Torts: Liab. for Physical & Emotional Harm §48 (Am. Law Inst. 2012).

Answer 7

(1) FoodStar (F) vs. AVX

Products liability applies to all participants in the products chain of production and distribution.[1118] Here, AVX was a member in the chain of distribution because AVX sold the lane-departure technology to car dealerships.

To recover under strict products liability, the plaintiff must demonstrate that (a) a defect existed in the product; a product is defective if it contains a manufacturing defect, design defect, or inadequate warning,[1119] (b) the defect caused the injury, and (c) the defect in the product existed at the time the product left the seller or distributor's possession.[1120] Here, AVX sent the technology to Car Dealership (C) with the defect in the program's code. AVX will argue that C's installation caused the defect, but this is a weak argument because C's mechanic installed the product correctly, tested it, and verified it worked properly. Thus, C did not modify the program's code between AVX's distribution and Bert's (B) use.

Manufacturing Defect

Even if reasonable care was exercised in the preparation and marketing of the product, a manufacturing defect exists if the product departs from its intended design.[1121] Here, AVX intended all its lane-departure technology to have proper code, but sent the technology to the dealership with a defect in the program's code. Thus, a manufacturing defect existed.

Design Defect

A product is defective in design if the foreseeable risks of harm posed by the product could have been reduced or avoided by the adoption of a reasonable alternative design, and the omission of the alternative design renders the product not reasonably safe.[1122]

Here, F will argue AVX should have used the lane-departure technology that updated when connected to the internet because competitors in the industry

---

1118. *Automobile Ins. Co. of Hartford Connecticut v. Murray, Inc.*, 571 F.Supp.2d 408, 427 (W.D.N.Y. 2008). See also Restatement (Third) of Torts: Prod. Liab. § 1 (Am. Law Inst. 1998).

1119. *Cooper v. Old Williamsburg Candle Corp.*, 653 F.Supp.2d 1220, 1224 (M.D. Fla. 2009).

1120. *Id.* at 1223.

1121. Restatement (Third) of Torts: Prod. Liab. § 2 (Am. Law Inst. 1998).

1122. *Id.*

were selling this design. Reasonable manufacturers likely realized that consumers failed to update the maps every six months and revamped the technology to include automatic updates that made the product safer. However, AVX will argue the alternative design was not reasonable because it would cost AVX three times more to manufacture the automatic-update technology. Higher expenses would hurt AVX's profit. Moreover, only some companies sold the automatic-update technology and not all companies. Thus, AVX's design was likely reasonable because other companies still required updates on the maps every six months.

Warning Defect

If an alternative design was not required, then F will argue AVX needed to warn consumers about the risks associated with missing an update. A warning defect exists if foreseeable risks of harm could have been reduced or avoided by reasonable instructions or warnings, and the omission of the instructions or warnings rendered the product not reasonably safe.[1123]

Here, F has a strong argument that the warnings were inadequate because they were buried in the middle of a 40-page manual. The details about the six-month update appeared on page 20 in 11-point font. A reasonable manufacturer would have distributed the warnings as a separate notice page, placed the warnings in larger text on the first page, or put a reminder to update the maps every six months on the cover of the manual.

Read and Heed

AVX will argue the warning was reasonable because AVX can assume a person purchasing the lane-departure technology would read the manual and follow instructions.[1124] A product bearing a warning, which would make the product safe for use if the warning is followed, is not defective or unreasonably dangerous.[1125] Thus, if the warning on page 20 was reasonable, then AVX could assume B would read and heed the instructions. However, if the warning was unreasonable, then there is a warning defect.

Foreseeable Misuse

AVX will argue the warning is irrelevant because B misused the product. Injury from the misuse of a product does not give rise to a strict liability claim

---

1123. *Id.*
1124. Restatement (Second) of Torts § 402A cmt. j (Am. Law Inst. 1965).
1125. *Id.*

if the misuse was beyond the products intended use and not reasonably fore-seeable.[1126] Here, AVX will argue that B relying on the lane-departure technol-ogy to drive the car while he napped was not foreseeable because it is common sense to not sleep while driving.

However, F has a stronger argument because AVX added a large warning on the title page that stated, "This lane-departure technology is a safety feature and should not be treated as an automatic-driver technology. Drivers must still keep their hands on the wheel and stay alert." The prominent warning suggests AVX expected people to misuse the product by relying on the technology to drive the car. Thus, B's misuse was likely reasonably foreseeable and will not absolve AVX from liability unless the warning against misuse was deemed adequate.

In conclusion, F will likely succeed in a products liability suit against AVX because several defects existed.

(2) FoodStar (F) vs. Car Dealership (C)

See rules above. (FoodStar v. AVX). Here, C was a member in the chain of distribution because C purchased the lane-departure technology from AVX, sold the product to consumers, and installed the product.

Warning Defect

See rules above. (FoodStar v. AVX: Warning Defect). F will argue C should have verbally explained the update process to B because C conducts the semi-annual updates to the technology's maps. However, C failed to tell B about the maintenance schedule and did not warn B about the risks associated with miss-ing an update. C will argue a dealership can reasonably rely on the customer to read the instruction manual provided with the technology. See rule and analysis above. (FoodStar v. AVX: Read and Heed). However, if AVX's warning was unrea-sonable, then C's defense will fail because C should have verbally warned B.

Foreseeable Misuse

C will argue it is not liable because B's misuse was not foreseeable. How-ever, this argument is weak. See rule and analysis above. (FoodStar v. AVX: Foreseeable Misuse). Here, compared to other members in the chain of distri-bution, C, as the retailer, commonly interacts with consumers. Thus, C should have known that consumers might forget to update the technology or rely on

---

1126. R. 3d of Torts: Prod. Liab. § 2 cmt. p, supra note 1121. See also *Port Authority of New York and New Jersey v. Arcadian Corp.*, 189 F.3d 305, 314 (3d Cir. 1999).

the technology to drive the car. B shared with C that he needed something to keep him safe when he fell asleep on the road. C should have realized B planned to use the technology inappropriately and clarified that the lane-departure technology did not transform his vehicle into a self-driving truck. A reasonable dealership would have spent time discussing the hazards of improper use and providing instructions on the updates.

In conclusion, C likely needed to verbally warn B about the risks.

(3) Joint and Several Liability

Here, Truck Company (T) is not a member in the chain of distribution because T is the consumer; B, an employee of T, purchased the technology. Thus, F cannot sue T under strict products liability. However, F can sue T under negligence. If F sues the defendants under negligence, then F can argue they are jointly and severally liable for F's harm.

Joint and Several Liability

Defendants are jointly and severally liable for any indivisible injury legally caused by their tortious conduct.[1127] If the jury determines the defendants caused an indivisible injury, then F can recover the full judgment from any of the liable defendants.[1128]

Here, F will argue the actions of the defendants worked in unison to cause F's harm. The technology stopped working because of the program error that was amplified by the lack of an update. AVX delivered the product with a program-code defect, and B did not update the maps because AVX and C failed to warn B about the risks associated with skipping an update. C also neglected to remind B that the lane-departure technology was a safety enhancement and not an automatic-driver technology. B, an agent of T, failed to read the manual, update the car, and inappropriately used the car while driving because he took a nap at the wheel. Thus, each defendant contributed to B veering off the road and ruining F's products in the car crash.

The defendants' best argument is that F's harm is divisible. If the jury agrees that each defendant's contribution can be separated into distinct percentages, then the defendants will not be joint and severally liable. F will need to collect

---

1127. Restatement (Third) of Torts: Apportionment Liab. § 12 (Am. Law Inst. 2000).

1128. Restatement (Third) of Torts: Apportionment of Liab. § A18 (Am. Law Inst. 2000).

the appropriate judgment according to the percentage of fault from each individual defendant.

Contribution

If joint and several liability applies, then F can collect the judgment from any defendant and the defendants must sue each other for contribution. If two or more defendants are liable for the same harm and one of the defendants discharges liability of the other by a settlement or judgment in a lawsuit with the plaintiff, then the defendant discharging liability is entitled to recover contribution from the other liable defendant.[1129] The defendants cannot recover more than the person's comparative share of responsibility.[1130] Here, F sued all three companies so it is unlikely they will need to file a separate lawsuit for contribution.

(4) Vicarious Liability

An employer is liable for the torts committed by employees acting within the scope of their employment.[1131] If the actor is an independent contractor, then the employer is not liable for the physical harm caused by the contractor or the contractor's servants.[1132] Here, T will argue B is not liable because he is an independent contractor.

Employer or Independent Contractor

To determine if an employee is an independent contractor, the court examines the following factors: (a) the employee's right to control the manner of performance; (b) the employee's opportunity for profit or loss; (c) the employees investment in the materials and labor used for the task; (d) if the services required a special skill; (e) the working relationship between the employer and alleged employee; and (f) if the service is an integral part of the employer's business.[1133]

Here, (a) T controlled B's manner of performance because T likely selected the clients, products, and delivery locations. However, B did have the freedom to choose various routes. (b) B would not profit from a timely delivery or suffer a loss from a failed delivery. F hired T and paid T the delivery fees. B was

---

1129. Restatement (Third) of Torts: Apportionment of Liab. § 23 (Am. Law Inst. 2000).
1130. *Id.*
1131. R. 3d of Agency § 2.04, supra note 1091.
1132. R. 2d of Torts § 409, supra note 1092.
1133. *Donovan v. DialAmerica Marketing, Inc.*, 757 F.2d 1376, 1382 (3d Cir. 1985).

simply T's agent. (c) B used T's truck, but installed his own technology in the vehicle, which suggests B invested some materials. However, T paid B a wage to drive the truck and B did not need to hire other employees. (d) Truck driving usually requires some certifications, but it does not require any specialized skills because most adults know how to drive. (e) B only worked three out of seven days in the week and received no benefits, which suggests B was temporarily working for T. However, (f) T's business was a delivery service using trucks. Thus, B's driving services were an integral part of T's business. In conclusion, more factors support that B was T's part-time employee.

Scope of Employment

If B is an employee, then T is only liable for torts committed within the scope of B's employment. T will argue B was on a frolic when the accident occurred, which is a pursuit of an employee's personal business unrelated to employment.[1134] B was driving to his daughter's ballet recital and would not start his shift until her recital was over. Thus, B was not officially working when he took a nap behind the wheel. T had no interest in the ballet recital.

However, F will argue B was taking a mere detour, which is a deviation for personal reasons that are still sufficiently related to employment.[1135] B was on his delivery route when he stopped at his daughter's ballet recital. Thus, B was driving in the direction of his next delivery and using T's truck, which means T was benefiting from B's actions even though B had not started his shift. If the B was not acting in the scope of employment because his shift did not begin, then T is not vicariously liable and F will need to sue B to recover damages.

1134. *Snodgrass v. Jones*, 755 F.Supp. 826, 829 (C.D. Ill. 1991).
1135. *Id.*

Answer 8

(1) Garner (G) v. Homeowner (H): Strict Liability

Abnormally Dangerous Activity

An actor who carries on an abnormally dangerous activity is subject to strict liability for physical harm resulting from the activity.[1136] Here, G suffered burns on his legs because the firecrackers lit his pants on fire. Thus, the firecrackers caused a physical harm. An activity is abnormally dangerous if (a) the activity creates a foreseeable and highly significant risk of physical harm even when reasonable care is exercised, and (b) the activity is not one of common usage in the community.[1137]

(a) Here, G will argue it is foreseeable that firecrackers could start a fire, especially in a residential area where neighboring yards have grass and other flammable materials. The risk of harm is significant because firecrackers are explosive and sparks can ignite a fire. H will argue he used reasonable care because he only used the firecrackers in his backyard. H avoided the front yard to minimize the disturbance. Firecrackers are safe because they use less gunpowder than fireworks and, if use appropriately, there is minimal risk of harm. For example, even in largely populated areas, people simply rope off an area for a firecracker display to prevent people from entering.

However, H's argument is weak because firecrackers can still start a fire in his backyard if they are not discharged safely. In conclusion, because firecrackers involve explosives and fire, there is likely a significant risk of harm.

(b) Here, H will argue firecrackers were used everyday during Luna New Year in his hometown because Luna New Year is the most popular holiday in Asia. However, G's argument is stronger because the applicable standard will be G's current neighborhood. H's neighbors' filed a nuisance lawsuit, which suggests daily firecracker displays to celebrate Luna New Year are not common in his residential area.

In conclusion, H will be strictly liable for the harm the firecracker caused G's leg because setting off firecrackers is likely dangerous and not a common activity.

1136. Restatement (Third) of Torts: Liab. for Physical & Emotional Harm § 20 (Am. Law Inst. 2010).
1137. Id.

Domestic or Wild Animals

An owner of a wild animal is subject to strict liability for physical harm caused by the wild animal.[1138] A wild animal includes animals that have not been generally domesticated and that are likely, unless restrained, to cause personal injury.[1139] A domestic animal includes animals devoted to the service of mankind at the time and in the place in which it is kept.[1140]

Here, G will argue Butch (B) is a wild animal because B is a mix of a husky and a gray wolf. Although a husky is a common breed of dog that is devoted to serving mankind as a pet, a gray wolf is a wild animal. Gray wolves are normally found in zoos and only interact with animal trainers. Gray wolves require some restraint and are not a species that freely interacts with members of the public. However, H will argue all dogs have animal instincts. Huskies can attack humans as easily as gray wolves. Thus, the amount of caution used around a stray husky would be the same as a gray wolf. Because B is a mixed breed, B might not be a wild animal.

Wild Animal Liability

If B is considered a wild animal, then H is subject to strict liability for any harm done by B, even if H exercised the utmost care to confine or prevent B from doing harm.[1141] Strict liability is limited to harm that results from a dangerous propensity that is a characteristic of the wild animal.[1142] Here, G's injury was a result of a wolf's dangerous propensity because B bit G. Wolves normally use their mouths to kill prey. Wolves are also territorial, which means B would naturally bite any intruders, such as G, who stepped on H's land. Thus, H is likely strictly liable for the dog bite.

Domestic Animal with Dangerous Tendencies

If the court determines that B is a domestic animal, then H is strictly liable for any physical harm caused by B's dangerous tendencies that H knew or had

---

1138. Restatement (Third) of Torts: Liab. for Physical & Emotional Harm § 22 (Am. Law Inst. 2010).

1139. *Id.*

1140. Restatement (Second) of Torts § 506 (Am. Law Inst. 1977).

1141. Restatement (Second) of Torts § 507 (Am. Law Inst. 1977).

1142. *Id.*

reason to know about.[1143] Here, because B never displayed aggressive behavior. H likely had no knowledge about B's dangerous tendencies. However, even domestic animals are territorial and will naturally protect themselves if someone intrudes on their land. Thus, H should have known B would bite intruders. G will argue H knew B was scared of firecrackers because H put B in his kennel before performing his evening firework ritual. H wanted to protect others from the dangerous actions that B might commit when the firecrackers began. Thus, it is likely H knew B would react aggressively if B was outside the kennel during the fireworks ritual.

In conclusion, H is likely strictly liable for G's injuries.

(2) Garner (G) v. Homeowner (H): Nuisance

Private Nuisance

A private nuisance is a non-trespassory invasion of another's interest in the private use and enjoyment of land.[1144] The invasion must be an unreasonable and substantial interference.[1145] Here, G will argue he cannot use and enjoy his land because the firecrackers cause loud noises and smoke everyday. The loud noises disrupt G's sleeping schedule, which unreasonably impacts his health and employment because G works the graveyard shift. H's neighbors have the right to peace and quiet in the evenings. However, H will argue the firecrackers only last for a brief period of time each year, only five minutes for seven days. H's ritual might interfere with G's enjoyment, but the interference is minimal because he sets off firecrackers at 7:00 PM, which is usually when people are awake and not sleeping. Thus, G's nuisance claim is invalid because G experiences heightened sensitivity compared to other neighbors, who do not sleep in the middle of the day.

In conclusion, H's argument will likely fail because even though G's complaint is related to his unique sleeping patterns, H's firecrackers interfered with the use and enjoyment of several neighbors in the area, including G.

1143. Restatement (Third) of Torts: Liab. for Physical & Emotional Harm § 23 (Am. Law Inst. 2010).

1144. Restatement (Second) of Torts § 821D (Am. Law Inst. 1979).

1145. *Cook v. Rockwell Intern. Corp.*, 273 F.Supp.2d 1175, 1201–1202. (D. Colo. 2003).

Public Nuisance

To recover damages in an individual action for a public nuisance, the plaintiff must have suffered harm of a kind different from that suffered by other members of the public.[1146] Here, G will argue he can bring an individual action under public nuisance because H's firecrackers disrupted G's sleeping schedule. No facts suggest other neighbors are complaining about the lack of sleep. However, this is a weak argument because the crux of G's claim is that the noise is interfering with the use and enjoyment of G's land. The other neighbors also find the noise annoying, which is the same harm G experienced. Thus, G will not be able to sue for public nuisance because G's harm is essentially the same as his neighbors' harm.

(3) Neighbors (N) v. Homeowner (H): Nuisance

Public Nuisance

See rule above. (Garner v. Homeowner: Public Nuisance). In order to maintain a proceeding to abate a public nuisance, the plaintiff must have authority as a public official or public agency to represent the state or a political subdivision in the matter, or have standing to sue as a representative of the general public, as a citizen in a citizen's action or as a member of a class in a class action.[1147] Here, N must find someone with standing to bring the claim and prove H's actions caused an unreasonable interference with a right common to the general public.[1148]

The court considers the following factors to determine if the interference was unreasonable: (a) if the conduct involves a significant interference with the public health, safety, or peace; (b) if the conduct is prohibited by a statute, ordinance, or administrative regulation, or (c) if the conduct is of a continuing nature or has produced a permanent or long-lasting effect.[1149] (d) The defendant must know or have reason to know that there is a significant effect upon the public right.[1150]

(a) N will argue H's actions caused a significant interference with the safety because firecrackers can start fires and firecracker smoke can negatively impact N's health by causing coughing or other illnesses. Moreover, the peace of their

---

1146. Restatement (Second) of Torts § 821C (Am. Law Inst. 1979).
1147. *Id.*
1148. Restatement (Second) of Torts § 821B (Am. Law Inst. 1979).
1149. *Id.*
1150. *Id.*

home is ruined because the noise is annoying. (b) No facts suggest any laws prevent H from setting off firecrackers at 7:00 PM in a residential area. (c) H will argue his firecracker ritual is not continuing in nature, but temporary. H's firecrackers last for a short period of time, five minutes, for one week in the year. Thus, the ritual will be over before the case is resolved. However, N will argue the firecrackers are continual in nature because H sets off firecrackers every year. N wants to stop the annual practice. Moreover, the smoke lingers, which means the effect lasts longer than the five minutes. (d) H will argue he had no reason to know his actions were problematic because no facts suggest anyone in the neighborhood told H his firecrackers negatively impacted the neighborhood. However, N will argue it is common sense that loud noises and smoke could annoy neighbors.

In conclusion, it is likely the court will find that H's action is disruptive because it happens every year and H will be liable for public nuisance and must stop the firecracker ritual.

Index